i2B

introduction2Business

Bassim Hamadeh, CEO and Publisher
Mieka Portier, Senior Field Acquisitions Editor
Sean Adams, Production Editor
Jess Estrella, Senior Graphic Designer
Alisa Munoz, Licensing Coordinator
Natalie Piccotti, Director of Marketing
Kassie Graves, Vice President of Editorial
Jamie Giganti, Director of Academic Publishing

Printed in the United States of America.

ISBN: 978-1-5165-3390-9 (pbk) / 978-1-5165-3391-6 (br) / 978-1-5165-4538-4 (al)

First Edition

Bonnie Chavez

Dedicated to . . .

Preston, Scarlett & Bennett

I hope that your lives will be filled with wonder and awe.
Always remain adventurous and seek to learn and grow each day.
Hold yourself up to highest standards possible and never accept anything less than your best effort in all that you do.
Remember to embrace the blessings in your life.
Make every moment count.

Contents

To Every Student who reads this Book . . .

> *"Nothing is truly learned until it is lived. Reason, experience, spirit—once these come together, the stage is set for alchemy. The wisdom inside you is like a spark that once lit can never be extinguished."*
>
> —Deepak Chopra
> "The Way of the Wizard"

I have had the most amazing opportunity to be a change agent, a "spark", as a Professor of Business for the last 30 years. Each day I am inspired by my students and humbled by the brief moments in time we spend together as part of our life's journey.

In writing this book I have put forth my best effort to keep it simple and live by the mantra "less is more". This book, your introduction2Business, is designed to provide you with a fundamental understanding of core business concepts. As I wrote each chapter I continually reminded myself of the following:

> *"… it's not just learning things that's important. It's learning what to do with what you learn and learning why you learn things at all that matters … Many of the things I'm supposed to know seem so useless that I can't see the purpose in learning them at all … You may not see it now … but whatever we learn has a purpose and whatever we do affects everything and everyone else, if even in the tiniest way."*
>
> —Norton Juster
> "The Phantom Tollbooth"

It is from my experience as a student, business owner, and college professor that I have attempted to write a textbook that is straightforward, concise, easy to comprehend, and meaningful. My hope is that you will find the book a modest, but useful tool in the process of transforming yourself into something greater than you ever imagined. The very essence of alchemy!

To The Great Teacher ...

This book is designed for and dedicated to you; the great teacher. It is designed for the teacher who seeks to share his/her passion and knowledge of business with every student who enters their class. It is dedicated to the great teacher who sees each day as an opportunity to inspire curiosity, engage greater student discourse, and facilitate student success. This book has been designed with you in mind. This means that I have attempted to write a book that provides students, by way of your guidance, with an incisive introduction2Business and an understanding of how business principles will impact their lives as they go out into the world.

With sincere respect and gratitude,

Professor, Business Administration
Department Chair, Business Administration
Santa Barbara City College

Chapter 1

Business in Free Markets

PROLOGUE

In any discussion of business it is important to first establish an understanding of the economic system in which business activities take place. Around the world today there are a variety of economic systems at work; each significantly affecting the standard of living of the citizenry and productive capacity of the economy. Unlike command economies, wherein the government determines what goods should be produced, how much should be produced and the price at which the goods are offered for sale, free market economies allow every individual to pursue their own self-interest and assume the risk associated with bringing a new idea, product, service, or business into the market. For any business to survive and prosper in a free market, where there is an abundance of competition, they must be capable of establishing and maintaining a unique competitive advantage.

> "Research indicates that a whopping 60 percent of an organization's competitive advantage is derived from internal advancements in knowledge and learning. As Ray Stata, former chairman of Analog Devices (and a pioneer in creating learning organizations) famously quoted in a 1995 edition of the The International Journal of Organizational Analysis: The rate at which individuals and organizations learn may become the only sustainable competitive advantage left."[1]

It is the result of competition in the marketplace that the best products and ideas will "win the day" and as a result produce a meaningful return on investment to the entrepreneur or investor. The free market ultimately determines the winners and losers based on the ability and capacity of the individual, or the individual firm, to efficiently meet the unique needs and demands of consumers in the market. It is through the prism of a market economy that we will examine the major functional areas of business.

Adam Smith, in his book entitled *"An Inquiry into the Nature and Causes of the Wealth of Nations"*, believed that it was essential for every individual, in order to earn money, to be capable of producing something of value. In Adam Smith's lasting imagery of capitalism he explained the basic elements of a free market still hold true today. In a now famous phrase espousing a new era of economic independence, Smith declares;

> "To prohibit a great people from making all that they can ... or from employing their industry in the way that they judge most advantageous, is a manifest violation of the most sacred rights of mankind.[2]

FREE ENTERPRISE

The free market economy, where the factors of production are owned and utilized by private citizens and businesses, is based on the premise that no one forces any person to create innovative new products, develop and implement operational efficiencies, or assume the risk of launching a new business. Free markets, or more specifically a ***Capitalist*** economic system, provide every individual with the opportunity to pursue any idea, assume any level of risk, and seek profit from their own individual initiative.

In spite of our relatively short 241-year history, America today enjoys a very high standard of living. The freedom and prosperity that we enjoy is the direct result of the principles espoused by the Founding Fathers who advocated for free enterprise and limited government. Free enterprise is based on the fundamental principle of voluntary exchange of goods and services between producers and consumers wherein both mutually benefit from this free exchange. The role of the government in a free market economy is to create an environment where individuals and organizations can create prosperity through meeting the needs of others. The Founding Fathers asserted that the right to life, liberty and the pursuit of happiness were granted by our Creator and not by our government. Only in a country where the government protects the personal and property rights of its citizens can free enterprise succeed and flourish.

> "Our Founding Fathers introduced the revolutionary idea that each person's desire to pursue their idea of happiness was not self-indulgence, but a necessary driver of a prosperous society. They created a government to defend that right for everyone. The pursuit of happiness became the driver of the entrepreneurial spirit that defines the American free market economy."[3]

Free enterprise, much like the principles espoused by the founders in the Declaration of Independence, is based on the fundamental assumption that "*... all men are created equal, that they are endowed by their Creator with certain unalienable Rights,*"[4] and as a result pursue their own self-interest in an effort to improve their standard of living and quality of life.

In economic terms the ***Standard of Living*** is measured by the relative cost of goods and services consumers are able to purchase with the money they have. We tend to equate a higher standard of living with a higher level of consumption, but in reality the key to long-term prosperity, and a higher standard of living, is the result of an increase in the level of productive capacity, as reflected in an increase in the Gross Domestic Product (GDP), provide the mechanism for people to find work, generate income, and subsequently purchase goods and services thus improving the overall productive capacity of the economy. The baseline measure of the standard of living is real national output per head of population or real GDP per capita. This is calculated by dividing real national income (Gross Domestic Product) by the total population.

> "The United States performs very well in many measures of well-being relative to most other countries in the Better Life Index. The United States ranks at the top in housing, and income and wealth. They rank above the average in health status, jobs and earnings, education and skills, social connections, personal security, subjective well-being, environmental quality, and civic engagement."[5]

Quality of Life is a more subjective, often intangible, measure and typically refers to the general well being of a society and those variables that lead to "satisfaction and joy". These variables include:

- Political freedom
- Equal Protection under the law
- Educational opportunities
- Right to privacy
- Freedom of religion
- Weather/Climate
- Recreational opportunities
- Aesthetic – Artistic, Cultural, Intellectual

CAPITALISM: THE CIRCULAR FLOW OF BUSINESS

Within a market economy business activities are based on a voluntary exchange between the consumer and individual businesses. Each provides the other with something of value and in return acquires something that he/she considers of greater value. *"Under our assumptions, therefore, the means of production and productive process have in general no real leader, or rather the real leader is the consumer. The people who direct business firms only execute what is prescribed for them by wants or demand and by the given means and methods of production. Individuals have influence only in as so far as they are consumers, only insofar that they express a demand."*[6]

The forces of ***Supply and Demand*** determine the amount of goods and services that are produced in the market. The flows of income and of expenditures are equal and as a result of this reciprocal relationship between businesses and consumers need each other to maintain their existence.

The circular flow illustrates how the interactions between consumers and individual businesses work within a free market. In a market economy ***Consumers*** determine what is produced, marketed, and consumed. Consumers do this by spending money on what they need and in turn ***Businesses*** produce and distribute goods and services that consumers need and will purchase. A business is any organization, regardless of its size, that seeks to make a profit, through the production and/or sales of goods and services. Businesses, when managed effectively, can create wealth and are essential to the growth and stability of the economy. Ultimately, businesses contribute to an improved standard of living and quality of life.

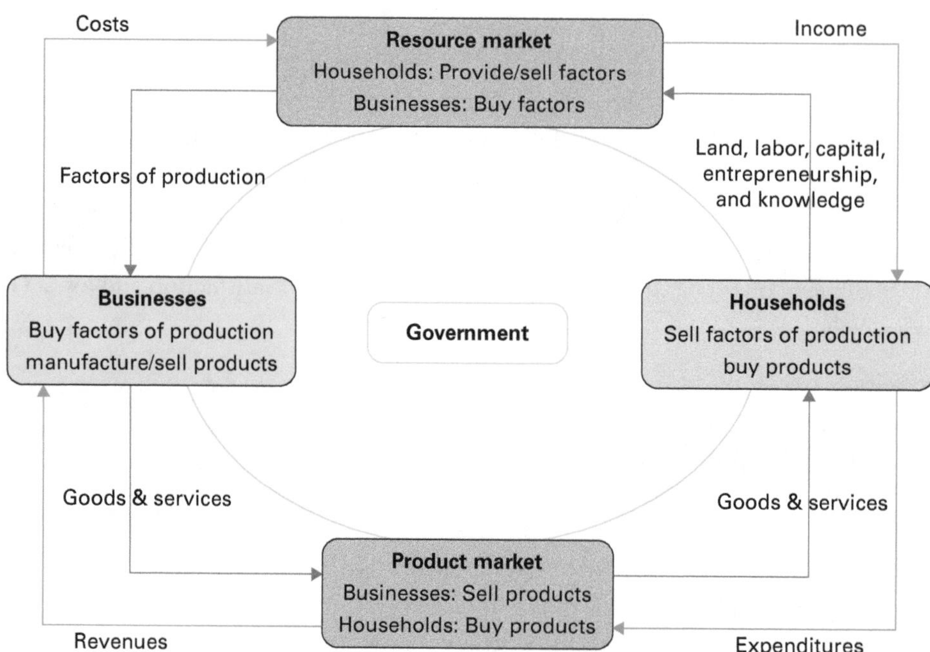

All of the activities within the circular flow serve as a catalyst for the movement of money—flows of payments from businesses to households and eventually to the government. The ***Government*** at the federal, state, and local levels influences the production and consumption of goods within the market by establishing tax rates and regulations that impact the interactions of consumers and businesses. Taxes represent the principal source of government revenue and are subsequently used for the public good—Defense, Education, Health Care, Social Security, Welfare, & Pensions.

The circular flow model clearly demonstrates that businesses are not the final owners of resources or products. Instead, private individuals own all for-profit businesses as well as all of the factors of production. In a free market, democratic society, the government ultimately does not own anything and instead is responsible to the people—who bear the consequences of policies formulated by the elected officials within the government.

Factors of Production

In every economic system there are scarce resources that individuals seek out and utilize in order to satisfy their unique needs and financial objectives. In addition these same scarce resources, the ***factors of production***, are what every business must acquire or utilize in order to produce and deliver goods and services to the marketplace. Businesses must efficiently utilize the factors of production and create a positive revenue stream, if it is their intent to produce consistent year-after-year profit margins. In a free and vibrant economy, wherein there exists a robust circular flow, the creation of a small business represents the first step toward the creation of wealth and a higher standard of living. The more dynamic and active the interaction between businesses and households within the circular flow, the more vibrant the economy and the utilization of the five factors of production.

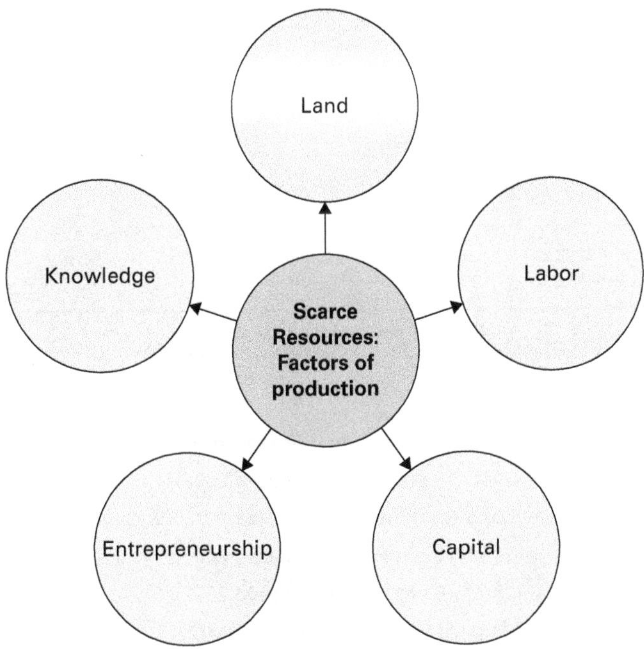

Land

From a business and economics perspective, Land does not simply represent soil or the earth's surface. Instead ***Land*** represents the natural resources which include; building sites, forests, mineral deposits, wildlife, farmland, and water. Land is considered a passive factor in production; since it simply exists. This category represents the contribution to production of what are often referred to as *"nonhuman resources as found in their original, unimproved form"*.[7] Natural resources require the application of capital and human resources (mental and physical labor) to be utilized (extracted, processed, refined) for the realization of their economic value.

Labor

The economic contributions of people represent the most vital component to any organization or economic system. In economics, labor is often defined as the measure of the work performed by human beings. Based on this definition labor represents the aggregate of all human physical and mental effort used in the creation and production of goods and services.

"Much of manufacturing in the United States centers on higher value-added activities that require highly-skilled workers ... Ironically, despite an ongoing recession and unemployment ... U.S. manufacturers face a significant talent shortage."[8]

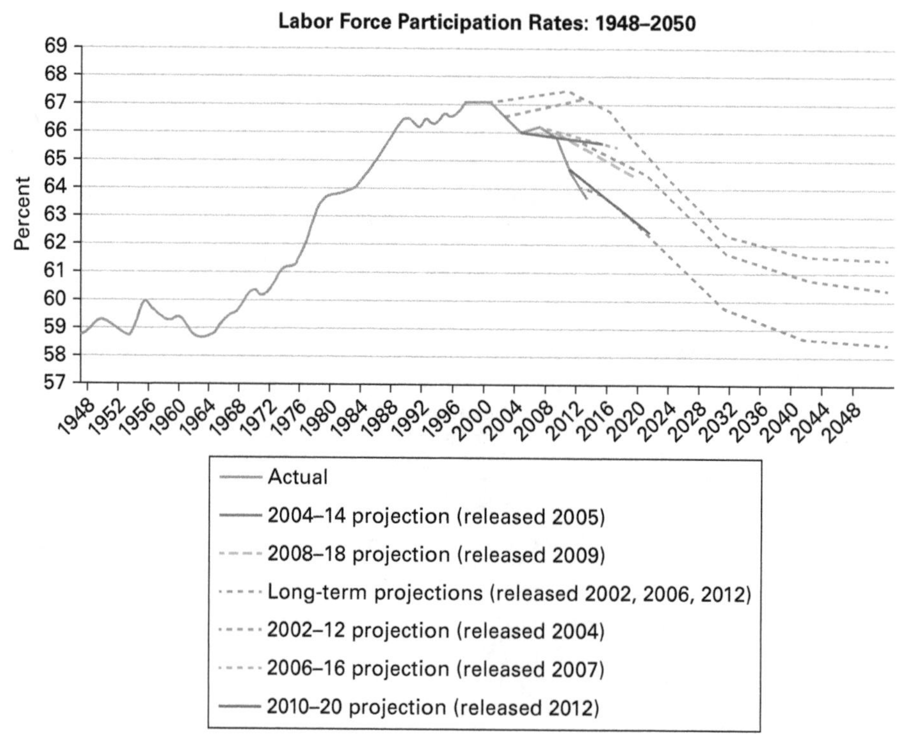

SOURCES: Actual LFP rate data from the Bureau of Labor Statistics/Haver Analytics; BLS projections data are from Table 3 in Toossi, 2002; Toossi, 2004; Toossi, 2005; Toossi, 2006; Toossi, 2007; Toossi, 2009; Toossi, 2012a; and from Toossi, 2012b.

Capital

To an economist, capital has several meanings - including the money raised to operate a business. But normally the term capital means investment in assets (machinery, plants and equipment, new technologies, factories and buildings) that can increase the productive capacity of a business to produce goods and services in the future. In this context, capital does not mean 'money' but instead the real assets that businesses purchase or hire, using money. Since money alone is not one of the basic inputs in the operational process capital itself does not constitute money.

Knowledge—Information

Rapid change and technological innovations place a premium on knowledge and information. Technology has revolutionized the means by which we communicate, access and store information, design and develop products, and market and distribute products.

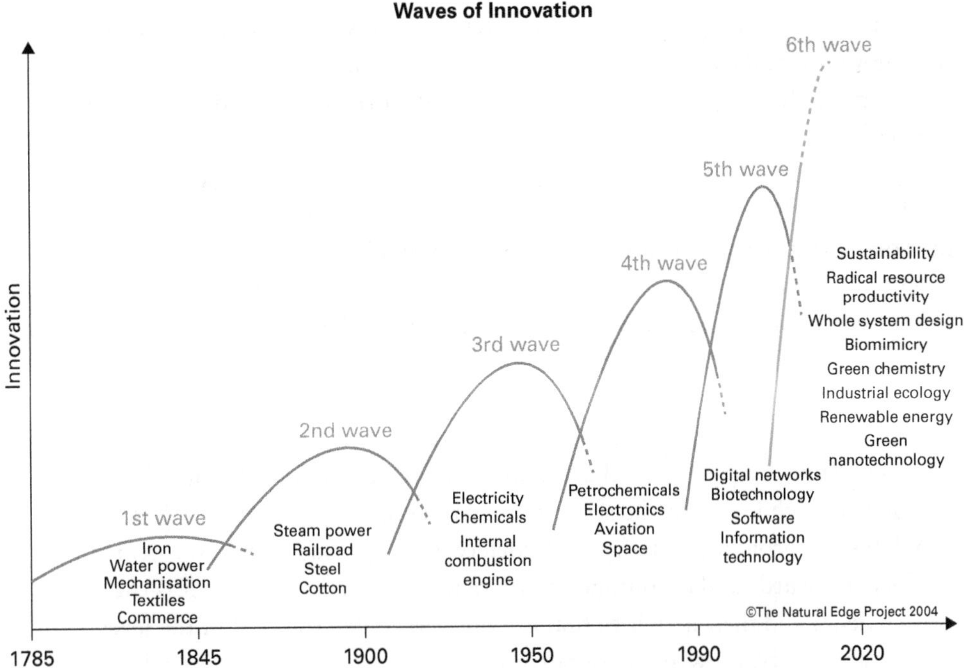

It is also essential to recognize the impact that social, educational, economic, and political forces alike will transform the future of all business endeavors. Changes in technology and networks will impact the acquisition of knowledge, shape human intelligence, reshape human interactions and communication, and transform existing business systems.

> "... harnessing information as a primary factor of production will mean recognizing and effectively planning for the four "V's" of data: volume, velocity, variety and veracity.
>
> - **Volume:** The sheer amount of data being digitized, maintained, secured, and then used. Knowing the organization's current needs and having a plan for its growth is fundamental.
> - **Velocity:** The speed at which data must be moved, stored, transformed, managed, analyzed or reported on in order to maintain competitiveness. This will vary by organization and application or usage.
> - **Variety:** The different types of data, from source (origin) to storage and usage, must be well understood because competitiveness requires access to the right types of data more than ever. From aged flat files to spatial and unstructured data, a plan must be in place.
> - **Veracity:** The truthfulness or quality of data can either lead to poor understanding and decisions that belie progress or deliver a powerful jolt of reality that fuels new insight and ideas. Ultimately, data quality may be the most important frontier."[9]

The 21st century economy will increasingly rely on knowledge and information to induce future innovation and expand future productivity. Managing our way into an unpredictable and rapidly changing future will rely more and more on knowledge as a critical factor of production.

Entrepreneurship

In the most general sense, an entrepreneur is any individual who assumes the financial risk required for the creation, development, and management of a new business venture. Successful entrepreneurs are able to acquire and organize the factors of production required to efficiently produce and deliver goods or services to the market/consumer.

> "Entrepreneurs occupy a central position in a market economy. For it's the entrepreneurs who serve as the spark plug in the economy's engine, activating and stimulating all economic activity ... A society is prosperous only to the degree to which it rewards and encourages entrepreneurial activity because it is the entrepreneurs and their activities that are the critical determinant of the level of success, prosperity, growth and opportunity in any economy. The most dynamic societies in the world are the ones that have the most entrepreneurs ..."[10]

THE ROLE OF THE ENTREPRENEUR

Entrepreneurs play a vital role in a market economy and are the spark that ignites all economic activity. The economic success within a nation is the result of encouraging and rewarding entrepreneurial initiative.

Entrepreneurs are individuals, who draw on personal initiative, carefully calculate ***risk***, and determine how to allocate and use scarce resources to develop new ideas, products, and services that solve problems, meet needs, and/or provide some value added benefit to various segments of the market. All risk that entrepreneurs assume is assessed against the backdrop of the potential ***profit*** that is likely to be generated as a result of their business activities.

The successful entrepreneur is not an uninformed risk-taker. Instead, the successful entrepreneur uses the information developed through experience, education, and meaningful research and analysis to determine the viability of a new venture. The decision to pursue a new business opportunity should always be based on a pragmatic assessment of the risk relative to the potential return.

In order to properly assess the risk or return of a new business venture well-informed entrepreneurs will develop a comprehensive business plan. A business plan, in its simplest form, will normally define the scope and purpose of a business, the associated risks, the strategies required to effectively compete, and the resources necessary to achieve the goals of the company.

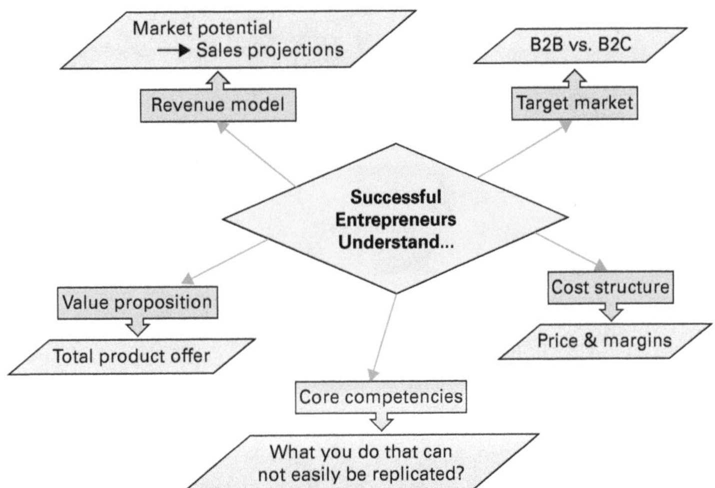

Entrepreneurship serves as a major contributing factor to a country's economic well-being, both in terms of economic growth as well as job creation. Entrepreneurs are responsible for a large share of the technological innovation in product development as well as advances in production processes. Entrepreneurship serves as a catalyst for a more robust economy with the development of new products and emerging technologies.

> "Why do entrepreneurship and innovation fuel economic growth? On the surface, the answer seems intuitive: entrepreneurs create businesses and new businesses create jobs, strengthen market competition and increase productivity. Here in the United States, entrepreneurism is part of our American identity and self-image. It's non-partisan, too; both sides of the political spectrum celebrate entrepreneurial small business as a fount of innovation and growth. Entrepreneurism is seen as a route to upward mobility—a way for average people to build wealth."[11]

THE BUSINESS ENVIRONMENT

All organizations operate in a dynamic and constantly changing world and are subject to powerful forces that are beyond their control. Managers must understand the implications of these forces in order to effectively assess the short- and long-term impact on their respective organizations. No business can survive without understanding how their interaction with the external environment will likely influence their plans, goals, and strategies.

In his book *"The Dance of Change: The Challenges to Sustaining Momentum in Learning Organizations"* Peter Senge states *"... if today's business organizations want to meet such external challenges of globalization, changing workforces, the evolving competition and new technologies, it is not enough to change strategies, structures and systems. Organizations, after all, are products of the ways that people think and interact. Sustaining any profound change process requires a fundamental shift in thinking and action. We need to think of sustaining change more biologically and less mechanistically. This requires patience as well as urgency. It requires a real sense of inquiry, a genuine curiosity about limiting forces."*

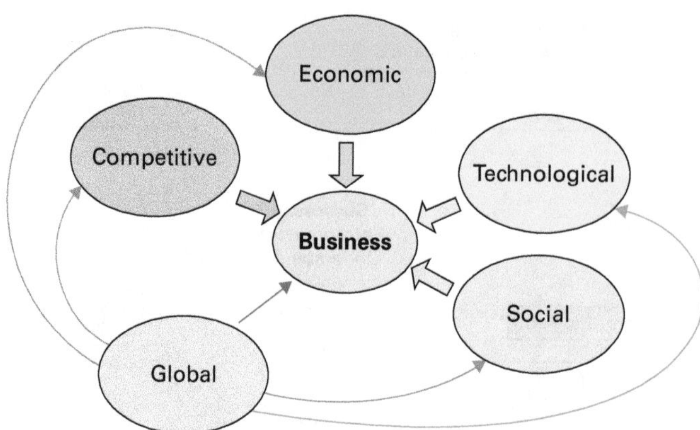

Economic Environment

The nature of the risk involved in creating a new business is in part determined by the economic system in which the business operates as well as the policies put into place by the government.

The role of the government in a market economy is a current point of discussion and debate among U. S. government officials and citizens within the private sector. Nonetheless, the primary role of the government in a market economy is to:

- Minimize taxes and regulations
- Allow for private ownership
- Pass laws that allow for the creation of enforceable contracts
- Establish a currency that is tradable in world markets
- Eliminate corruption whenever possible

"Economic freedom is the fundamental right of every human to control his or her own labor and property. In an economically free society, individuals are free to work, produce, consume, and invest in any way they please, with that freedom both protected by the state and unconstrained by the state. In economically free societies, governments allow labor, capital and goods to move freely, and refrain from coercion or constraint of liberty beyond the extent necessary to protect and maintain liberty itself. How do you measure economic freedom?"[12] The ten components of economic freedom are:

Business Freedom
Fiscal Freedom
Monetary Freedom
Financial Freedom
Freedom from Corruption

Trade Freedom
Government Spending
Investment Freedom
Property Rights
Labor Freedom

In addition, the state of the economy, whether in a period of economic contraction or expansion, will affect businesses and their capacity to sustain revenues and generate future profits. Businesses do not operate in a vacuum but instead are a part of a dynamic and unpredictable economy where politics, legal constraints, global trade, consumer confidence, and business cycles all impact the success of every company. It is imperative that every business owner or manager understand the economic forces affecting their business as part of their decision making process in order to remain competitive and viable.

Technological Environment

Technology is most often associated with computers, networks, telecommunications and other digital tools. However technological advancements in the last decade have rapidly improved the efficiencies of business and industry as well as create improved capabilities for transforming inputs (resources) into outputs (goods/services). Technological innovation continues to reduce production time and costs resulting in the greater supply of goods and services; often at significantly lower prices. Managers within organizations need to be aware and capable of integrating new technologies within their organizations as a means of creating a sustainable competitive advantage.

Technology affects the lifestyle and consumption patterns of consumers, stimulates the creation of new industries, radically changes existing industries, and creates entirely new products and markets.

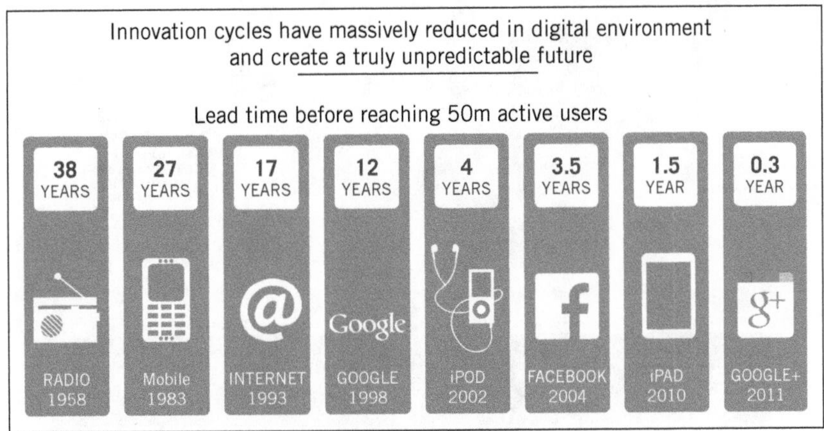

Organizations that are stagnant and fail to embrace new technologies are less likely to survive the turbulent and rapid change that has now become the norm. The following business activities are typically improved as a result of advancements in the technological environment:

- Information Management (availability, timeliness, relevance)
- Buying and selling of products (e-commerce, social networking)
- Inventory Control (Bar codes, QR codes, Just-in-Time, consumption patterns)
- Communications Systems (computers, modems, cellular phones, networks)
- Customer Relations (database programs, delivery, product development)
- Production Processes (Computer Integrated Manufacturing)
- Product Development and Design (3D Printers)

Social Environment

All business activities, and more specifically marketing management and human resource management, are influenced by the basic beliefs, values, norms, customs, and lifestyle patterns of people within society. With the growing diversity of the population in the United States, and throughout the world, it is incumbent that every organization understands the implications of the shifting demographics and social trends that will impact their employees, customers, and stakeholders.

The United States continues to be a country with an array of different cultures and a continuously changing demographic landscape. ***Demography*** represents an area of study that measures the changing characteristics of the population and includes such common factors as age, gender, income, physical condition, ethnicity, occupation, and marital status.

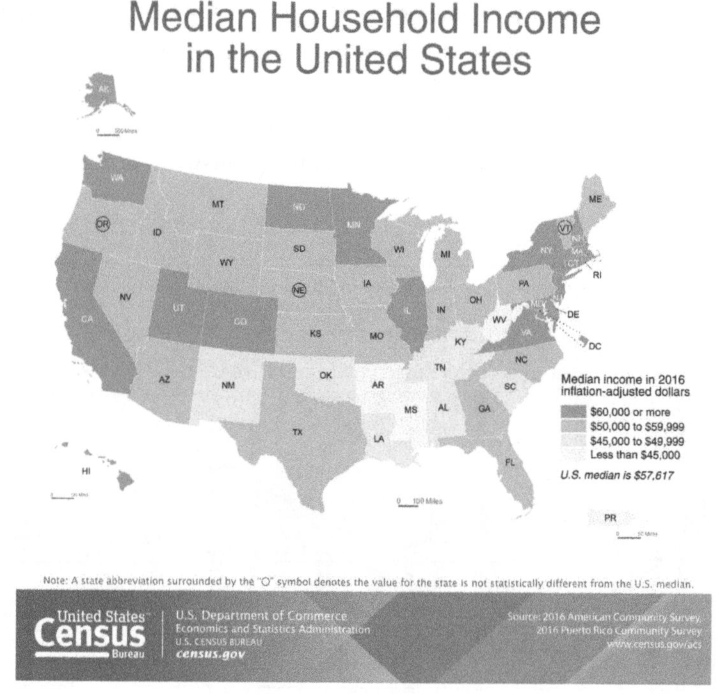

In a dynamic and globalized world, changes in societies, markets and organizations has become an important strategic concern. Societies around the world are becoming more diverse with one culture merging and blending with and into another. The resultant effect of the merging of societies is a loss of cultural identity and cultural norms making it even more difficult to predict consumer behavior and/or manage a diverse workforce. From a competitive point of view, it is essential for every organization to embrace a multicultural society and understand the complexity of a shifting social landscape.

> "The U.S. population will be considerably older and more racially and ethnically diverse by 2060, according to projections released today by the U.S. Census Bureau. These projections of the nation's population by age, sex, race and

Hispanic origin, which cover the 2012-2060 period, are the first set of population projections based on the 2010 Census.

"The next half century marks key points in continuing trends—the U.S. will become a plurality nation, where the non-Hispanic white population remains the largest single group, but no group is in the majority," said Acting Director Thomas L. Mesenbourg.

Furthermore, the population is projected to grow much more slowly over the next several decades, compared with the last set of projections released in 2008 and 2009. That is because the projected levels of births and net international migration are lower in the projections released today, reflecting more recent trends in fertility and international migration.

According to the projections, the population age 65 and older is expected to more than double between 2012 and 2060, from 43.1 million to 92.0 million. The older population would represent just over one in five U.S. residents by the end of the period, up from one in seven today."[13]

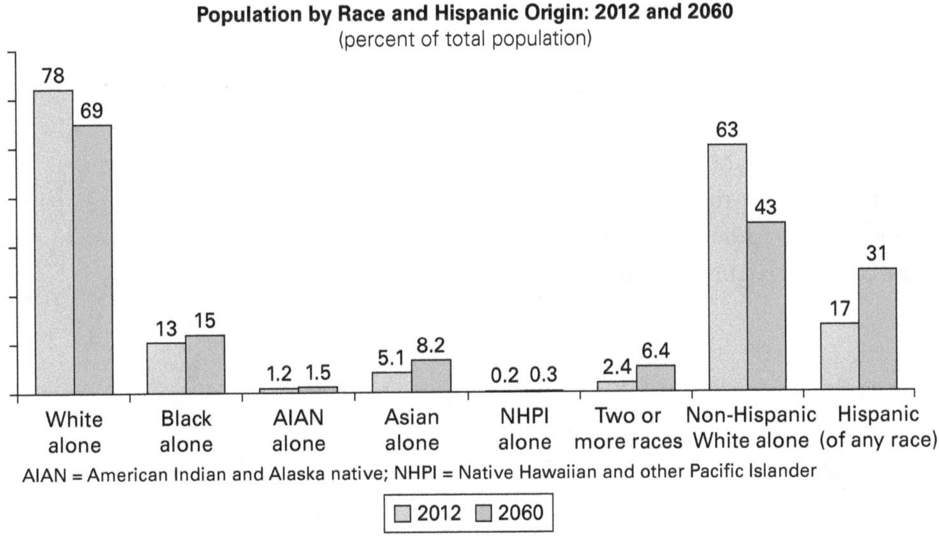

Competitive Environment

The competitive environment in business is somewhat analogous to a competitive environment in sports. When a sports team prepares for a game they typically scout the competition, develop a game plan, allocate resources, and carefully examine the conditions on the playing field. In most instances the home team typically has an advantage due to their intuitive understanding of the subtle nuances on the playing field. In order to effectively compete, the visiting team will spend considerable time studying the playing field in order to diminish the competitive advantage of the home team. In business, like sports, it is important to understand the nuances of the playing field and more importantly the external forces that will influence the success or failure of each company competing for market share and profit.

Regardless of the size and scope of a business, it is essential that management understand the nature of the competitive environment and the unique forces affecting the organization's ability to create and sustain a meaningful competitive advantage.

The four different classifications of competitive environments is based on the unique dynamics of each category and provides important insights regarding the potent variables that ultimately affect an organization's success within the marketplace.

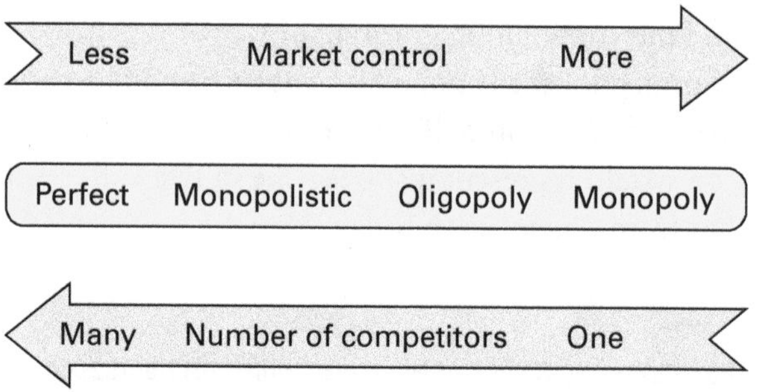

Perfect Competition is characterized by an ease of entry and exit into an industry. This creates a competitive environment wherein there are numerous competitors; each with an insignificant share of the market. Each firm is normally too small to affect a change in the price of products due to the fact that they sell homogeneous products that are "perfect" substitutes for each other. It is rare to find a pure example of perfect competition but there are some close approximations in agricultural markets.

Monopolistic Competition represents a market structure where a large number of companies sell similar products with some distinguishing features (e.g. packaging, quality, logo, brand name, etc.) to a large segment of diverse consumers. Each firm makes independent decisions about price and output, based on how it intends to position its product, the specific characteristics of its target market, and the associated costs of production. In monopolistic competition new entrants can easily enter into the market and successfully carve out a share of the revenue stream. The key to successfully competing in a monopolistic competitive environment is contingent upon an organization's ability to differentiate it product from a large number of similar products. The restaurant industry provides the best example of a monopolistic competitive environment.

Oligopolistic Competition consists of a small number of relatively large firms that comprise an industry where:

1. Companies produce similar products.
2. Relative size and extent of market control creates interdependence among firms within an industry.
3. The largest firms in the industry often influence prices.
4. Significant financial barriers restrict entry into the market.

The products produced by the firms in an oligopoly are often nearly identical and, therefore, the companies, which are competing for market share, are interdependent as a result of market forces.

A **Monopoly** is a market structure characterized by an absence of competition, or an absence of any competing products, where a single company or group owns all of the productive capacity for a given type of product or service. Monopolies were deemed illegal as a result of federal legislation with the passage of the Sherman Antitrust Act of 1890 and the Clayton Antitrust Act of 1914. The Clayton Act enhanced the Sherman Act and included further clarification on issues involving price discrimination, price fixing and unfair business practices.

Monopolies are formed under certain conditions, including:

1. Exclusive ownership or use of a scarce resource, such DeBeers Consolidated Mines who owns the majority of all worldwide diamond production.
2. Government grants a firm monopoly status, such as the United States Post Office.
3. Existence of patents or copyright giving a firm the exclusive right to sell a product or protect their intellectual property, such as Microsoft's 'Windows' brand.
4. When firms merge to give them a dominant position in a market.

Competing in the 21st Century?

For a business to compete in the future it will require more than technology or information about marketplace trends; those are readily available to any business. What is less common, but essential, is an understanding of marketplace trends and their competitive implications. Management's understanding of their organization's competitive environment will determine what strategies will be required and how they will need to be executed. Making quality products will not be enough to compete in the 21st century global market. To successfully compete, at a minimum, organizations must:

- Exceed the expectations of the customer.
- Provide speed in the delivery of goods and services.
- Embrace and understand the rapid change of product development, patterns of individual behavior, and innovation.
- Acknowledge the organization's moral and social responsibilities in the global marketplace.
- Restructure the organization to meet the needs of diverse employees.
- Engage in sustainable business practices as a means of preserving the natural environment.

Global Environment

The tectonic shift occurring in the global economic environment, from developed to developing economies, and the rapid growth in the number of consumers in emerging markets, are the global developments that businesses around the world must now consider in their strategic planning process. Combining these shifts in global economic activity with evolving technologies, greater access to information and markets, and expanding global labor markets, means that a myopic view of the world is equivalent to "sticking your head in the sand".

Globalization was the buzzword of the 1990s, and in the next century, it is evident that the effects of globalization will continue to reshape business in the 21st century and beyond. Essentially, globalization refers to the growth of trade and investment, accompanied by the growth in international competition, and the integration of economies around the world. The following chart illustrates the effects of GDP growth of countries around the globe.

OECD Interim Economic Outlook Real GDP Growth Projections

Year-on-year, %

	2016	2017		2018	
		Interim EO projections	Difference from November EO	Interim EO projections	Difference from November EO
World	3.0	3.3	0.0	3.6	0.0
United States	1.6	2.4	0.1	2.8	–0.2
Euro area	1.7	1.6	0.0	1.6	–0.1
Germany	1.8	1.8	0.1	1.7	0.0
France	1.1	1.4	0.1	1.4	–0.2
Italy	1.0	1.0	0.1	1.0	0.0
Japan	1.0	1.2	0.2	0.8	0.0
Canada	1.4	2.4	0.3	2.2	–0.1
United Kingdom	1.8	1.6	0.4	1.0	0.0
China	6.7	6.5	0.1	6.3	0.2
India[1]	7.0	7.3	–0.3	7.7	0.0
Brazil	–3.5	0.0	0.0	1.5	0.3
G20	3.1	3.5	–0.1	3.8	0.0
Rest of the world	2.3	2.7	–0.1	3.2	0.0

Note: Difference in percentage points based on rounded figures.
1. Fiscal years starting in April.

Global GDP growth is projected to pick up modestly to around 3½ per cent in 2018, from just under 3% in 2016, boosted by fiscal initiatives in the major economies. The forecast is broadly unchanged since November 2016. Confidence has improved, but consumption, investment, trade and productivity are far from strong, with growth slow by past norms and higher inequality.[14]

To ignore the new global realities is equivalent to eliminating new market opportunities with millions of potential consumers who are now possess both the purchasing power and connectivity in a digital world.

According to Punnett (2004) the globalization concept is based on a number of relatively simple premises:

- *Technological developments have increased the ease and speed of international communication and travel.*
- *Increased communication and travel have made the world smaller.*
- *A smaller world means that people are more aware of events outside of their home country, and are more likely to travel to other countries.*
- *Increased awareness and travel result in a better understanding of foreign opportunities.*
- *A better understanding of opportunities leads to increases in international trade and investment, and the number of businesses operating across national borders.*

BUSINESS: WHY YOU SHOULD CARE

Business, as an academic discipline, provides you with an understanding of your place in the world. Whether it is your intention to become a mechanic, computer programmer, engineer, marine biologist, artist, or entrepreneur, your ability to understand the basic principles of business will serve as a catalyst for your future success. Whatever your professional/career goals, you will likely work for a nonprofit or for-profit organization. Regardless of the nature of the enterprise, your understanding of basic business principles will provide you with a greater understanding of how your organization develops products and services that add value to the lives of your customers. Whether you are attempting to solicit donations from donors to save the ocean or sell a customer a new pair of shoes, you need to understand the forces at work that influence the exchange of money. This voluntary process of exchange is the very essence of business.

ENDNOTES

1. Scott Mautz, "Science Says This is the Key to Sustainable Competitive Advantage (and It's Easy to Blow Off)," Inc. 7 May 2017, 18 April 2017 <https://www.inc.com/scott-mautz/science-says-this-is-the-key-to-sustainable-competitive-advantage-and-its-easy-t.html?cid=search>

2. "The Concise Encyclopedia of Economics." Library of Economics and Liberty <http://www.econlib.org/library/Enc/bios/Smith.html>

3. Kimberly Amadeo, "What Is the American Dream Today," The Balance 17 Feb. 2017, 27 March 2017 <https://www.thebalance.com/what-is-the-american-dream-today-3306027>

4. United States. Library of Congress. Primary Documents in American History: Declaration of Independence. June 2013. Aug. 2012 <http://www.loc.gov/rr/program/bib/ourdocs/DeclarInd.html>

5. "United States: How's Life?" OECD 2015. 4 Jan 2017 <http://www.oecdbetterlifeindex.org/countries/united-states/>

6. Schumpeter, Joseph. The Theory of Economic Development. New Brunswick: Transaction Publishers, 1983.

7. Brun, Michael. "Factors of Production." Encyclopedia of Business and Finance, 2nd ed. 2007. *Encyclopedia.com.* 24 Oct. 2011 <http://www.encyclopedia.com>.

8. "Make: An American Manufacturing Movement." Council on Competitiveness. 2011. Compete: Council on Competitiveness. 1 Dec 2011 <http://www.compete.org/images/uploads/File/PDF%20Files/USMCI_Make.pdf>

9. Savitz, Eric. "The New Factors of Production and the Rise of Data-Driven Applications." Forbes 31 Oct. 2011. <http://www.forbes.com/sites/ciocentral/2011/10/31/the-new-factors-of-production-and-the-rise-of-data-driven-applications/2/>

10. Tracy, Brian. "The Role of the Entrepreneur." Entrepreneur 20 June 2005. <http://www.entrepreneur.com/article/78478>

11. Sappin, Ed. "7 Ways That Entrepreneurs Drive Economic Development." Entrepreneur 20 Oct 2016. <https://www.entrepreneur.com/article/283616>

12. Miller, Terry, and Holmes, Kim R. 2011 Index of Economic Freedom. The Heritage Foundation and The Wall Street Journal, 2011. < http://www.heritage.org/index>

13. United States. Department of Commerce. U.S. Census Bureau Projections Show a Slower Growing, Older, More Diverse Nation a Half Century from Now. Dec. 2012. 29 May 2013 <https://www.census.gov/newsroom/releases/archives/population/cb12-243.html>.

14. OECD, Interim Economic Outlook. 7 March 2017 <http://www.oecd.org/eco/economicoutlook.htm>

SOURCES

1. Fig. 1.3: Data from the Bureau of Labor Statistics/Haver Analytics.

2. Fig. 1.4: Source: http://www.thirdway.org/report/an-american-kodak-moment. Copyright © 2004 by The Natural Edge Project.

3. Fig. 1.7: Adapted from: https://www.tnooz.com/article/consumer-technology-development/.

4. Fig. 1.8: Source: https://www.census.gov/library/visualizations/2017/comm/income-map.html.

5. Fig. 1.9: Source: United States Census Bureau.

6. Fig. 1.11: Copyright © 2012 Depositphotos/Maxym.

7. Fig. 1.12: Source: http://www.oecd.org/eco/economicoutlook.htm. Copyright © 2018 by Organisation for Economic Co-operation and Development (OECD).

Chapter 2

Economics

The Creation of Wealth

PROLOGUE

An understanding of the complex nature of the economic system in which businesses operate is fundamental to understanding how the forces within the economy influence the choices made both by the consumer and businesses. Economic literacy gives people the tools for understanding their world and how to interpret economic events that will either directly or indirectly affect them. In addition, an understanding of economics allows young people to make more intelligent decisions as consumers and producers, comprehend the impact of government policies that influence and shape society, and lastly recognize how and why a free market contributes to a higher standard of living and quality of life.

> "At the heart of economics is a scientific mystery ... a scientific mystery as deep, fundamental and inspiring as that of the expanding universe or the forces that bind matter ... How is order produced from freedom of choice?"[1]
>
> —Vernon Smith, Nobel Laureate

Economics is the social science that studies how society chooses to employ scarce resources to produce goods and services and distribute them for consumption among various competing groups and individuals. There are two major areas of study in economics: Microeconomics and Macroeconomics. Both of these areas encompass numerous important topics, including but not limited to: the concept of supply and demand, market equilibrium, capitalism vs. socialism, unemployment, economic development, international trade and finance, fiscal and monetary policy, and the national debt. A fundamental understanding of how these topics play a central role in your life will provide you with the insight and knowledge necessary to make better choices of how to use your time, money and political voice.

> "A society that puts equality - in the sense of equality of outcome - ahead of freedom will end up with neither equality nor freedom. The use of force to achieve equality will destroy freedom. On the other hand, a society that puts freedom first will, as a happy byproduct, end up with both greater freedom and greater equality. Freedom means diversity but also mobility. It preserves the opportunity for today's less well off to become tomorrow's rich, and in the process, enables almost everyone, from top to bottom, to enjoy a richer and fuller life."[2]
> —Milton Friedman, Nobel Laureate

ECONOMICS: THE ROLE OF THE GOVERNMENT?

If you are so inclined to do so and listen to the voices in the media today you will hear pundits, politicians, and business leaders discussing what role the government should play in the economy? As you might expect different people will have different answers. Based on America's economic success it seems fair to conclude that the economy operates best when the government leaves businesses and individuals to succeed, or fail, based on merit, in an open, free, and competitive market. But exactly how "free" are businesses in America's free enterprise system? The answer is; "not completely." The abundance of government regulations influences virtually every aspect of business operations of both small and large organizations. Every year, the government produces more and more new regulations, often spelling out in explicit detail exactly what businesses can and cannot do. "For example, the number of final rules published each year is generally in the range of 2,500-4,500, according to the Office of the Federal Register." In America today the debate about when, and how extensively, the government should intervene in business affairs continues to be a source of much disagreement.

> "As governments, we stumble from crisis to crash program, lurching into the future without a plan, without hope, without vision."
> —Alvin Toffler, The Third Wave

There are three broad classifications of economic systems at work in the world today. These systems are unique from each other based on the nature and level of control exercised by the government. These three systems are classified as Command, Market, and Mixed Economies.

Command Economies

A command economy is one in which the coordination of economic activity is governed, not by a market mechanism, but by directives from within the government.

> In 1848 Karl Marx and Friedrich Engels authored The Communist Manifesto, which "set the stage for the inauguration of command economies. Marx and Engels argued that society is defined by the struggle between the working class,

> or proletariat, and the owners of capital, or bourgeoisie. Because the latter sought to exploit the former, the answer was to take away their power and replace it with that of the state."[3]

Command economies are planned and directed by agents of the government where resources are allocated to factories by the state through a central planning mechanism. This type of economic system is unresponsive to the needs of consumers and/or rapid changes in market conditions. The government largely decides what goods and services will be produced, who will have access to the products and services, and at what rate the economy will grow.

Instead of leading to greater efficiency command economies often produce too much of one thing and not enough of another. Central planning ignores information about consumers' needs and the demand patterns within the market. As a consequence of this isolation from market forces the government determines what to produce and sets the prices for products/goods in the market without any consideration of the laws of supply and demand. Without any ability to measure or control demand the rationing of goods in the market often becomes necessary. Countries like China, Belarus, Libya, Cuba, and North Korea are examples of centralized, "command economies" where the people within these countries have limited access to goods and services.

Market Economies

In a free-market system, decisions about what to produce and in what quantities are decentralized; or more simply stated, determined by the forces within the market. Consumers send signals to producers regarding what to produce and how much to produce through the market mechanism of price. Economists consider price from two distinct areas of study; Supply & Demand, and in theory, when quantity supplied equals quantity demanded, the most competitive price for a good can be determined.

> "The market economy is the social system of the division of labor under private ownership of the means of production. Everybody acts on his own behalf; but everybody's actions aim at the satisfaction of other people's needs as well as at the satisfaction of his own. Everybody in acting serves his fellow citizens. Everybody, on the other hand, is served by his fellow citizens. Everybody is both a means and an end in himself, an ultimate end for himself and a means to other people in their endeavors to attain their own ends."[4]

In a market economy, individuals can readily exchange goods and services at market-determined prices. Consumers will buy products when they believe the value derived is equal or better than the price required by the seller. When consumers believe that price equals value they are then ready to engage in the exchange process wherein they exchange money for goods and services.

KEY ECONOMIC THEORIES

Thomas Malthus: Economics—The "Dismal Science"

Often dubbed as the "prophet of gloom and doom", Thomas Malthus was best known for his pessimistic predictions regarding the future of humanity. His major contribution to economic thought came in his essay "The Principles of Population." In this essay Malthus predicted that the demand for food inevitably becomes much greater than its supply; that man, sooner or later ... [would] run up against himself; that the population of mankind will eventually outstrip man's ability to supply himself with the necessities of life." According to Malthus an increase in the population would lead to an oversupply of labor and cause a subsequent fall in the price paid for labor. At the same time, the growing demand for food and other provisions would cause an increase in the cost of survival as well as a lack of food and other resources.

Adam Smith: The Economic Theory of Wealth Creation

Known as the Father of Economics, Smith formulated the first modern theory of economics, called the Classical School, in 1776. Smith theorized that people who acted in their own self-interest produced goods and wealth that benefited all of society. Smith stated that "*... the combination of self-interest, private property, and competition among sellers in markets will lead producers as by an* ***invisible hand*** *to an end that they did not intend, namely, the well-being of society*".

The central thesis of Adam Smith's book, *The Wealth of Nations*, is that capital is best employed for the production and distribution of wealth under conditions of governmental noninterference, or laissez-faire, and free trade. In Smith's view, *"freedom was vital to the survival of any economy"*, especially the freedom to:

- *Own land*
- *Work hard (if they had the incentives for doing so)*
- *Seek economic reward*
- *Keep the profits from working the land or owning a business*

John Maynard Keynes: Keynesian Economics

John Maynard Keynes closely examined the problem of prolonged depression in his major work, *The General Theory of Employment, Interest, and Money* (1936). In Keynes' view, the inherent instability of the marketplace required government intervention. Keynes advocated that the best way to pull an economy out of a recession is for the government to borrow money and increase demand by infusing the economy with capital to spend. Since business investment inevitably fluctuated, it could not be depended upon to maintain a high level of employment and a steady flow of income throughout the economy. He asserted that a market-driven economy was "inherently unstable".

Keynes proposed that government spending must compensate for insufficient business investment in times of recession. Keynes came to believe that such a program would increase national purchasing power as well as foster employment in complementary industries.

ECONOMIC SYSTEMS

There is no "pure" economic system operating in the world today and most systems could be characterized as "command economies or market economies". Each economic system is differentiated based upon the amount of government intervention and control within the market. Whether a command economy or market economy the role of the government ultimately determines how each of the following questions will be answered:

- What is produced?
- What amount is produced?
- What is the method of output distribution?
- What is the rate of economic growth?

Capitalism

In a capitalist system, individuals and firms have the right to own and use wealth to earn income and to sell and purchase labor for wages with little or no government control. Capitalism allows production and distribution capacities to be privately owned and operated for profit. Individual businesses decide what to produce, how much to pay employees, how much to charge for their goods and services, and whether to produce certain products or import those goods.

There are four *"Basic Rights"* guaranteed to the citizenry within a capitalistic, free market system. These rights are:

- *Right to Private Property*—This grants each individual the right to own, use, buy, sell, and bequeath property.
- *Right to Profit after Taxes*—This guarantees that the investor/owner in a business has the right to all profits, after taxes, earned by the business.
- *Right to Freedom of Choice*—Citizens are free to choose their occupation, what they purchase, education, and how they invest their money.
- *Right to Freedom of (Fair) Competition*–The public, not the government, sets the rules regarding the nature of competitive markets.

"You cannot help the poor by destroying the rich.
You cannot lift the wage earner up by pulling the wage payer down.
You cannot further the brotherhood of man by inciting class hatred.
You cannot build character and courage by taking away
people's initiative and independence.
You cannot help people permanently by doing for them, what they
could and should do for themselves."

—William J. H. Boetcker

Socialism

Socialism is founded on the basic belief that economic inequality is bad for society and that the government's role is to reduce inequality by creating programs that benefit the poor. Such programs include: free public education, free or subsidized health care, social security, and higher taxes on the rich.

Under a socialist economic system, individuals own their individual human capital and the government owns most other, non-human resources, and most of the major factors of production are owned by the state. Land, factories, and major machinery are publicly owned. This distribution of profit is designed to create equality and reduce the disparity in wealth among the citizenry within the country. There are however opportunities for entrepreneurial ventures and the pursuit of profit.

> "In Kurt Vonnegut's 1961 short story 'Harrison Bergeron,' published in the volume *Welcome to the Monkey House*, Vonnegut writes 'the government forced each individual to wear 'handicaps' to offset any advantage they had, so that everyone could be truly and fully equal.'
>
> We can see as well that this vision of equality is not actually fair. It is not fair to the beautiful to force them to wear ugly masks. It is not fair to the productive to deprive them of what they have produced, merely to make them equal to others who have produced less. As Vonnegut's story shows, putting social limits on the success that people are allowed to achieve with their own talents and abilities makes for an ugly society, harshly restrictive on its best lights who have the most actually to give to the benefit of all.
>
> Finally, this vision of equality as a social goal, with equal incomes and wealth for all, is severely counterproductive economically, and so makes for a poor society as well. Pursuing such a vision would require very high marginal tax rates on anyone with above average production, income and wealth, which experience as well as theory shows us leads to less production."[5]

Communism

In a communist system all economic decisions are made by the state and all of the factors of production are owned or controlled by the state/government. Karl Marx, an economist and philosopher, believed that capitalism was destructive and caused the "factory owners" to exploit laborers for profit. Such actions, according to Marx, would gradually depress wages, increase unemployment, and serve to hasten a prolonged period of economic decline. Marx believed, as expressed in his book, *Critique of the Gotha Program,* that a society in which the people, without regard to class, owned all of the nation's resources and contributed "according to his ability, to each according to his needs".

Marx's theories about society, economics and politics, collectively known as Marxism, asserted that societies progress through class struggles: conflicts between the ownership class that controls production and a *"proletariat"* that serves as the primary source of labor for production. He called capitalism the *"dictatorship of the bourgeoisie,"* believing that such a system was run by the wealthy for their own benefit.

A communist economic system is based on the principle of an even distribution of ownership of property among every member of the population. The government takes on a central planning role both directing the production and consumption of goods and services. Because of the immense power of the state, small businesses are almost nonexistent resulting in a shortage of the basic goods and services necessary to sustain a modest standard of living for a majority of the population. Since there is no competition workers are paid the same and as a consequence there is an absence of innovation and productivity.

Mixed Economies

A mixed economy is an economic system that includes both private and government control reflecting characteristics of both capitalism and socialism. The United States, like most advanced democracies in the world today, can most accurately be classified as a mixed economy. This usually means that individuals exercise a great deal of control over their economic lives and make most economic decisions in the marketplace.

Mixed economies exhibit many of the same characteristics of a command economy in strategic areas including but not limited to: welfare, defense, energy production, healthcare, international trade, and transportation. All of these programs are funded by the federal government in an attempt to safeguard its people and its markets. The government's role in these areas depends upon the priorities of the citizens. It is obvious that in a mixed economy the government plays a more significant role in the oversight of market activity and the allocation and distribution of resources. In theory, a mixed economy has most of the benefits of wealth creation that free markets allow plus the benefits of government oversight and social programs.

COMPETITIVE ENVIRONMENTS WITHIN FREE MARKETS

There are four different classifications of competitive environments. Each is unique and provides important insights regarding the dynamic variables that ultimately affect an organization's success within the marketplace. The four classifications are:

TYPE OF COMPETITION	NUMBER OF COMPETING FIRMS	EXAMPLES
Perfect	Many	Agriculture
Monopolistic	Many	Retail
Oligopolistic	Few	Utilities
Monopoly	One	Varied

FREE MARKETS: HOW PRICES ARE DETERMINED

Microeconomics: Supply & Demand

Microeconomics involves the study of individual behavior (individuals, firms and government agencies that compose the larger economy) and their willingness to purchase (demand) goods and produce (supply) goods at a specific time for a specific price. The most basic laws in economics are the law of supply and the law of demand. In reality almost every economic occurrence is the result of the interaction of these two laws.

> "Market exchange works because people value things differently. The planned economy rests on the unlikely assumption that everyone can agree what to produce, and how. The price system reflects the imbalance of demand and supply, and automatically steers resources to where they are most needed - without the need for planners to discover, understand, and correct the imbalance. Competition is not a textbook 'given' but a dynamic process; in which people constantly search to discover the cheapest mix of resources to produce the most desired outputs." —F. A. Hayek

The Economic Concept (Law) of Supply

The law of supply is a fundamental economic theory that refers to the quantity of goods a producer is willing and able to sell at a specific price. A firm's profitability depends upon its ability to price goods equal to the market price; the price at which demand equals supply. The law of supply states that all other factors remaining constant (*ceteris paribus*) the higher the price of a product, the greater the quantity supplied. Generally speaking, suppliers' costs affect the quantity of products they are willing to offer in the market during any period of time. There are several other factors that result in a shift in the supply curve and can include changes in the price of substitute and/or complementary goods, the number of suppliers in the market, operational costs, and changes in technology.

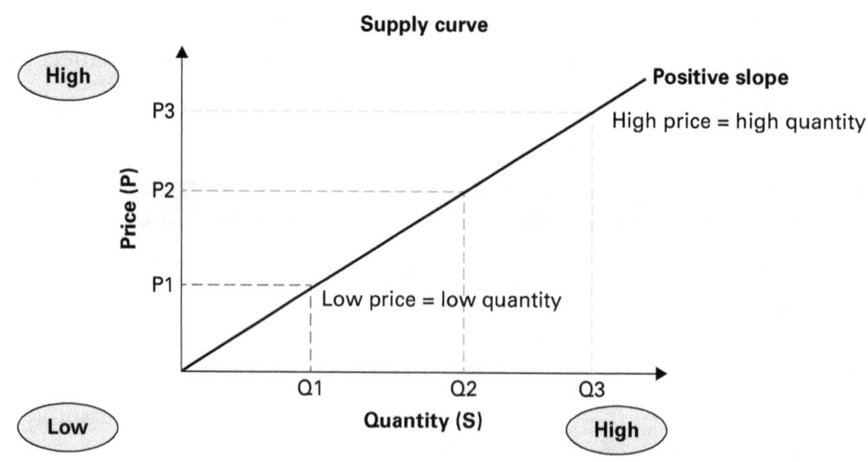

The supply curve represents a ***positive slope*** illustrating the positive relationship of price and quantity; the quantity of products supplied increases as the price increases. Higher prices mean that producers of goods and services can achieve greater profits resulting in increased capital and capacity allowing producers to expand their productive capacity and supply of products. This increased supply will ultimately satisfy the existing demand such that any additional production must be met with new demand in order for the price increases to be sustained.

The Concept (Law) of Demand

When economists refer to demand they are referring to changes in the quantity of a good or service that is demanded at successively different prices. The quantity of a good demanded in a given time period increases as its price decreases. This is based on the assumption that nothing else changes (*ceteris paribus*). The demand slope illustrates the relationship between different prices and quantities demanded at each price point. Most demand curves are downsloping or are referred to, as a ***negative slope,*** meaning that as the price decreases the quantity consumers demand will increase.

Within every market there are a group of products that maintain a relatively fixed demand pattern. Some products remain in constant demand regardless of changes in the price. Demand for these goods is called ***inelastic*** indicating that changes in the price of a particular product will not change or affect the level of demand. If the demand for a good is sensitive to price changes, it is called ***elastic,*** and is an important factor when establishing a pricing strategy for a new product in the market. A number of factors influence the ***price elasticity of demand*** of a particular good and include: its importance, the availability of substitutes, and the percentage of our income that it costs us to purchase.

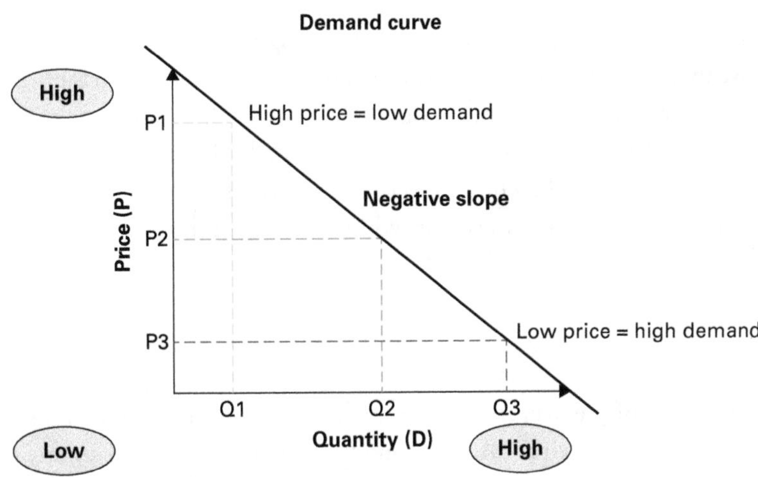

Equilibrium (Market) Price

Market equilibrium is reflected in the price at which the quantity demanded and the quantity supplied is equal. It is the prevailing market price at which a good or service can be bought. How much an individual consumer is willing to pay at a specific point in time for certain goods and services, demand, is based on the total of all individual consumer's demand for goods and services. Conversely, the amount of goods and services each producer is willing to produce, supply, is based on the price of a product or service at a specific point in time and represents the total of all individual producers' willingness to supply for goods and services. Therefore the Equilibrium Price represents the point in time where Supply equals Demand and is determined by market forces within the economy and the interaction between the consumer and producer.

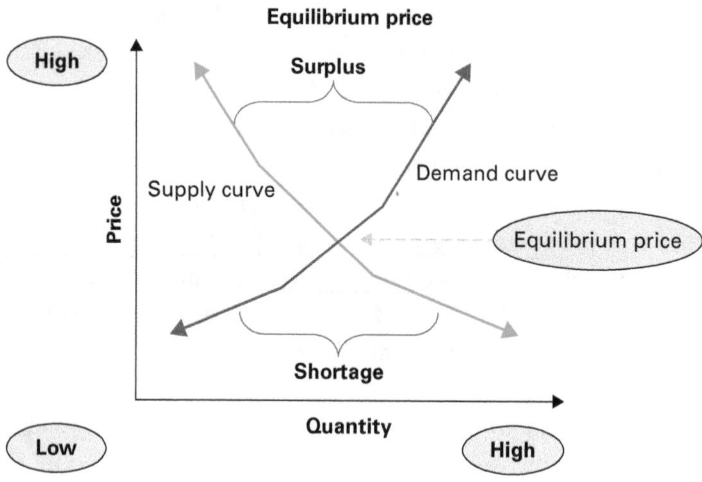

THE AMERICAN ECONOMY

"Despite facing challenges at the domestic level along with a rapidly transforming global landscape, the U.S economy is still the largest and most important in the world. The U.S. economy represents about 20% of total global output, and is still larger than that of China. Moreover, according to the IMF, the U.S. has the sixth highest per capita GDP (PPP). The U.S. economy features a highly-developed and technologically-advanced services sector, which accounts for about 80% of its output."[6]

Macroeconomics

This involves the study of the overall operation of an economy and the various components that affect the standard of living. Macroeconomics focuses on the economy as a whole, while in microeconomics the focus is on the factors that affect the decisions made by firms and individuals.

Macroeconomics examines broad-based economic phenomena such as changes in unemployment, national debt, gross domestic product, and inflation. The importance of macroeconomics is illustrated in the following Bureau of Labor statistics:

Consumer Price Index
May 12, 2017
On a seasonally adjusted basis, the Consumer Price Index for All Urban Consumers increased 0.2 percent in April after falling 0.3 percent in March. The index for all items apart from food and energy rose 0.1 percent in April after declining 0.1 percent in March.

Employment Cost Index
April 28, 2017
Compensation costs increased 0.8 percent for civilian workers, seasonally adjusted, from December 2016 to March 2017. Over the year, compensation rose 2.4 percent, wages and salaries are up 2.5 percent, and benefits rose 2.2 percent.

Employment Situation
May 05, 2017
Total nonfarm payroll employment increased by 211,000 in April, and the unemployment rate was little changed at 4.4 percent. Job gains occurred in leisure and hospitality, healthcare and social assistance, financial activities, and mining.

Producer Price Index
May 11, 2017
The Producer Price Index for final demand advanced 0.5 percent in April. Final demand prices edged down 0.1 percent in March and climbed 0.3 percent in February. In April, the final demand services index increased 0.4 percent, and prices for final demand goods rose 0.5 percent.

Productivity and Costs
May 04, 2017
Productivity decreased 0.6 percent in the nonfarm business sector in the first quarter of 2017; unit labor costs increased 3.0 percent (seasonally adjusted annual rates). In manufacturing, productivity increased 0.4 percent and unit labor costs increased 2.1 percent.

Real Earnings
May 12, 2017
Real average hourly earnings increased 0.1 percent in April, seasonally adjusted. Average hourly earnings increased 0.3 percent, and CPI-U increased 0.2 percent. Real average weekly earnings increased 0.4 percent over the month.

U.S. Import and Export Price Indexes
May 10, 2017
The price index for U.S. imports advanced 0.5 percent in April, after ticking up 0.1 percent the previous month. Higher fuel prices and nonfuel prices both contributed to the increase in April. U.S. export prices rose 0.2 percent in April following a 0.1-percent advance in March.[7]

MAJOR ECONOMIC INDICATORS

Gross Domestic Product (GDP)

The gross domestic product is the most important economic indicator and represents the broadest measure of economic activity. The GDP signals the direction of overall aggregate economic activity within the country and directly impacts all other economic indicators. GDP represents the sum of all goods and services produced within a nation's boundaries in a given year. The GDP can increase for two distinct reasons:

- It can increase because more goods and services are actually being produced. (Real GDP)
- It can increase because prices of goods and services have risen.

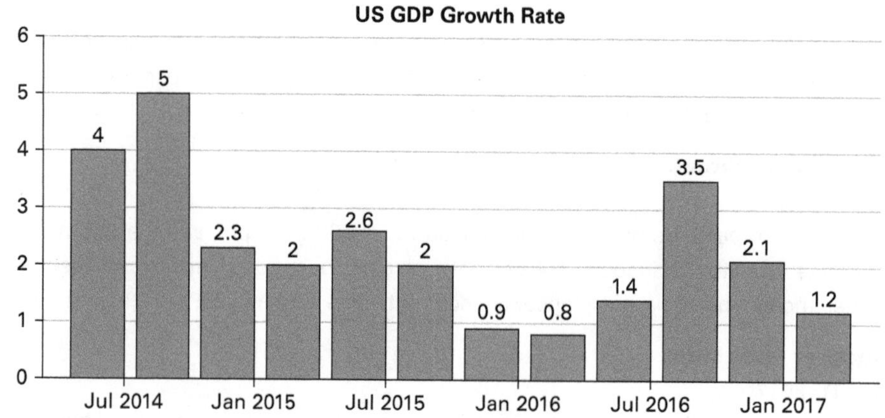

Inflation

Inflation is the result of rising prices caused by a combination of excess consumer demand and increases in the costs of raw materials, human resources, and other factors of production. The rate of inflation reflects the rate at which the price for goods and services is rising, and, subsequently, purchasing power is declining.

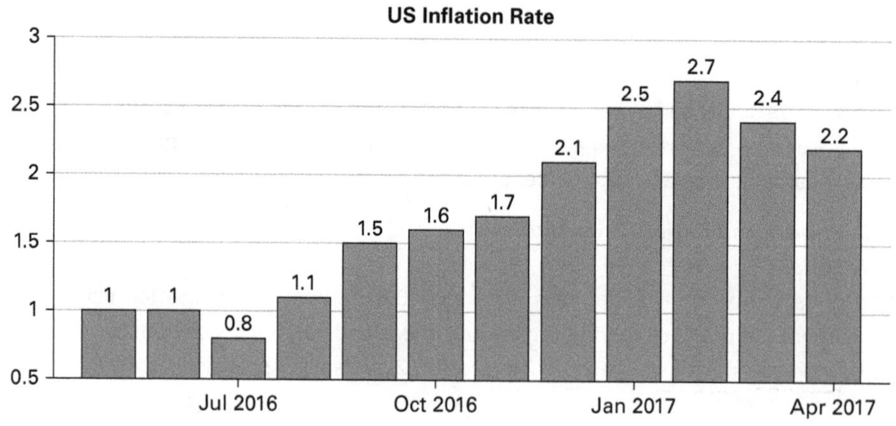

***Cost-push inflation** develops as a result of increasing costs of production factors, which in turn decrease the amount of total production in the economy. Because there are fewer goods being produced, supply diminishes, and demand for these goods remains consistent, the prices of finished goods increase (inflation).*

***Demand pull inflation** occurs when total demand for goods and services exceeds the total available supply. This type of inflation is often monetary in origin due to the loosening of the money supply by the Federal Reserve causing demand to grow faster than the ability of the economy to supply goods and services. The phrase that is often used is that there is "too much money chasing too few goods".*

Deflation

This situation is characterized by falling prices as a result of overproduction of goods that consumers cannot afford to buy. A persistent decline in prices can create a whole series of negative repercussions including, but not limited to, declining profits, business failure, shrinking employment and incomes, and increasing defaults on loans by companies and individuals.

Consumer Price Index (CPI)

The most common measure of inflation is the Consumer Price Index. The CPI measures the monthly average change in the price of goods and services. The federal Bureau of Labor Statistics (BLS) calculates the CPI monthly based on the prices of a "market basket" of goods most commonly purchased by the average urban American family.

"The CPI represents all goods and services purchased for consumption by the reference population (U or W) BLS has classified all expenditure items into more than 200 categories, arranged into eight major groups. Major groups and examples of categories in each are as follows:

- Food & Beverages (breakfast cereal, milk, coffee, chicken, wine, full-service meals, snacks);
- Housing (rent of primary residence, owners' equivalent rent, fuel oil, bedroom furniture);
- Apparel (men's shirts and sweaters, women's dresses, jewelry)
- Transportation (new vehicles, airline fares, gasoline, motor vehicle insurance);
- Medical Care (prescription drugs and medical supplies, physicians' services, eyeglasses and eye care, hospital services);
- Recreation (televisions, toys, pets and pet products, sports equipment, admissions);
- Education & Communication (college tuition, postage, telephone services, computer software and accessories);
- Other Goods & Services (tobacco and smoking products, haircuts and other personal services, funeral expenses).

Also included within these major groups are various government-charged user fees, such as water and sewerage charges, auto registration fees, and vehicle tolls. In addition, the CPI includes taxes (such as sales and excise taxes) that are directly associated with the prices of specific goods and services. However, the CPI excludes taxes (such as income and Social Security taxes) not directly associated with the purchase of consumer goods and services."[8]

Producer Price Index (PPI)

The Producer Price Index measures the average price change over time in the selling prices received by domestic producers of goods and services. It measures the prices for goods at the wholesale level.

Unemployment

The national unemployment rate is computed solely from the Current Population Survey (CPS) of about 60,000 households conducted by the Census Bureau. Residents of selected households are interviewed about their work experience. From these responses, the Bureau of Labor Statistics then estimates the size of the labor force and the number of people who are jobless. This includes the number of citizens, 16 years old or older, who are unemployed and are attempting to find a job within the prior four-week period.

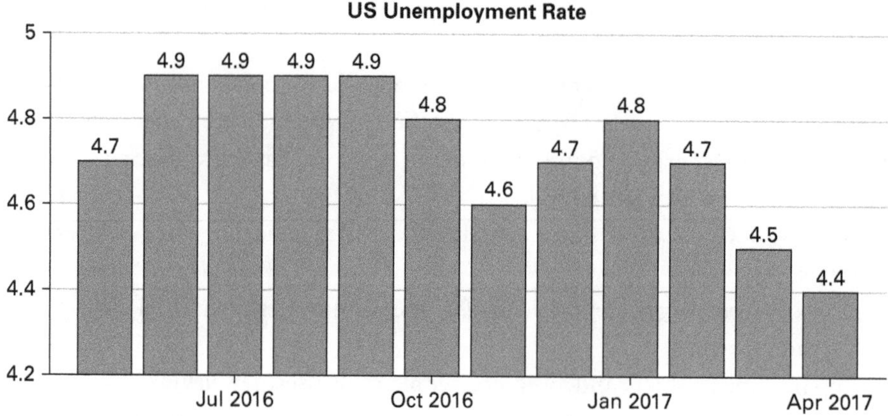

Types of Unemployment

Frictional Unemployment

This is a temporary condition wherein an individual is between jobs or transitioning into the labor market (college graduate) and actively seeking employment.

Structural Unemployment

A condition resulting from individuals possessing skills that are no longer in demand. This represents the most difficult form of unemployment to overcome and requires individuals with outdated skills to seek new training/education.

#9

Cyclical Unemployment

This occurs when the number of workers demanded falls short of the number of persons supplied. It is caused by changes in the economy (expansion vs. contraction) that result in layoffs and the displacement of skilled workers.

Seasonal Unemployment

Unemployment due to seasonal changes (summer versus winter) or changes in the labor supply (students seeking summer employment).

BUSINESS CYCLES

Economic growth within the economy is not a static or even stable process. Instead, the economy goes through changes, which are often classified as "boom or bust". Historically, from 1947 until 2011 the United States' average quarterly GDP Growth was 3.28 percent reaching an historical high of 17.20 percent in March of 1950 and a record low of –10.40 percent in March of 1958.[9]

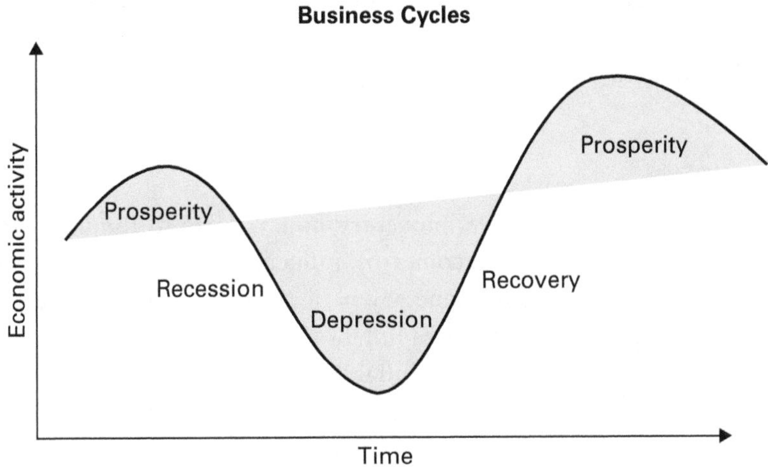

During a period of economic **prosperity** unemployment remains low, strong consumer confidence contributes to expanding consumer purchases, and business expansion increases. A **recession** is a cyclical contraction within the economy that lasts for six months or longer. Businesses experience a slowdown in production, postpone expansion plans, reduce inventories, and often reduce the size of their workforce. A **depression**, in theory, is a continued downward spiral of the economy over an extended period of time. During the "Great Depression" of 1929, the unemployment rate was 25% and total U.S. economic output fell from $103 billion to $55 billion. In a **recovery** the economy is characterized by declining unemployment, increasing business activity, and increasing consumer demand.

GOVERNMENT POLICY: REGULATING THE ECONOMY

The role of government in the economy extends beyond its basic role as a regulator of specific industries. The government also oversees the rate of growth of economic activity, seeks to maintain optimal levels of employment, and, to the extent to which it can, preserve stable prices. The federal government has two main tools for achieving these objectives: ***fiscal policy***, through which it determines the appropriate level of taxes and spending; and ***monetary policy***, through which it manages the supply of money. The Federal Reserve, created in 1913, is the independent U.S. central bank, and manages the money supply and use of credit (monetary policy), while the president and Congress adjust federal spending and taxes (fiscal policy).

> "Private enterprise has no press agent. Government does. Every government agency will inform you that anything bad that happens is the result of forces outside its control. But anything good that happens—who do you suppose produced that? If it weren't so tragic, it would be amusing to read the annual reports of the Federal Reserve System from its inception. Every year of prosperity, the Federal Reserve report says, 'Thanks to the wise and farsighted policy of the Federal Reserve, the United States had a good year.' Every year of recession or depression, the Federal Reserve report reads, Despite the best efforts of the Federal Reserve System, events beyond our control...."[10] —Milton Friedman "Economic Myths and Public Opinion"

Monetary Policy

Administered by the Federal Reserve, monetary policy refers to the use of money and credit controls to alter economic outcomes by influencing the availability and cost of money. The underlying objective of monetary policy is to influence the performance of the economy as reflected in such factors as inflation, economic output, and employment. The Federal Reserve, in fact, can't control inflation or influence productivity and employment directly; instead, it affects them indirectly, mainly by raising or lowering short-term interest rates.

Monetary Policy is established by the Federal Open Market Committee (FOMC) which consists of twelve members—the seven members of the Board of Governors of the Federal Reserve System; the president of the Federal Reserve Bank of New York; and four of the remaining eleven Reserve Bank presidents, who serve one-year terms on a rotating basis. The FOMC meets eight times per year to set key interest rates, such as the the federal funds rate (prime rate) and discount rate, as well as decide whether to increase or decrease the money supply, which the Fed does by buying and selling government securities (Treasury Notes, Treasury Bills, Treasury Bonds, U.S. Savings Bonds, etc.)

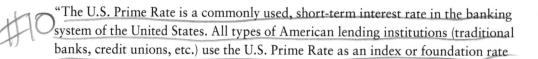

> "The U.S. Prime Rate is a commonly used, short-term interest rate in the banking system of the United States. All types of American lending institutions (traditional banks, credit unions, etc.) use the U.S. Prime Rate as an index or foundation rate

for pricing various short-term loan products. A consistent U.S. Prime Rate also makes it easier and more efficient for individuals and businesses to compare similar loan products offered by competing banks.

Fiscal Policy

This involves the government's actions designed to maintain economic stability by increasing or decreasing revenues (taxes) and expenditures (entitlements). Often referred to as government "tax and spend" policy, fiscal policy can be either expansionary or contractionary. It is expansionary when taxation is reduced or public spending is increased with the aim of stimulating total spending in the economy. Expansionary policy might occur when the government feels the economy is not growing fast enough or unemployment is too high. Contractionary policies are designed to reduce government spending and increase tax revenues as a means of slowing down economic activity by taking money out of the "purse" of the consumer.

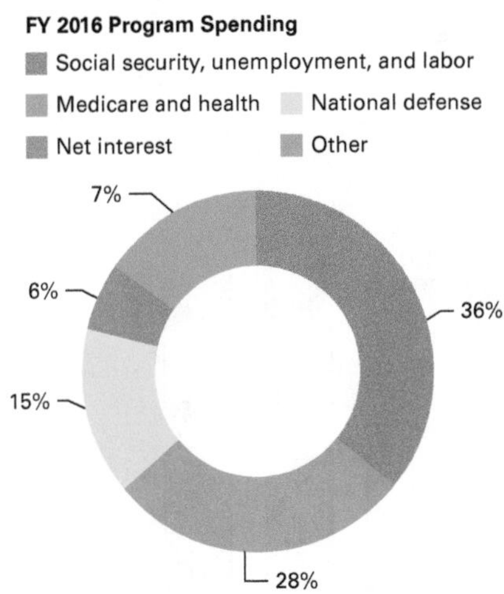

Spending Overview

- Spending on Social Security, unemployment, and labor in 2016 was about 37% of all outlays that year. This was greater than average when compared to budgets from other years. *(Average proportion = 35%)*
- Medicare and general health spending was about 28% of all outlays that year. This was one of the highest proportions spent when compared to budgets from other years. *(Average proportion = 14%)*
- Spending on national defense was about 15% of all outlays that year. This was less than average when compared to budgets from other years. *(Average proportion = 22%)*
- As for spending on net interest, the government dedicated about 6% of all its outlays that year to paying down its accumulated debt. This was less than average when compared to budgets from other years. *(Average proportion = 8%)*
- All other programs (agriculture, energy, commerce and housing credit, community and regional development, etc.) made up approximately 14% of national spending in 2016.

Federal Deficit

A deficit is created when the government spends more money than it receives from the taxes it collects. When this happens the government must borrow money to compensate for the deficit. The effects of the current deficit include:

- *A decline in private investment.*
- *An increase in foreign debt.*
- *An increase in inflation.*
- *Higher taxes.*
- *An expanding National Debt.*

The National Debt

The national debt represents the sum total of the U.S. Government's financial obligations. To access up-to-the minute debt information, use the following web site: *http://www.brillig.com/debt_clock/*

> "Government debt and budget deficits are both set to spiral higher in the coming three decades if current patterns hold, according to new projections released Thursday by the Congressional Budget Office.The report warns that the rising debt and deficits risk another crisis. 'The prospect of such large and growing debt poses substantial risks for the nation and presents policymakers with significant challenges,' it said.
>
> Due largely to increases in Medicare and Social Security costs, the federal debt will reach 150 percent of gross domestic product in 2047, the CBO report said.
>
> The total current debt held by the public of $14.3 trillion is 77 percent of GDP. The current total debt level of $18.8 trillion is about 101 percent of GDP (the CBO computes debt to GDP based on public debt). The debt-to-GDP ratio would rise to 89 percent in 2027, according to current projections."[11]

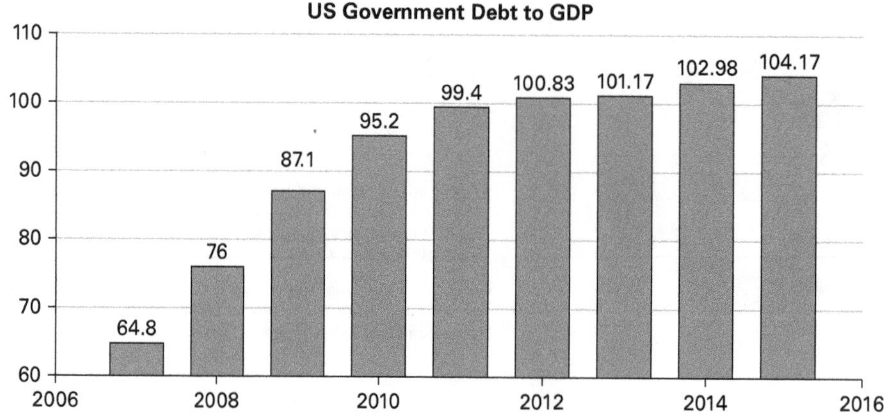

ECONOMICS: HOW IT WILL AFFECT YOUR LIFE

As a college student your understanding of basic economics may not be a priority or have any obvious relevance in your daily life. Paying rent, finding a job, buying text-books, or completing class assignments are of much greater importance to you as you attempt to get through each day. However, the condition of the economy, and your understanding of changes in the economy, has a direct impact on your life. As you know economics is the study of choices and why and how we make them. The pursuit of self-interest, the creation of a new business, and your desire to improve your life are all impacted by the state of the economy. In order to make better decisions, especially those decisions involving your future, your understanding of economics will be essential as you attempt to create wealth and a achieve a higher standard of living.

ENDNOTES

1. Smith, Vernon. Papers in Experimental Economics. New York: Cambridge University Press, 1991.
2. Friedman, Milton and Rose Friedman, Free to Choose: A Personal Statement. Florida: Harcourt, 1980.
3. Maxfield, John. "What is a Command Economy?" Motley Fool 31 Aug 2015. 17 May 2017 <https://www.fool.com/investing/general/2015/08/31/what-is-a-command-economy.aspx>
4. Mises, Ludwig von, Human Action: A Treatise on Economics, 4th Revised. Irvington-on-Hudson, New York; The Foundation for Economic Education, 1996. <http://www.econlib.org/library/Mises/HmA/msHmA.html.>
5. Ferrara, Peter. "Fallacies of Economic Equality that Promote Poverty." Forbes 7 Jul 2011. 11 Jun 2013 <http://www.forbes.com/sites/peterferrara/2011/07/07/fallacies-of-economic-equality-that-promote-poverty/>
6. "U.S. Economic Outlook." Focus Economics. 2 May 2017 <http://www.focus-economics.com/countries/united-states>
7. United States. Bureau of Labor Statistics. Major Economic Indicators. May 2017. <https://www.bls.gov/bls/newsrels.htm#major>
8. United States. Bureau of Labor Statistics. Consumer Price Index. <http://www.bls.gov/cpi/>
9. United States. Bureau of Economic Analysis. United States GDP Growth Rate. <http://www.tradingeconomics.com/united-states/gdp-growth>
10. From The Collected Works of Milton Friedman, compiled and edited by Robert Leeson and Charles G. Palm."Economic Myths and Public Opinion" by Milton Friedman The Alternative: An American Spectator 9, no. 4, January 1976, pp. 5–9 © The American Spectator Reprinted in: Milton Friedman, Bright Promises, Dismal Performance: An Economist's Protest, pp. 60–75. New York: Harcourt Brace Jovanovich, 1983. Originally published in a slightly different version as "Myth and Reality in Contemporary Public Opinion," Widening Horizons (Rockford College) 11 (March 1975): 1–6. <http://miltonfriedman.hoover.org/friedman_images/Collections/2016c21/AmSpectator_01_1976.pdf>
11. Cox, Jeff. "Debt and deficits are going to explode in the next 30 years, CBO says". CNBC. 30 Mar 2017. <http://www.cnbc.com/2017/03/30/debt-and-deficits-are-going-to-explode-in-the-next-30-years-cbo-says.htm>

SOURCES

1. Fig. 2.5: Source: Bureau of Labor Statistics.
2. Fig. 2.6: Source: tradingeconomics.com/U.S. Bureau of Economic Analysis.
3. Fig. 2.7: Source: tradingeconomics.com/U.S. Bureau of Labor Statistics.
4. Fig. 2.8: Source: tradingeconomics.com/U.S. Bureau of Labor Statistics.
5. Fig. 2.10: Source: http://federal-budget.insidegov.com/l/119/2016#Spending&s=47xnQz.
6. Fig. 2.11: Source: Tradingeconomics.com/U.S. Bureau of Public Debt.

Chapter 3

Business Ethics & Corporate Social Responsibility

PROLOGUE

It is not uncommon to read articles today wherein the media hold large corporations accountable for business practices that are deemed unethical or socially irresponsible. In fact, large corporations are often held to a higher standard than individual citizens because these same corporations seek profit from their business activities.

> "Companies are expected not only to obey the law or meet certain standards within their own businesses but also to ensure high standards across their supply chains. Large companies are expected to go further still, helping to solve major economic, environmental, and social problems—even those unrelated to their businesses. Moreover, as the expectations of citizens have increased, so has their power to scrutinize. Digital communication has enabled individuals and nongovernmental organizations (NGOs) to observe almost every activity of a business, to rally support against it, and to launch powerful global campaigns very quickly at almost zero cost. High expectations and scrutiny are here to stay. Successful companies must be equipped to deal with them."[1]

In today's business environment a greater number of companies are developing a formal code of ethics in an attempt to ensure that the organization and all of its employees understand and abide by ethical standards that advance ethical business practices. These codes of ethics, and the words written in a formal code, are of no value to the organization unless the intent is reflected in the actions of the people who represent the organization.

A business will likely be judged as either ethical or unethical based on the decisions and actions of the people who lead, manage, and work within each respective organization. It is often the case where an employee's behavior is the byproduct of the values, moral standards, and behaviors modeled by the managers of the organization.

Social responsibility goes beyond a company's code of ethics and the individual judgment of what is "right and wrong." Social responsibility requires every organization to consider what voluntary obligation it has to the well-being of society. It focuses on the policies an organization adheres to that take into account the needs of each stakeholder group whether they are investors, employees, customers, competitors, the community at-large, and/or the natural environment.

Today organizations must work to continuously build relationships with their stakeholders based on principles of fairness, honesty, openness and moral integrity. To ignore these basic principles is to contribute to their own demise.

> "Everybody has a view about a corporation's role in society. I do, too. I believe social responsibility begins with a strong, competitive company. Only a healthy enterprise can improve and enrich the lives of people and their communities. That's why a CEO's primary social responsibility is to assure the financial success of the company. Only a healthy, winning enterprise has the resources and capability to do the right thing."[2] —Jack Welch

ETHICS

If this were an ethics course we would likely learn about the great ethicists of history such as Socrates, Nietzsche, Mill, and Kant. However, our focus involves ethics in business and its relationship to societal norms (normative discipline) and those standards of appropriate and proper ("normal") behavior. Based on the premise that ethics is a normative discipline, business ethics is therefore the study of organizational standards of conduct and moral judgment. Ethics requires organizations to go beyond simply obeying the law and requires an organization to abide by the moral standards accepted by society. The morality and ethics of the modern workplace is ultimately determined by the values, norms, and standards of behavior of the leaders within the organization. It is the confluence of these values, norms, and standards of behavior, while in pursuit of profit, that tests the morality of the organization and their core values.

ETHICAL DILEMMA

In a "perfect world" business owners, managers, and employees would strive to maintain the moral high ground and choose principle over profit. However within a business setting, individuals are required to make decisions affecting their own well-being versus the well-being of organizational stakeholders. Each decision made by owners, employees and managers involves not only a personal decision, but also a decision on behalf of, and in the name of, the organization. An "ethical dilemma" exists when employees and managers must choose between two or more equally unsatisfactory alternatives that require serious consideration of numerous other factors such as values, laws, standards, various stakeholders, and profits. An ethical dilemma can also be defined as a situation wherein you as an individual have to decide if you should act in a way that might help another person even though doing so might go undermine your own self-interest.

In such a setting choosing the moral high ground requires that the individual (manager) choose principle over profit. Not easy!

Money vs Morals

When faced with an ethical dilemma it is appropriate to ask the following questions:

- *Is it legal? (Am I violating the law or company policy?)*

  A commonly accepted view holds that a business fulfills its ethical and social responsibilities simply by obeying the law. From this perspective, an ethically responsible business makes decisions that merely adhere to the precepts of the law and requires no further consideration or responsibility.

- *Is it balanced? (Does my decision create a Win-Win for all stakeholders?)*

  Ethically responsible business decision-making looks beyond the needs and concerns of stockholders and considers the impact that decisions will have on a wide range of stakeholder groups. In a general sense, a business ***stakeholder*** will be anyone affected, for better or worse, by the decisions made within the firm.

- *How will it make me feel about myself? (Have I compromised my personal values?)*

  We can think of values as the underlying beliefs that determine what decision an individual will make when confronted with a difficult ethical dilemma. Acts and decisions that seek to promote the welfare of all stakeholders are acts and decisions based on ethical values.

MAKING ETHICAL CHOICES

In 1958 American psychologist Lawrence Kohlberg hypothesized that an individual's development of moral standards passed through stages that can be grouped into three moral levels and six stages. Kohlberg's stages of moral development were an attempt to explain the development of moral reasoning based on the following three levels of morality:[3]

Three Levels of Moral Development

Level 3: Postconventional

Follows self-chosen principles of justice and right. Aware that people hold different values and seeks creative solutions to ethical dilemmas. Balances concern for individual with concern for common good.

Level 2: Conventional

Lives up to expectations of others. Fulfills duties and obligations of social system. Upholds laws.

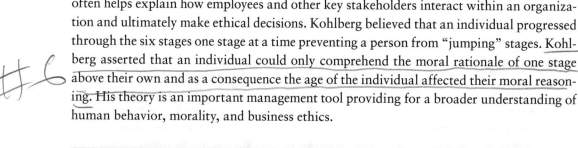

Level 1: Preconventional

Follows rules to avoid punishment. Acts in own interest. Obedience for its own sake.

	Level 1	Level 2	Level 3
Leadership Style:	Autocratic/coercive	Guiding/encouraging, team oriented	Transforming, or servant leadership
Employee Behavior:	Task accomplishment	Work group collaboration	Empowered employees, full participation

Kohlberg's theory on the development of morality has been widely influential in the fields of psychology, management, leadership and business ethics. His moral development theory often helps explain how employees and other key stakeholders interact within an organization and ultimately make ethical decisions. Kohlberg believed that an individual progressed through the six stages one stage at a time preventing a person from "jumping" stages. Kohlberg asserted that an individual could only comprehend the moral rationale of one stage above their own and as a consequence the age of the individual affected their moral reasoning. His theory is an important management tool providing for a broader understanding of human behavior, morality, and business ethics.

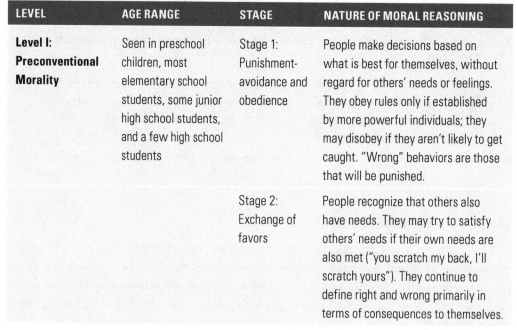

LEVEL	AGE RANGE	STAGE	NATURE OF MORAL REASONING
Level I: Preconventional Morality	Seen in preschool children, most elementary school students, some junior high school students, and a few high school students	Stage 1: Punishment-avoidance and obedience	People make decisions based on what is best for themselves, without regard for others' needs or feelings. They obey rules only if established by more powerful individuals; they may disobey if they aren't likely to get caught. "Wrong" behaviors are those that will be punished.
		Stage 2: Exchange of favors	People recognize that others also have needs. They may try to satisfy others' needs if their own needs are also met ("you scratch my back, I'll scratch yours"). They continue to define right and wrong primarily in terms of consequences to themselves.

Level II: Conventional Morality	Seen in a few older elementary school students, some junior high school students, and many high school students (Stage 4 typically does not appear until the high school years)	Stage 3: Good boy/girl	People make decisions based on what actions will please others, especially authority figures and other individuals with high status (e.g., teachers, popular peers). They are concerned about maintaining relationships through sharing, trust, and loyalty, and they take other people's perspectives and intentions into account when making decisions.
		Stage 4: Law and order	People look to society as a whole for guidelines about right or wrong. They know rules are necessary for keeping society running smoothly and believe it is their "duty" to obey them. However, they perceive rules to be inflexible; they don't necessarily recognize that as society's needs change, rules should change as well.
Level II: Postconventional Morality	Rarely seen before college (Stage 6 is extremely rare even in adults)	Stage 5: Social contract	People recognize that rules represent agreements among many individuals about appropriate behavior. Rules are seen as potentially useful mechanisms that can maintain the general social order and protect individual rights, rather than as absolute dictates that must be obeyed simply because they are "the law." People also recognize the flexibility of rules; rules that no longer serve society's best interests can and should be changed.
		Stage 6: Universal ethical principle	Stage 6 is a hypothetical, "ideal" stage that few people ever reach. People in this stage adhere to a few abstract, universal principles (e.g., equality of all people, respect for human dignity, commitment to justice) that transcend specific norms and rules. They answer to a strong inner conscience and willingly disobey laws that violate their own ethical principles.

SOURCES: Colby & Kohlberg, 1984; Colby et al., 1983; Kohlberg, 1976, 1984, 1986; Reimer, Paolitto, & Hersh, 1983; Snarey, 1995.

Ethical Decision Making: Four Key Rules

The challenge for managers making ethical decisions is to take into account the claims of all stakeholders affected by his/her decision. Whenever a stakeholder approach is taken the difficulty in making an ethical decision becomes much more difficult. At the heart of every ethical decision is the question: Who has the greatest stake? Do managers make decisions that are designed to benefit shareholders, or do managers have a larger responsibility to protect the interests of investors, employees, consumers, or even the natural environment? To make ethical decisions and ensure that they take into account all of the respective stakeholders, managers can use four ethical rules to evaluate the effects of their business decisions. The four key rules for making ethical decisions[4] include:

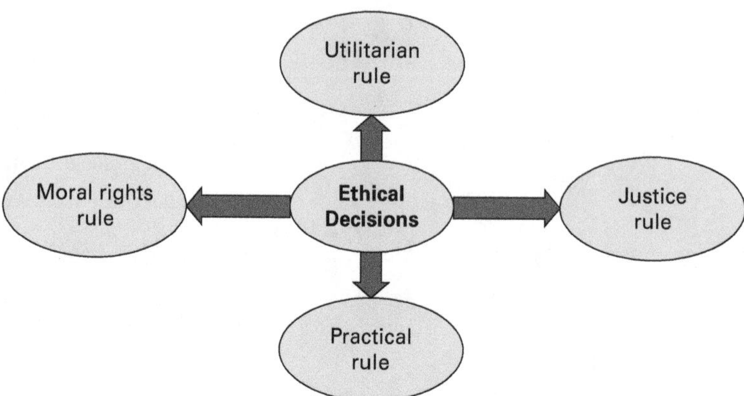

Utilitarian Rule

Jeremy Bentham and John Stuart Mill first conceived utilitarianism in the 19th century in an attempt to help legislators determine which laws were morally best. Bentham and Mill submitted that ethical actions are those that provide the greatest balance of good over evil. Using the utilitarian approach requires managers to first identify the various courses of action available. Once all alternative actions have been identified it is then necessary to ask who will be affected by each action and what benefit or harm will be derived from each. Lastly, when attempting to make an ethical decision, a manager would seek to produce the greatest good for the greatest number of people. Conversely, a manager would seek to create the least amount of harm.

Moral Rights Rule

> "The second important approach to ethics has its roots in the philosophy of the 18th-century thinker Immanuel Kant and others like him, who focused on the individual's right to choose for herself or himself. According to these philosophers, what makes human beings different from mere things is that people have

> dignity based on their ability to choose freely what they will do with their lives, and they have a fundamental moral right to have these choices respected. People are not objects to be manipulated; it is a violation of human dignity to use people in ways they do not freely choose."[5]

Using this approach it is the goal of a manager attempting to ensure, maintain, or protect the fundamental rights and/or privileges of each individual. For managers their ethical decisions are based on the evaluation of their decisions against the fundamental rights of every individual, including but not limited to, the right to life, freedom, health and privacy of the person. Managers using this approach would likely attempt to uphold the rights of all stakeholders.

Justice Rule

This approach is designed to ensure that an ethical decision benefits (or harms) people and/or groups in an impartial and equitable allocation of outcomes. *"The basic moral question in this approach is: How fair is an action? Does it treat everyone in the same way, or does it show favoritism and discrimination?"*[6]

Definitions of justice are often based on the principle that relevantly similar cases (persons) be treated alike. For managers "relevantly similar" is not always self-evident and as a result questions about justice are based on relevant characteristics by which people are to be considered equal or unequal. This is a recurring challenge for college professors when attempting to determine what actions are fair and appropriate when an individual student requests an exemption or accommodation based on their unique circumstances. The challenge in using this approach is to determine what are the appropriate rules or procedures used for making such a judgment.

Practical Rule

This approach is based on the principle that a manager, having had to resolve an ethical dilemma, would have no hesitation in communicating his/her decision to people outside the organization because the average person in society would think the decision was both moral and reasonable.

CORPORATE ETHICAL STANDARDS: TWO PERSPECTIVES

Ferrell and Fraedrich[7] describe two types of ethics programs, compliance and values-based (also known as integrity based). "The compliance-based system uses legal terms, training, rules of conduct, and penalties for noncompliance. The values-based system relies upon self-policing and motivation, rather than coercion. 'The company's values are seen as something to which people willingly aspire,' note Ferrell and Fraedrich. Ethicists sometimes refer to these two forms of ethics as the 'carrot and stick.' Values-based ethics are a 'carrot' that the organization pursues willingly, while compliance-based ethics are a 'stick' used to beat ethics into the organization."[8]

Compliance-Based Ethics emphasizes the prevention of unlawful behavior by increasing control and by penalizing wrongdoers. The intent of this approach is to avoid legal intervention and/or punishment. The areas where businesses seek to remain compliant normally involve employee wages, health benefits, retirement, employment rights, and safety. A purely compliance-based culture tends to be rules-driven, meaning that rules are the basis for every decision. This invites a legalistic view, rather than an ethical view, where obedience to the letter of the law is the objective; if it's legal it's ethical. In a compliance-based culture there exists a mentality that all that is required is to just do what the law dictates. This approach has a tendency to cause employees and managers to "bend" the rules or make plausible interpretations of the rules to justify desired conduct resulting in behaviors that are legal but undesirable.

Values-Based Ethics is based on an organization's guiding values and creates an environment, organizational culture, which supports ethically sound behavior and stresses a shared sense of accountability among employees. Values-based organizations are driven by core ethical beliefs and convictions, values about what is right and good, which serve as the underpinning for the development of company rules and policies. Thus, rules and policies are built upon traditional ethical values such as honesty, respect, fairness and responsibility.

2017 World's Most Ethical Companies

"The Ethisphere Institute, a global leader in defining and advancing the standards of ethical business practices, today announced 124 companies spanning five continents, 19 countries and 52 industry sectors as the 2017 World's Most Ethical Companies honorees.

Since 2007, Ethisphere has honored those companies who recognize their role in society to influence and drive positive change in the business community and societies around the world. These companies also consider the impact of their actions on their employees, investors, customers and other key stakeholders and leverage values and a culture of integrity as the underpinnings to the decisions they make each day.

The 124 2017 honorees span five continents, 19 countries and 52 industry sectors. Among the 2017 list are 13 eleven-time honorees and 8 first time honorees.

'We are honored to be recognized as one of the World's Most Ethical Companies for 11 consecutive years,' said **Kao Corporation** President and CEO, Michitaka Sawada. 'For 130 years, we have upheld the value of integrity passed down from Kao's founder. As a core value, we positioned integrity as the foundation of the Kao Group Mid-term Plan 2020 (K20), which started from this year. This integrity continues to be embraced as K20 guides the group's daily business activities.'

'We've always been committed to demonstrating the highest level of integrity, ethical business practices and social responsibility in everything we do,' said **Petco** CEO, Brad Weston. 'It's an honor to continue receiving this distinguished recognition and a direct reflection of our commitment to doing the right thing for people and pets.'

'Companies are the bricks of modern society. In order to make positive change happen throughout the world, ethics must be a core of private enterprise,' said **illycaffe S.p.A.** Chairman, Andrea Illy. The Ethisphere Institute's work is inspiring and helping companies prioritize meaningful investments that push them to be the best."[9]

CORPORATE SOCIAL RESPONSIBILITY

The concept of social responsibility has evolved from a nebulous "do-gooder" image to one of "social steward" with an expectation that an organization has an obligation to provide for the well-being society. Society has continually redefined its expectations of business owners and continues to hold all organizations to higher behavioral standard.

"I'm not sure it's a new development, but the amount of power and influence that these customers are now able to exercise has increased substantially and therefore it has become a top-level management issue. When consumers can leverage channels like the Internet to connect with one another and to identify and distribute information about companies, all of a sudden there is a shift in power toward the consumer or other stakeholder organizations."[10]

Leaders of public corporations are often judged solely by the profits they generate for shareholders and the rise in their company's stock price. However, the debate over the importance of doing good has heated up as many corporate leaders have broadened the scope of their perspective to address the needs of other constituent groups who may not have a financial stake in the company. Social responsibility involves a firm's obligation to improve its positive effects on society and reduce its negative effects. This means that social responsibility has become an integral part of an organization's mission and requires that management consider the social and economic effects of its decisions on all its stakeholders. Organizations must be committed to participating in activities that are designed to contribute to the well-being of society; yet at the same time pursue bottom line success.

Social Responsibility: Stakeholders

The idea that every business has a fundamental responsibility towards its stakeholders is hardly a novel concept, although there is both agreement and disagreement on what precisely the nature and scope of the responsibility involved should be. Agreement exists in the notion that some stakeholders are able to wield more power than others; wherein disagreement exists regarding the precise nature of the responsibility demanded by each stakeholder group.

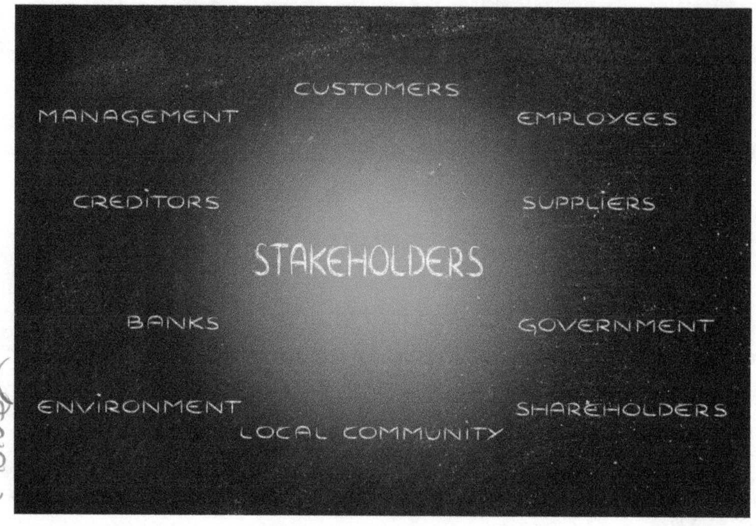

Stakeholders represent a person or entity other than an owner, stockholder, or creditor who potentially has a stake in the company and its operations. Stated another way, a stakeholder can be defined as any entity that may be impacted by the use and allocation of resources within your company. Stakeholders are made up of five distinct groups:

Customers—Businesses must produce goods and services that satisfy customers and add value to their lives. Most customers have an expectation that the product or service they buy will be made available at a reasonable price and at the appropriate quality and safety level. The conflict is obvious since the desires of the customer must be balanced with the needs of the financial stakeholders who seek a return on their investment.

Investors—Being socially responsible to investors sometimes requires difficult trade-offs, which influence profits, competitiveness, and management benefit. Ultimately, a business is responsible for making money for its investors while attempting to insure that it acts on behalf of the interests of all other stakeholders.

Employees—Businesses have several responsibilities to their employees, which include: the creation of employment opportunities, job security, and fair reward/compensation. "If you want employees to take a vested interest in the bigger picture, treat them like stakeholders. When you create an environment in which "jobs" are regarded more like "investments," employees will show up with passion, productivity, and focus, making your company more profitable."[11]

Society—Business has several responsibilities to society: to create new wealth, to promote social justice, building a community that goes beyond charitable contributions and improving overall environmental quality by making its own environment a better place.

Environment—Every business, regardless of its size or location, has a responsibility to insure that it protects the natural environment and conserves natural resources. In addition, today's companies have an even greater responsibility to reduce pollution and contamination while at the same time implementing new sustainable business practices that decrease the impact on the environment by harmful chemicals, materials, and waste generated by processes to manufacture goods and services. Sustainable businesses invest time and energy to carefully examine their internal manufacturing processes for the purpose of determining what processes may be harmful to the environment. The intended result of such an examination is new "green" processes that can perform at the same or a better level and, preferably, at a lower cost.

A NEW SOCIAL CONTRACT: SUSTAINABILITY

In recent years, the business community has made great progress in corporate social responsibility by adhering to a new ***social contract.*** A social contract, according to Thomas Hobbes, exists in society when "People agree, for example, not to harm one another and not to break their promises."[12] In business, the new social contract puts sustainability at the center of the strategic planning process and requires organizations and their management teams to address a range of social, environmental, market, and technological trends.

> "Traditional business models aim to create value for shareholders, often at the expense of other stakeholders. Sustainable businesses are redefining the corporate ecosystem by designing models that create value for all stakeholders, including employees, shareholders, supply chains, civil society, and the planet."[13]

In the 1990's John Elkington[14] developed a new perspective for measuring the performance of businesses in corporate America: "People, Profit, Planet". He proposed a new "accounting framework", called the triple bottom line (TBL), wherein a new set of criteria, beyond the traditional ***economic*** measures of profits, return on investment, and shareholder value, now included the natural ***environment*** and ***social*** dimensions.

The social bottom line measures your business' profits in human capital and your standing with the community in which you locate your business. Social variables refer to social dimensions of a community or region and would include measurements of education, equity and access to social resources, health and wellbeing, quality of life, and social capital. A company's social bottom line is increased when they create policies that are designed to create fair and beneficial labor practices and through community involvement.

The Triple Bottom Line approach to environmental sustainability takes into account the impact your business has on the planet. Sustainability measures would, at a minimum, measure the effects of an organization on water quality, energy consumption, use of natural resources, pollution, and land use. Controlling your environmental bottom line means that systems would need to be put into place so that it becomes possible to manage and monitor consumption, waste and emissions.

In the Triple Bottom Line approach, economic sustainability is measured in terms of how much of an impact your business has on the economy and community. The business that strengthens the economy through job creation and rising personal incomes also must pursue its traditional profits and improving organizational efficiency.

SOCIAL PERFORMANCE

As businesses increasingly invest in corporate social responsibility (CSR), it is important for these organizations to accurately assess their impact on different stakeholders—the ultimate beneficiaries of CSR programs. The Social Performance of every company can be approached and evaluated from one of three broad perspectives (dimensions):

Corporate Philanthropy (Voluntary, Integrity Based)

Businesses that engage in philanthropy do so with the intention of making the world a better place. By engaging in voluntary acts of giving something back to their communities, either through charitable contributions of money, time, or resources, philanthropy enriches the lives of people in the communities in which they conduct their business activities.

Corporate Responsibility (Required, Compliance Based)

This approach to the social performance of an organization is based on the concept that an organization has an obligation to conduct its business based on pre-existing legal guidelines as well as to take into account the welfare of its various stakeholders (i.e. hiring minorities, making safe products, protecting the natural environment). Corporate responsibility based on a compliance-based approach is often associated with the "cost of doing business" and ultimately creates value for the organization by protecting the company's reputation as well as reducing the potential risk of litigation.

Corporate Policy (Voluntary, Elements of Mission & Strategic Plan)

This approach encompasses the position (philosophy) that a firm takes on social and political issues. Typically, most companies who formulate policies affecting their social performance do so only after a careful analysis of all internal and external factors affecting a firm's mission and strategic plans. Corporate policy, formulated by top-level management within the organization, is a set of broad guidelines, outlining the firm's response and/or strategy to changing conditions within the business environment.

The Honest Company: Corporate Policy

"At Honest, giving back drives who we are and what we do. It is in our brand DNA and informs every piece of our business and operations, and we believe that it is our responsibility to do our part to help create a healthy and sustainable future for all.

This deep sense of purpose is passionately demonstrated in our actions and service to our families, our planet, and to our communities as we strive to create long-term value and positive social impact.

Everyday, your product purchases help support our Social Goodness work, allowing us to fund access to safe products and advances research and education that ultimately drives positive social impact we all can be proud of. Together we CAN make it better![15]

MEASURING SOCIAL PERFORMANCE

Historically a company's social performance was measured by the creation of new employment opportunities and its contributions to the economy. Today, social responsibility extends beyond the economy and employment and requires an organization to engage in actions that promote concern for the natural environment, maintain the privacy of the consumer, embrace and encourage cultural diversity, and advance altruistic behavior by every member of the organization. The social performance of a company is assessed through the process of a social audit.

A ***Social Audit*** requires organizations to engage in a systematic evaluation of the business activities within the company to determine the organization's effect on society and their progress in developing and implementing programs that are socially responsive and responsible.

Mission Statement

"UNDER AMOUR MAKES YOU BETTER"

"Many companies spend significant time and effort developing a mission statement — complete with vision, values, goals, and strategies. Ask managers whether their firm's mission statement lives in the company day-to-day or whether it lies neglected in someone's desk drawer. In too many instances, the truthful answer is: "The vision is more rhetoric than real."

This is not because the company's managers are neglectful or "bad people." Indeed, most managers would say they are doing their best to exemplify the values in these documents and achieve the vision. However, in-depth investigations of company practices, even in the best of firms, frequently reveal large gaps between stated values and daily practices.

> We propose that auditing a company's core operating practices by using a responsibility audit may help to bridge this rhetoric-reality gap. Such an audit assesses a company's overall performance against its core values, ethics policy, internal operating practices, management systems, and, most importantly, the expectations of key stakeholders — owners, employees, suppliers, customers, and local communities. Such audits alert companies to responsible business practices that will help them simultaneously 'do well (financially) and do good (socially)'."[16]

ETHICS: THE HARD REALITIES OF BUSINESS

In business, just as in life, we are often faced with making difficult decisions. Normally, we attempt to make decisions that are pragmatic, thoughtful, and serve to advance our own best interest. These decisions, we would hope, are made with the goal of doing as little harm as possible to the people and environment around us. However, we live in a world where the shades of gray are ever more subtle when making ethical decisions, and in the context of making money, are extremely precarious. The reality is that money changes people and will often cause an individual to compromise their ethics and later serve as a feeble rationale for their actions.

The hard reality for every business, large and small, is that it must make a profit to survive or it will perish. What will you do if faced with an ethical dilemma in the future? How will you respond when your integrity and ethical standards are put to the test? Will you "do the right thing," even at your own peril, or will you fall prey to the pressure to survive, compromising your own ethical standards? Your actions in these moments of crisis will ultimately define your organization and more importantly your legacy as a human being. Choose well.

ENDNOTES

1. Browne, J., & Nuttall, R. "Beyond corporate social responsibility: integrated external engagement". McKinsey&Company. March 2013. <http://www.mckinsey.com/insights/strategy/beyond_corporate_social_responsibility_integrated_external_engagement>

2. Welch, Jack and John A. Byrne, Jack: Straight From the Gut, New York: Warner Books, 2001.

3. Kohlberg, Lawrence; T. Lickona, ed. *"Moral Stages and Moralization: The Cognitive-Developmental Approach"*, Moral Development and Behavior: Theory, Research and Social Issues. Holt, Rinehart, and Winston, 1976, pp. 31–53.

4. Cavanaugh, G.F., Moberg, D.J. and Velasquez. "The Ethics of Organizational Politics." Academy of Management Review 6 (1981): 363–74

5. Velasquez, Manuel et al. "Thinking Ethically: A Framework for Moral Decision Making." Issues in Ethics. Markkula Center for Applied Ethics. Santa Clara University. V7 N1 (Winter 1996). 18 June 2013 <http://www.scu.edu/ethics/practicing/decision/thinking.html>

6. ibid

7. Ferrell, O.C., John Fraedrich, and Linda Ferrell. Business Ethics: Ethical Decision Making & Cases. Ohio: South-Western 2011

8. Anthony, Dan. "Explain Compliance-Based Ethics." Chron 21 June 2013. 21 June 2013. <http://smallbusiness.chron.com/explain-compliance-based-business-ethics-243.html>.

9. "2017 World's Most Ethical Companies: Honorees" Ethisphere. 2017. <http://worldsmostethicalcompanies.ethisphere.com/honorees/>

10. Holstein,William. "Fine-Tuning Corporate Social Responsibility." Bloomberg Businessweek 3 Apr 2008 <http://www.businessweek.com/managing/content/apr2008/ca2008043_500367.htm>

11. Spiegelman, Paul. "Deliver Value to Your Employees—Your Most Important Stakeholders." Inc. 18 July 2011. 12 May 2013 <http://www.inc.com/articles/201107/beryl-companies-paul-spiegelman-deliver-value-to-employees-your-most-important-stakeholders.html>.

12. Rachels, James and Stuart Rachels. "The Social Contract Theory", The Elements of Moral Philosophy. McGraw-Hill Education, 2015, p 87.

13. Whelan, Tensie and Carly Fink. "The Comprehensive Business Case for Sustainability". Harvard Business Review 21 Oct 2016. 30 June 2017. <https://hbr.org/2016/10/the-comprehensive-business-case-for-sustainability>

14. John Elkington, "Towards the Sustainable Corporation: Win-Win-Win Business Strategies for Sustainable Development," California Management Review 36, no. 2 (1994): 90–100.

15. "Honest to Goodness". The Honest Company <https://www.honest.com/social-goodness>

16. Waddock, Sandra and Smith, Neil. "Corporate Responsibility Audits: Going Well by Doing Good." MIT Sloan Management Review Winter (2000) 15 Jan 2000 <http://sloanreview.mit.edu/article/corporate-responsibility-audits-doing-well-by-doing-good/>.

SOURCES

1. Fig. 3.2: From: Richard Daft, Management, 8th ed., pp. 146. Copyright © 2008 by Cengage Learning, Inc.

2. Fig. 3.5: Copyright © 2014 Depositphotos/Faithie.

3. Fig. 3.6: Copyright © RadioFan (CC BY-SA 3.0) at https://commons.wikimedia.org/wiki/File:Mission_statement.png.

Chapter 4

Entrepreneurship

The Emergence of the Human Spirit

PROLOGUE

> "A legendary hero is usually the founder of something—the founder of a new age, the founder of a new religion, the founder of a new city, the founder of a new way of life. In order to found something new, one has to leave the old and go on a quest of the seed idea, a germinal idea that will have the potential of bringing forth that new thing."[1]

Entrepreneurs are, as Joseph Campbell states so eloquently, legendary heroes who bring forth the next new thing. Stated another way, entrepreneurs are those individuals who dare to dream, assume risk, and most importantly bring new products and ideas to the market. Entrepreneurs are founders, they build new businesses and subsequently create jobs, increase competition within the market, and through the development of technological innovation improve productivity and new product creation. Entrepreneurs seek profit from opportunities that normally go unnoticed by large hierarchical organizations and seek to create new ventures with a sustainable competitive advantage by producing goods and services that fill those gaps in the marketplace that have been overlooked by large corporate entities.

Societies throughout the world today are discovering that economic prosperity is the result of increased entrepreneurial activity.

> "Countries around the world are struggling to create economic opportunities for their citizens and entrepreneurship has grown in its appeal. Entrepreneurs create the enterprises and jobs that expand economies and they are the front of new innovations that improve productivity and increase standards of living.
>
> But entrepreneurship is much more than jobs and economic growth. A culture of entrepreneurship is a culture of empowerment, which helps to lower the barriers that in many places exclude women, young people, and minorities from economic and political participation."[2]

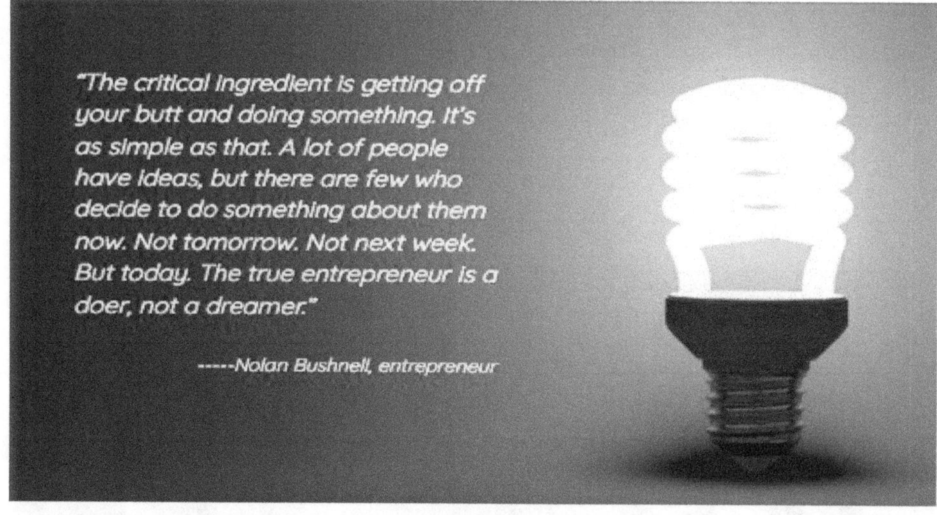

"The critical ingredient is getting off your butt and doing something. It's as simple as that. A lot of people have ideas, but there are few who decide to do something about them now. Not tomorrow. Not next week. But today. The true entrepreneur is a doer, not a dreamer."
-----Nolan Bushnell, entrepreneur

The level of success, prosperity, and growth in any economy is largely dependent upon motivated individuals who seek to carve out their own path and form a new business. The most vibrant societies in the world today are those wherein the government encourages and nurtures future entrepreneurs while at the same time creates an economic and legal environment that supports and motivates entrepreneurs. Where governments around the world create laws that allow for business owners to retain the majority of the profit produced in their entrepreneurial venture there exists a growing economy with a higher standard of living; "... the affirmative link between economic freedom and long-term development is unmistakable and robust. Countries that allow their citizens more economic freedom achieve higher incomes and better standards of living. People in economically free societies have longer lives. They have better health and access to more effective education.

They are able to be better stewards of the environment, and they push forward the frontiers of human achievement in science and technology through greater innovation."[3]

> "The entrepreneurial spirit has been a key source of America's greatness since the nation's founding over two hundred years ago. In addition to being the primary engine of our economic growth and prosperity, the entrepreneurial spirit is inextricably linked to the inalienable rights enshrined in the Declaration of Independence, including liberty and the pursuit of happiness. As Winston Churchill once said, "America is an idea, not a place." Central to the American idea is the notion that individual dignity necessarily includes the freedom to work hard, be creative and get ahead in life without interference by the state. As such, entrepreneurship has historically been seen in America as a fundamental expression of the human spirit."[4]

ENTREPRENEURS: DOMINANT CHARACTERISTICS

There are seven major themes that have emerged regarding the dominant characteristics of successful entrepreneurs. They are:

- Commitment and determination
- Courage
- Leadership
- Opportunity obsession
- Tolerance for risk, ambiguity and uncertainty
- Creativity, self-reliance and adaptability
- Motivation to excel[5]

> "It's hard to recall how our entrepreneurial spirit first began. We met in tenth grade and quickly became friends. At the time, we didn't realize we shared an entrepreneurial nature—formal schooling stifled it, and taking an entrepreneurial approach to our activities got us reprimanded. School taught us that fitting in was safer, requiring us to stay in line, defining us by our classes and grades, and weeding out any behavior considered disobedient."[6]
>
> —Nick Friedman & Omar Soliman, Founders of College Hunks Hauling Junk

IMPROVING YOUR CHANCES FOR SUCCESS: "KNOWLEDGE IS POWER"

Sir Francis Bacon

Know Your Business

Get the best education and experience before you start. Few people are prepared to succeed as entrepreneurs and as a result lack any practical knowledge about their industry, market, consumers (target market), competitive environment, start-up costs, cash flow, break-even point, or potential profits. The axiom, knowledge is power, is an important principle to keep in mind prior to starting any new business.

Prepare a Comprehensive Business Plan

Planning is designed to replace; "Here's what I think" with "Here's what I know". Writing a business plan is essential when creating any new business, especially if it is the first attempt by an entrepreneur at starting a new business. A well-written business plan is a roadmap that outlines what the company hopes to achieve and how it plans on achieving its stated goals and objectives.

Ideally, a business plan should be written prior to hiring your first employee, signing any contracts, or deciding what strategies you will utilize to generate sales revenues in your business. Research and thoughtful planning are essential in writing a realistic, practical, and useful business plan. Remember, a business plan is not meant to be an "end-all be-all" for a company, but a road map providing clarity and purpose for the entrepreneur. No matter how well written, no business plan can anticipate all the unforeseen elements that will undoubtedly arise when attempting to form a successful new venture. The process of writing a plan is often more important than the plan itself. Every entrepreneur must begin the planning process by asking the following four fundamental questions:

- Where am I now?
- Where do I want to go?
- Where am I in relation to where I want to go?
- How do I get there?

Continuously Manage Your Company's Financial Resources

Managing financial resources enables a new business venture to obtain capital for growth, efficiently allocate resources, maximize the return on investment of the business, and monitor the activities of the business through an intelligent analysis of accounting documents. Such management requires a well-written, comprehensive financial management plan clearly outlining the assets, debts and the current sales projections, and future profit potential of your business. Remember, cash is your most valuable resource.

> "Business analysts report that poor management is the main reason for business failure. Poor cash management is probably the most frequent stumbling block for entrepreneurs. Understanding the basic concepts of cash flow will help you plan for the unforeseen eventualities that nearly every business faces.
>
> **Cash vs. Cash Flow**
>
> Cash is ready money in the bank or in the business. It is not inventory, it is not accounts receivable (what you are owed), and it is not property. These can potentially be converted to cash, but can't be used to pay suppliers, rent, or employees.

Profit growth does not necessarily mean more cash on hand. Profit is the amount of money you expect to make over a given period of time, while cash is what you must have on hand to keep your business running. Over time, a company's profits are of little value if they are not accompanied by positive net cash flow. You can't spend profit; you can only spend cash.

Cash flow refers to the movement of cash into and out of a business. Watching the cash inflows and outflows is one of the most pressing management tasks for any business. The outflow of cash includes those checks you write each month to pay salaries, suppliers, and creditors. The inflow includes the cash you receive from customers, lenders, and investors."[7]

Understand Financial Statements

The financial statements in your business are the most reliable indicators of the small business's health. If you do not understand how financial statements are used, how they can benefit you and your business, how to get the most out of them, how others view them, or how they are created, then you have significantly depleted your ability to effectively manage the operations of your venture. In virtually every instance, every decision you make in your business has some financial consequence that requires a fundamental understanding of the four basic financial statements: Income Statement, Statement of Owner's Equity, Balance Sheet, and Statement of Cash Flow. To intelligently use financial statement information you must be able to, at a minimum, examine and understand trends in key financial data, financial data across companies within your industry, and key financial ratios. It is the result of this type of analysis that business owners can evaluate the operational performance of their company.

> "Financial statements are the instrument panel of the business that reports on managerial success or failure, and that flashes warning signals of impending difficulties. To be able to read that panel, you must understand the gauges and their calibrations to make sense out of the data it conveys. In other words, you must understand accounting and financial relationships to interpret the data in the panel."[8]

Learn to Manage People Effectively

A business is comprised of what people do. People are the heart of every business and the quality of the people determines the success of the business. The complex activities that make things happen in a business are comprised of the actions of the owner, manager, employees, customers, competitors, creditors, and public. It is a critical error in judgment to believe that a business is only about its strategic plan, marketing position, cash flow, production schedules, or profit margins.

It is not unusual for investors to base their investment decisions on the character of the individual involved in the enterprise. They know that the experience, skills, and resolve of the team members can significantly impact on the long-term success of the company more than the product or the service.

Set Your Business Apart from the Competition

Differentiate your company and products by ensuring you add value to your customer. In order to convince your customers that you are different from competitors it is essential to exceed their expectations in every aspect of your business. At a minimum this includes customer service, convenience, speed, and quality that your company provides. In addition you should position your business by creating a unique selling proposition that merges all marketing efforts into a unified message insuring that your customers understand what to expect when they establish a relationship with your company.

> "How would you feel if you entered a doctor's office and found yourself walking on blood-stained carpets? I constantly asked my partners this question ... At times, it seemed as if 90 percent of what I did while traveling store to store was 'cleaning up the blood'. I looked at each and every Kinko's location from the customer's perspective ... Retail is detail".[9]

LEADING CAUSES OF SMALL BUSINESS FAILURE

The importance of small businesses in the U.S. economy suggests that an understanding of why small businesses fail (or are successful) is crucial to the stability and health of the U.S. economy.

Entrepreneurship is linked to the creation of jobs, increases in productivity, improvement of living standards, and economic growth in the United States in general.[10] Small businesses help create new jobs, introduce new products and provide specialized expertise to large corporations and represent about 99 percent of employers, employ about half of the private sector workforce and are responsible for about two-thirds to three-quarters of the net new jobs.[11]

Unfortunately, according to the U.S. Small Business Administration, over 50% of small businesses fail in the first year and 95% fail within the first five years.[12] "Businesses with fewer than 20 employees have only a 37% chance of surviving four years (of business) and only a 9% chance of surviving 10 years", reports Dun & Bradstreet and of these failed businesses, only 10% of them close involuntarily due to bankruptcy and the remaining 90% close because the business was not successful, did not provide the level of income desired, or was too weak to continue.[13]

> "All our successes are the same. All our failures, too.
> We succeed when we do something remarkable.
> We fail when we give up too soon.
> We succeed when we are the best in the world at what we do.
> We fail when we get distracted by a task we don't have the guts to quit."[14]
>
> Seth Godin
> The Dip

NEW VENTURE ASSESSMENT: ASKING THE RIGHT QUESTIONS

New start-up companies can enhance their chances for success if they engage in a systematic, critical analysis of the following:

- Start-Up Costs
- Financing Requirements
- Market Potential
- Profit Potential
- Return on Investment
- Economic Trends
- Legal Requirements
- Opportunities & Risks

The assessment process for a new business normally includes a careful review of the following critical questions:

- Who are my customers?
- Where are they located?
- At what price will they buy my product/service?
- In what quantities will they buy my product/service?
- Who are my competitors? What are their strengths and weaknesses?
- What is my competitive advantage?

NEW VENTURE ASSESSMENT: THREE CRITICAL TESTS

Prior to investing the time and energy to write a formal business plan the new entrepreneur should consider whether their plan can "pass" the following three tests:

- *The Reality Test* proves that:
    - A market really does exist for your product or service.
    - There is strong demand for their business (product/service) idea.
    - You can actually produce/deliver the product based on the cost estimates in the plan.
    - The product/service offers customers something of value.
- *The Competitive Test* evaluates:
    - A company's position relative to its customers.
    - Management's ability to create a sustainable competitive advantage.
    - The quality, skill, and experience of the venture's management team
- *The Value Test* proves that:
    - A venture offers investors or lenders an attractive rate of return or a high probability of repayment.

BUSINESS PLANNING: DO I REALLY NEED A BUSINESS PLAN?

In the not too distant past there was widespread consensus among academics, business consultants, and investors that a business plan was essential for every business startup in order to improve its chances for success. However, *"A study completed by Babson College would suggest that at least for those who are not seeking outside funding, having a formal business plan before starting a small business or not having one at all really made no difference in the ultimate success of the business."*[15] The formal planning process seems to run counter to what is at the heart of the entrepreneurial spirit: the capacity to learn and adapt through experience.

CREATING A BUSINESS PLAN: WHY DO IT?

The business planning process has so much to teach an aspiring entrepreneur about their prospective new business. A business plan is essentially a developmental tool for the organization and its founders. Among the many benefits of a business plan is that it:

- Provides a 360 degree perspective which enables the entrepreneur/business owner to critically analyse the viability, potential for the growth and sustainability of a new/existing company.
- Clarifies the company's vision and mission thereby instilling a sense of commitment and common purpose among all members of the company.
- Helps the founders of the company gain a more thorough understanding of the opportunities and challenges in their market and industry. This allows for the creation of the most effective strategies and tactics necessary to effectively respond to customer needs.

- Defines the planning and evaluation guidelines necessary to successfully manage the ongoing venture.
- Determines who your competition is and how you will differentiate your products, services and create a meaningful value proposition.
- Assists the new entrepreneur in securing needed financial resources.
- Establishes the basis for evaluating company performance and growth.

Major Components of a Business Plan

Executive Summary	The executive summary should highlight your overall plan and therefore be the last section you write. However, it is the first document to be viewed in your business plan.
The Industry, Company & Products or Services	The product(s) or service(s) Entry and growth strategy
Market Research & Analysis	Target market and sales projections Competitive advantages Costs, profitability, and harvest potential

The Economics of the Business	Gross and operating margins Profit potential and durability Fixed, variable, and semi-variable costs Months to breakeven Months to reach positive cash flow
Marketing Plan	Overall marketing strategy (4 P's)
Design & Development Plan	Product improvement and new products Proprietary issues
Manufacturing & Operations Plan	Operating cycle Regulatory and legal issues
Management Team	Key management personnel Management and ownership Other investors Board of directors Supporting professional advisors and services
Overall Schedule	It sets the plan into practical, concrete terms, with timelines, deadlines, and milestones.
Critical Risks, Problems & Assumptions	A credible business plan includes a description of the risks and the consequences of adverse outcomes relating to your industry, your company, your product's market appeal, and the timing and financing of your startup.
Appendices	Supporting Documents

BUSINESS PLAN: FINANCING THE NEW VENTURE

Financing for a new start-up is a difficult process often resulting in disappointment. Acquiring the necessary financing represents one of the most difficult aspects of launching a new business with only two broad categories of funds available to the new entrepreneur. ***Equity*** financing essentially represents the sale of assets in your company to a buyer, who then has an equity interest (ownership) in the business. ***Debt*** financing represents a loan, a legally binding obligation, normally secured with real assets, that must be repaid at a specific point in time in the future. When starting a new business an entrepreneur has only a limited number of potential sources of equity and debt funding.

Equity

- Personal Savings
- Family & Friends

  "If you can't finance your business out of your own pocket, by maxing out your credit cards or taking out a second (or third or fourth) mortgage on your home, you'll have to seek funding from the people who know and love you. That means approaching the "three Fs"—family, friends and fools—for the funds."[16]

- Bootstrapping
  This approach to funding a new startup entails using one's personal income when available combined with the lowest possible operating costs and speeding up inventory turnover. Lastly this approach often requires new entrepreneurs to use a cash-only approach in selling their products or services.
- Venture Capitalists
  Venture Capital is available to early-stage, high-growth, high risk, startup companies. Venture capital firms generate a return on their investment through an eventual realization event, such as an IPO or sale of the company's stock or assets.
- Investment Angels
  Angel investors typically invest their own funds, unlike venture capitalists, and as a consequence bear extremely high risk. As such, they require a very high return on investment of 20% to 30% over a holding period of normally five to seven years.

Debt

- *Commercial Banks*
  Banks are generally reluctant to offer long-term loans to small firms. The SBA **guaranteed lending program** encourages banks and non-bank lenders to make long-term loans to small firms by reducing their risk and leveraging the funds they have available. Most commercial banks also provide small businesses with access to traditional term loans, lines of credit, and revolving lines of credit.
- *Small Business Administration* http://www.sba.gov/
  The SBA is a secondary source of capital for the small business owner and becomes a viable option only after all private lending options have been exhausted. The SBA offers a variety of loan programs to eligible small businesses that cannot borrow from conventional lenders. Here is a list of recommendations when submitting a loan request from the SBA:

Loan Application Form

"Forms vary by program and lending institution, but they all ask for the same information. You should be prepared to answer the following questions. It's a good idea to have this information prepared before you fill out the application:

- Why are you applying for this loan?
- How will the loan proceeds be used?
- What assets need to be purchased, and who are your suppliers?
- What other business debt do you have, and who are your creditors?
- Who are the members of your management team?
- Personal Background

Either as part of the loan application or as a separate document, you will likely need to provide some personal background information, including previous addresses, names used, criminal record, educational background, etc."[17]

- **Guaranteed Loans**—Banks and other lending institutions offer a number of SBA guaranteed loan programs to assist small businesses. While SBA itself does not make loans, it does guarantee loans made to small businesses by private and other institutions. The 7(a) Loan Program in which the SBA guarantees to repay 75 to 85 percent of small-business commercial loans up to $750,000.
- **Microloans**—The Microloan program provides loans up to $50,000 to help small businesses and certain not-for-profit childcare centers start up and expand. The average microloan is about $13,000. The U.S. Small Business Administration provides funds to specially designated intermediary lenders, which are nonprofit community-based organizations with experience in lending as well as management and technical assistance. These intermediaries administer the Microloan program for eligible borrowers. The money from these loans can only be used as working capital or for the purchase of inventory, supplies, furniture, fixtures, machinery and/or equipment. Proceeds cannot be used to pay existing debts or to purchase real estate.

- SBIC's

  The SBIC Program is one of many financial assistance programs available through the U.S. Small Business Administration. The structure of the program is unique in that SBICs are privately owned and managed investment funds, licensed and regulated by the SBA, that use their own capital plus funds borrowed with an SBA guarantee to make equity and debt investments in qualifying small businesses. Only companies defined by SBA as "small" are eligible for SBIC financing. Generally, the SBIC Program defines a company as "small" when its net worth is $18.0 million or less and its average after-tax net income for the prior two years does not exceed $6.0 million.

  The U.S. Small Business Administration does not invest directly into small business through the SBIC Program. Most SBICs are formed by small groups of local "angel" investors, although many SBICs are owned by commercial banks. Banks can invest up to 5% of their capital and surplus in an SBIC. The SBIC operations are separate from their regular banking operations. For every dollar an SBIC raises, the government will allow them to raise 3 additional dollars in SBA guaranteed debt - up to $105.2 million in matching funds per SBIC.[18]

SELECTING THE APPROPRIATE LEGAL STRUCTURE: SEEK THE ADVICE OF THE EXPERTS

When starting a new business one of the most important decisions to be made involves selecting the appropriate legal structure. Determining the appropriate legal structure for your new company will ultimately have a profound effect on the rights and duties of the owners as well as the longevity of any new business. This decision will impact many different areas of a new business, including taxation, reporting requirements, legal liability, and available sources of capital. Selecting the appropriate business structure will help determine the best way to treat income and assets as well as minimize the risk associated with operating a new business venture. Because of the important implications of determining the optimal legal structure of a new business every entrepreneur should seek the advice and counsel of a skilled attorney and accountant.

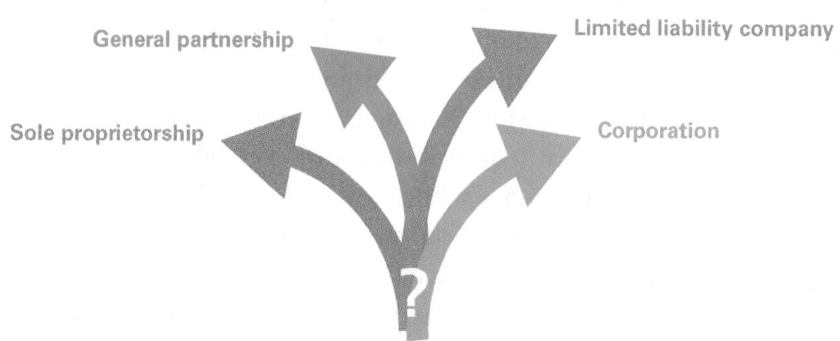

There are a series of important considerations that every entrepreneur should take into account when attempting to determine the most advantageous legal structure for a new business. "*When choosing a business entity, you should consider: (1) the degree to which your personal assets are at risk from liabilities arising from your business; (2) how to best pursue tax advantages and avoid multiple layers of taxation; (3) the ability to attract potential investors; (4) the ability to offer ownership interests to key employees; and (5) the costs of operating and maintaining the business entity.*"[19]

MAJOR FORMS OF BUSINESS OWNERSHIP

A ***Sole Proprietorship*** is merely an extension of the owner and as a consequence there is no legal distinction between the owner and the business. "You are the business and the business is you!" If you decide tomorrow to get a truck, and call yourself John's Junk Removal, you've just created a sole proprietorship without really going through any formal process!!

However, if you are the sole member of a domestic limited liability company (LLC), you are not a sole proprietor. You can operate a sole proprietorship under your own name, or under another name you've chosen with the provision that there are no other legal designations such as LLC or Inc. No forms or filing is required and all tax liability is the specific responsibility of the owner on an individual basis. Any debt or other liability is solely the responsibility of the proprietor to the full extent of all his/her personal and business assets.

Advantages

Control
Minimal Startup Costs
Easy to form/Dissolve
Flexibility

Disadvantages

Unlimited liability
Limited Resources
Management Deficiencies
Not a separate legal entity

A ***General Partnership*** is comprised of two or more owners, called partners. The formation of a partnership, either by written or oral agreement, requires a voluntary "association" of persons who assume ownership of the business. In a general partnership each partner has the legal right to participate in the management decisions within the business and share in the profits of the business. Additionally a general partner, regardless of the amount of their investment, assumes/shares unlimited personal liability for all the obligations of the business. All the debts of the business are the debts of the general partners. If the assets of the business are insufficient to pay the claims of its creditors, the creditors may seek financial remedy from one or more of the partners to pay the claims using their individual, non-business assets. Thus, a partner may have to pay more than his/her share of the partnership's liabilities.

Advantages

- Ease of formation
- Minimal Startup Costs
- Complementary skills
- Expanded financial capacity

Disadvantages

- Unlimited liability
- Not a legal entity
- Personality conflicts
- Difficult to terminate/transfer interest
- You are liable for your partner's torts (negligence) and contracts made in the ordinary course of business.

A ***Limited Partnership*** consists of at least one general partner and one or more limited partners. In many respects a limited partnership is similar to a general partnership, with one fundamental distinction. Limited partnerships have one or more partners who cannot participate in the management and control of the partnership's business. A partner who has such limited participation is considered a "limited partner" and does not generally incur personal liability for the partnership's obligations. A limited partnership is recognized as a legal entity only after a *Certificate of Partnership* is filed with the Secretary of State within the state in which it operates.

Uniform Partnership Act

> "Each state (with the exception of Louisiana) has its own laws governing partnerships, contained in what's usually called "The Uniform Partnership Act" or "The Revised Uniform Partnership Act" (or the "UPA" or "Revised UPA"). These statutes establish the basic legal rules that apply to partnerships and will control many aspects of your partnership's life unless you set out different rules in a written partnership agreement."[20]

When there is an absence of any formal document specifying the nature of the relationship between partners in a business all legal issues that may emerge are resolved using the Uniform Partnership Act (UPA) or the Revised Uniform Partnership Act (RUPA). The UPA/RUPA defines three key elements of any general partnership:

- Common ownership
- Shared profits and losses
- The right to participate in managing the operations of the business.

All partnerships should be regulated with partnership agreements that conform to the UPA/RUPA. Your partnership agreement should, at the very least, specify how business decisions will be made, disputes will be resolved, and issues of liquidation/buyout will be determined. This agreement is essential if for some reason you encounter difficulties with one or more of the partners or if someone wants out of the partnership. Additionally, the agreement should address the purpose of the business and the authority and responsibility of each partner. It's a good "rule of thumb" to consult an attorney experienced with small businesses for help in drafting the agreement.

General Partnership: ***Articles of Partnership Agreement***

At a minimun, prior to forming a partnership, in order to minimize the possibility of internal conflict between the partners, the following issue should be included in an Articles of Partnership Agreement.

- Contributions—the amount and time of contributions to be made by each partner should be specified.
- Management and control—identify whether some or all partners will manage and control the partnership.
- Profit and loss—specify how the profits and losses will be allocated to the partners.
- Distributions—indicate when distributions of cash or property will be made.
- Partner's responsibilities and duties—describe each partner's responsibilities and duties.
- Duration of the partnership—indicate the life of the partnership along with any events that may cause the partnership
- Death of a partner—identify how a partner's interest will be valued if the partner dies.
- Withdrawal—identify how a partner's interest will be valued if the partner withdraws from the partnership.
- Admission of new partners—indicate the process for admitting new partners into the partnership.
- Right of first refusal—specify that the partnership or individual partners will have the right to purchase a withdrawing partner's interest before the partner can offer to sell the interest to someone outside the partnership.
- Continuation of the partnership—identify the criteria to enable the partners to continue the partnership if an event causing the dissolution of the partnership occurs.

Corporations issue stock to their shareholders, who invest equity capital in the corporation with the presumption that they will earn a return on their investment. That profit may take the form of dividends paid by the corporation or increased market value of the company. The shareholders, who elect a board of directors to represent their interests, subsequently select the managers necessary to run the day-to-day operations of the business, own the corporation. Consequently, ownership and management of a corporation may be completely separate. A corporation has a life separate from its owners and its managers.

Advantages

Limited financial liability
Specialized management skill
Expanded financial capacity

Disadvantages

Costly to form/dissolve
Double Taxation
Legal Restrictions

Types of Corporations

Closed (Private) Corporations—Comprised of very few shareholders, set by state law (35 in California), whose shares are not available for sale to the general public. In the typical closed corporation, the controlling shareholders are also the managers within the business and as a result may legally be permitted to dispense with the board of directors and manage the close corporation as if it were a partnership.

> "A corporation owned and operated by a few individuals, often members of the same family, rather than by public shareholders. Close corporations are regulated by state close corporation statutes, which usually limit the number of shareholders to 30 or 35 shareholders and require special language in the articles of corporation. In exchange for following these requirements, state law usually permits close corporations to function more informally than regular corporations. For example, shareholders can make decisions without holding meetings of the board of directors and can fill vacancies on the board without a formal vote of the shareholders."[21]

Conventional (C) Corporation—Recognized by the state as a *"legal person"*, a corporation has the authority to act independently of, and assume liabilities separate from, its owners. What this means for the corporation's owners (stockholders) is that they are not liable for the debts or obligations of the corporation beyond their original investment.

A corporation not only limits the stockholders liability, it enables many people to share in the profits of a business "without working there or having other commitments". In addition its profits are taxed separately from its owners under subchapter C of the Internal Revenue Code.

Nearly all the shareholders of publicly held corporations are merely investors who are not involved in the management of the corporation. In most cases, the law requires a C corporation to report its financial operations to the state attorney general. Because a corporation is treated as an independent entity, a C corporation does not cease to exist when its owners or shareholders change or die. Shareholders elect a board of directors to make the business decisions essential to maintain the well-being of the organization as well as oversee all company policies. Professional managers who often own small percentages of the corporation manage the day-to-day operations of conventional corporations.

Subchapter S Corporation, or S Corporation—A special type of close corporation. It is treated nearly like a partnership for federal tax purposes. Its shareholders report the earnings or losses of the business on their individual federal income tax returns. This means that an S Corporation's profits are taxed only once—at the shareholder level. Thus, electing S Corporation status eliminates the double-taxation penalty of incorporation. S corporations became less attractive in the early 1990s for two reasons: (1) Tax law changes increased the top tax rate on the owners of S corporations to 39.6 percent—nearly six percentage points higher than the top rate on a C corporation's earnings; and (2) states were passing new legislation creating limited liability companies that had much the same appeal.

Limited Liability Company

A Limited Liability Company (LLC) is similar to an S Corporation without all of the special eligibility requirements. LLC's have all the flexibility of partnerships with the same kind of liability protection provided by a corporate structure. Limited Liability Companies (LLCs) have become the most popular choice for small to medium-sized businesses when compared to corporations or partnerships. Often described as the combination of a partnership and a corporation, the LLC combines a corporation's liability protection with a partnership's tax flexibility. All 50 states and the District of Columbia now recognize LLCs. Other benefits of an LLC are listed below.

- Limited personal liability for business debts and obligations. Liability does not extend beyond the member's capital contributions to the business.
- No shares of stock are issued in an LLC and each member owns an interest in the business as designated by the "Articles of Organization" which are similar to the "Articles of Incorporation" or "Articles of Partnership".
- Members may transfer their interest only with the unanimous written consent of all remaining members.
- The lifespan of an LLC is 30 years. Dissolution occurs only if all members choose/agree to dissolve the business.

- Owners/members are not required to be U.S. citizens or permanent residents
- Simplified record keeping (annual meetings and minutes are not required).
- Pass-through taxation wherein the owners (also known as "members") report their share of profits or losses in the company on their individual tax returns.

ENTREPRENEURSHIP: WE ARE ALL ENTREPRENEURS!

Like many college students, in the midst of a journey of exploration and discovery, you are often asked: What is your major? What type of work/career are you pursuing? These questions are unnerving, for good reason, and your responses to these questions may be some of the most significant you will make in your adult life. For most college students the pursuit of a college education represents a logical step in a career path leading to employment. Just ask your parents.

Far too often a large percentage of college students never dream of building their own business. Somehow they have convinced themselves that entrepreneurship is exclusively for those individuals who are capable of taking risks, organizing resources, capable of dealing with uncertainty, or gifted with greater creativity. However, most students engage in daily small acts of entrepreneurship without ever thinking that their actions are entrepreneurial. Entrepreneurship involves an awareness and assessment of a current situation, seeking alternative solutions to everyday problems, formulating plans and strategies for accomplishing your goals, and looking for new ways to make your life better. In your daily life you engage in these very same processes.

It is essential that each and every student begin to look at the world through the prism of an entrepreneur's eye. Look for new opportunities, seek new knowledge that is meaningful rather than simply designed to fill academic units, challenge old assumptions, and dare to put yourself to the ultimate test of building a business. Being an entrepreneur is about doing something you have never done before. Grab this opportunity with both hands and shake up your world. You are selling yourself short if you do not see yourself as an entrepreneur, or better yet, a "legendary hero".

ENDNOTES

1. Campbell, Joseph. The Hero with a Thousand Faces. California: New World Library, 2008.
2. "Celebrating Entrepreneurship around the World." CIPE. 2012. Center for International Private Enterprise. 12 Nov 2012 <http://www.cipe.org/blog/2012/11/12/celebrating-entrepreneurship-around-the-world/#.Uc9tlhb3D-a>.
3. Miller, Terry and Anthony B. Kim. 2017 Index of Economic Freedom: The Growth Impact of Economic Freedom. The Heritage Foundation.com. 2017. <http://www.heritage.org/index/book/chapter-1>
4. "Enterprise and Free Markets." The Heritage Foundation.com 2011-02-18 <http://www.heritage.org/Initiatives/Enterprise-and-Free-Markets>
5. Spinelli, S. and Abrams, R.J. Personal Entrepreneurial Strategy. McGraw-Hill 2013 <http://mhanswers-auth.mhhe.com/management/entrepreneurship/personal-entrepreneurial-strategy#seven-themes->
6. Friedman, Nick, and Soliman, Omar. Effortless Entrepreneur: Work Smart, Play Hard, Make Millions. New York: Three River Press, 2010
7. "The Importance of Cash Management" Reuters 2 Apr 2009. 6 May 2013 <http://www.reuters.com/article/2009/04/02/businesspropicks-us-findlaw-importance-o-idUSTRE5313U120090402>.

8. Cabrera, Bay. “Understanding Financial Statements.” Entrepreneur 7 Jun 2013. 15 Jun 2013 <http://www.entrepreneur.com.ph/growyourbusiness/article/understanding-financial-statements>.

9. Orfalea, Paul. Copy This! How I turned Dyslexia, ADHD, and 100 square feet into a company called Kinko’s. New York: Workman Publishing Company Inc. 2007.

10. Baumol, W.J, 1993, Entrepreneurship, management and the structure of payoffs, Cambridge. MA:MIT Press

11. Small Business Economic indicators, Office of Small Business Advocacy, US Small Business Administration, Washington D.C, June 2003 (Available from www.sba.gov)

12. Ibid

13. “Some of the Reasons Why Business Fail and How to Avoid Them.” Entrepreneur Weekly, Issue 36, 3-10-96.

14. Godin, Seth. The Dip: A Little Book That Teaches you When to Quit and When to Stick. New York: The Penguin Group, 2007

15. Duermyer, Randy. “Do You Really Need a Business Plan?: Can You Start a Small Business Without a Formal Business Plan?” the balance 10 Aug 2016. 6 Jul 2017 <https://www.thebalance.com/do-you-really-need-a-business-plan-1794226>

16. Ennico, Cliff. “Accepting Money From Friends & Family.” Entrepreneur 6 May 2002. 1 Jul 2013 <http://www.entrepreneur.com/article/51542>.

17. United States Small Business Administration. Business Loan Application Checklist. 29 Mar. 2012. <http://www.sba.gov/content/business-loan-application-checklist>

18. United States Small Business Administration. The SBIC Program: Seeking SBIC Financing for Your Small Business. 29 Mar. 2012 <http://archive.sba.gov/aboutsba/sbaprograms/inv/esf/inv_sbic_financing.html>

19. *How to Choose the Right Business Entity.* Nationwide Incorporators, 2017. <https://www.nationwide-incorporators.com/article-how-to-choose-right-entity>

20. Laurence, Beth. “Creating a Partnership Agreement: Put the terms of your partnership in writing to protect your business.” NOLO: Law for All. 2013. <http://www.nolo.com/legal-encyclopedia/creating-partnership-agreement-29906.html>.

21. Definition provided by Nolo’s Plain English-Law Dictionary, published by NOLO: Law for All <http://www.nolo.com/dictionary/close-corporation-term.html>.

SOURCES

1. Fig. 4.1: Copyright © Seattle City Council (CC by 2.0) at https://commons.wikimedia.org/wiki/File:Jeff_Bezos_at_Amazon_Spheres_Grand_Opening_in_Seattle_-_2018_(39262177384).jpg.

Chapter 5

Management

Maximizing Human Potential

PROLOGUE

It may be a rather simplistic statement but management at its most basic level is an interpersonal process comprised of working with people, and other scarce resources, to achieve organizational goals and objectives. However, such a definition does little to explain the significance of management, and managers, and the complex and multidimensional responsibilities of today's modern manager. Management is both a circular and continuous process of interrelated activities designed to simultaneously produce efficient and effective outcomes. In other words, management is about achieving results by mobilizing the talents and abilities of people! Like a professor in the classroom, a coach in the gym, or a manager in a retail store, managers achieve success as a result of their ability to inspire and harness the willing participation of the people who work under their leadership and supervision. A manager, professor or coach is successful only to the extent that the people they manage are successful. The ongoing challenge for any individual who assumes the role of manager is to bring together a diverse group of individuals, all with unique needs and expectations, and instill in each individual a common sense of purpose and commitment, provide them with the training and resources necessary to perform their individual jobs, and empower each employee to perform at the highest level possible.

The primary responsibility of management is to improve the ability of organizational members to efficiently utilize its scarce resources to achieve the vision, mission and goals of the organization. Effective managers utilize four key resources: human resources, material resources, informational resources, and financial resources to achieve the goals and objectives of the organization.

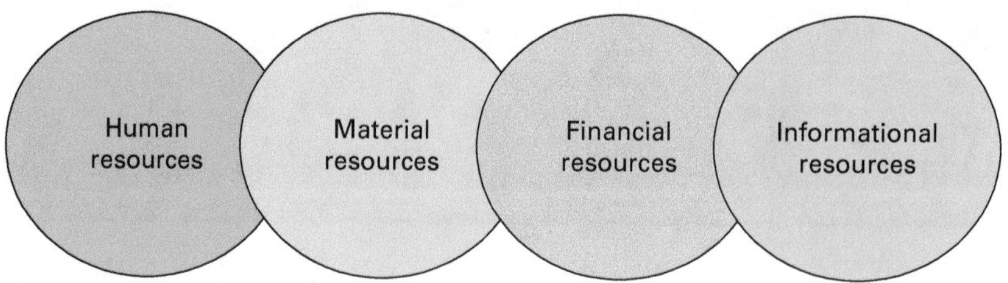

In order to achieve their goals organizations rely on their management teams, and individual managers, to carry out the four critical management functions of planning, organizing, leading, and controlling. Today's successful managers just don't "boss" people; instead they create a vision and actively sell their new and innovative ideas to the members of the organization in an ethical and responsible manner. However, effective management is not a naturally occurring event but instead the result of experience, training, education, as well as trial and error.

MANAGEMENT: DYNAMIC FORCES IN A CHANGING ENVIRONMENT

The transformational change coming will soon make the way we work almost unrecognizable. In an era of evolving technologies, business models, demographics, and workplace attitudes change is occurring exponentially in its pace and scope. A number of changes have prompted managers to restructure their organizations and their approach to management. A short list of some of the most significant changes facing managers in the 21st century involve:

- *Global Political Instability*
- *Global Economic/Business Crisis*

- *Greater Government Intrusion and Regulation*
- *Shifting Social Norms & Values*
- *Changing and Diverse Workforce*
- *Constantly evolving "Disruptive Technologies"*[1]

These changes require a shift in the old management paradigm built upon the principles of hierarchy, command and control, and specialization to a new model based on a systems approach where collaboration, synergism, innovation, self-managed teams and an organic structure are the new standard. Managers, in the face of all of the changes in the workplace, must now be able to:

- Establish and articulate a purposeful vision.
- Recognize the unique needs of consumers in the marketplace.
- Utilize big data and advanced analytics as a means of understanding customer patterns, correlations and preferences.
- Efficiently allocate and utilize scarce resources.
- Utilize technology to improve processes throughout the organization.
- Anticipate and plan for changes in the market, industry, and economy.
- Understand the nature and scope of their core competencies.
- Build trust and collaborative relationship with all members of the organization.

Executives are shifting away from downsizing and outsourcing toward innovation, scenario planning and pricing optimization. But nearly 60 percent of them remain concerned that the effect of the recession on consumer behavior will linger for at least three more years. The question is: What will it take for companies to accelerate faster than the competition?"[2]

MANAGEMENT SKILLS

In his 1974 article in the Harvard Business Review entitled, "Skills of an Effective Administrator", social psychologist Robert L. Katz, described *"three basic developable skills"* required to carry out the *"administrative processes"* by managers based on their level of administrative responsibility. In order to carry out these important responsibilities managers must possess the knowledge and skill necessary to insure the success of the organization. These are three commonly accepted skills[3] necessary to be an effective manager:

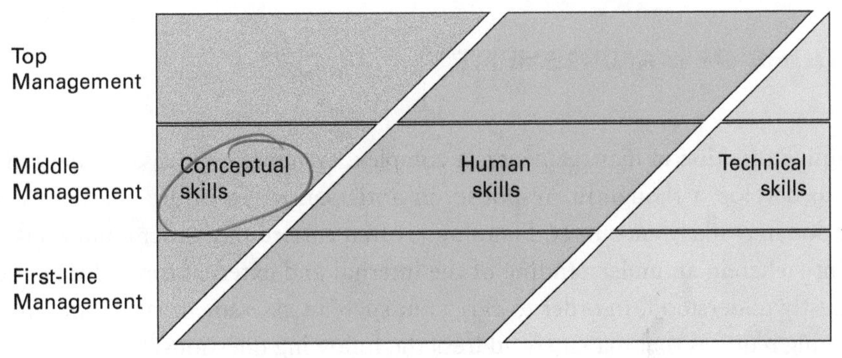

Conceptual Skills

Conceptual skills refer to the ability of a manager to think creatively, analyze complex situations, understand cause and effect, and solve complex problems. A manager's conceptual skills allow him/her to see the big picture and understand the interdependence of all aspects of an organization. Additionally, conceptual skills provide managers with an understanding and awareness of the forces outside their organization (political, economic, competitive, social, technological) that will directly or indirectly impact their ability to successfully compete and/or create a meaningful competitive advantage. In the business world, these skills are considered a prerequisite for individuals seeking top-level management positions.

Human Relations Skills

Also referred to as interpersonal skills, these skills allow managers to work effectively with and through people. This includes the ability to lead, inspire, delegate tasks, resolve conflicts, and empathize with people on a day-to-day basis while vigorously pursuing organizational objectives. Leaders who have the ability to maintain, and facilitate, good human relations in their teams are likely to be more successful. Some studies suggest that it may be more important for leaders to be knowledgeable and skilled in human relations, individual motivation, and group processes, than to be highly proficient in the subject matter under discussion. "Great leaders move us. They ignite our passion and inspire the best in us. When we try to explain why they are so effective, we speak of strategy, vision, or powerful ideas. But the reality is much more primal: Great leadership works through emotions. No matter what leaders set out to do—whether it's creating strategy, mobilizing teams to action—their success depends on how they do it. Even if they get everything else right, if leaders fail in this primal task of driving emotions in the right direction, nothing they do will work as well as it could or should."[4]

Technical Skills

Often referred to as task-related skills, front line managers must possess specific knowledge or ability related to various functional areas within the organization. In order to be able to direct, train, and evaluate the work of employees in manufacturing, accounting, marketing, or technical support, front line managers must possess expert knowledge in the functional area over which he/she has oversight authority.

FUNCTIONS OF MANAGEMENT

Planning

The planning function of management is a complex, systematic process wherein managers attempt to develop a thoughtful response, in anticipation, to future challenges that the organization may likely encounter. Planning is often carried out under conditions of great uncertainty wherein an understanding of the internal and external forces for change must be manifestly understood. In order to carry out such an assessment, at a minimum, effective planning requires that managers address the following questions:

- *What goals and objectives are most appropriate?*
- *How will resources be allocated?*
- *What future trends will impact the organization?*
- *What are the best strategies needed to compete and win in the marketplace?*

In addition, planning requires managers to consider four fundamental questions that examine both internal and external forces for change. The four fundamental questions are:

- *What is the situation now?*
- *Where do we want to go?*
- *How can we get there from here?*
- *What obstacles do we have to overcome?*
- *What opportunities do we need to act on?*

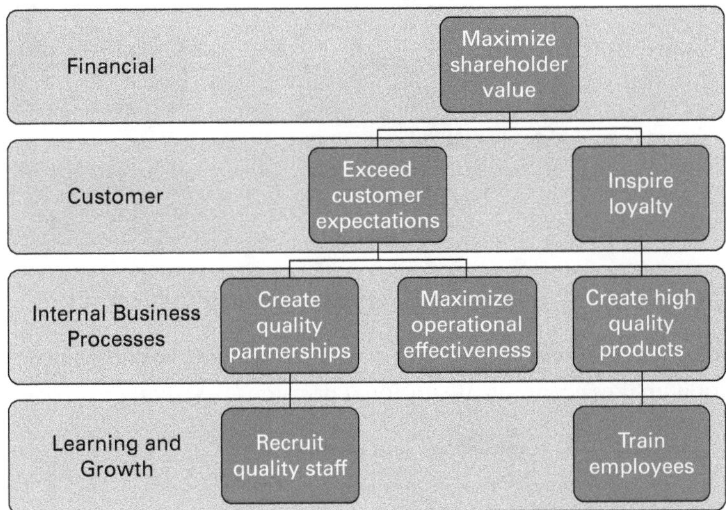

In order to address these questions and develop effective responses to forces outside and inside the organization, top managers conduct a SWOT analysis in order to identify the prevailing strengths, weaknesses, opportunities, and threats facing the organization.

SWOT Analysis

A SWOT analysis is a comprehensive assessment of the strengths, weaknesses, opportunities, and threats affecting the planning process within the organization. This strategic planning tool is used to identify the organization's internal strengths and weaknesses and the external environment's opportunities and threats. When examining the internal environment the firm is attempting to identify its core competencies that are unique to it and what resources, capabilities, and knowledge it has that can be used to exploit market opportunities. The process also requires managers to identify the internal weaknesses and/or deficiencies within the organization that diminish the competitiveness of the firm. An analysis of the external environment is conducted in order to identify the challenges, emerging trends, and changes in the environment that represent potential opportunities and threats. One of the most significant challenges facing managers when conducting a

SWOT analysis is the collection of current market information in a timely fashion and transforming it into usable knowledge that may be leads to the creation of a viable plan that will facilitate a sustainable competitive advantage.

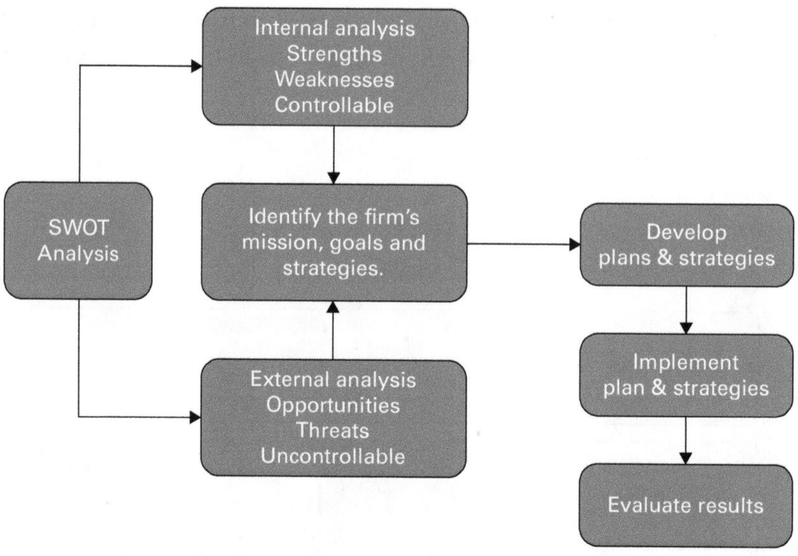

Decision Making: A Manager's Primary Responsibility

#6

According to the *classical model*[5] of decision making a manager, having access to all of the relevant information, makes economically rational decisions based on four basic assumptions.

1. *Problems are precisely formulated and defined.*
2. *All alternatives and results can be accurately identified.*
3. *All criteria for evaluating alternatives have been established.*
4. *The decision maker is both logical and rational.*

The basic premise of the model is that once a manager recognizes the need to make a decision, they then should be capable of generating a series of credible alternatives necessary to make the right choice. The right choice in this instance is the one that produces the greatest economic benefit for the organization. A rational decision provides a structured and sequenced approach to decision making and brings logic, rather than personal preference, to the decision-making process.

Decision Making—A Rational Process

> "Good decision makers know that the most important, and most difficult, part of decision making is not making the decision. That's often quite easy. The most difficult and most important part is to make sure that the decision is about the right problem. . . Every decision is risky: it is a commitment of present resources to an uncertain and unknown future. Ignore a single element in the process and the decision will tumble down like a badly built wall in an earthquake. But if

> the process is faithfully observed and if the necessary steps are taken, the risk will be minimized and the decision will have a good chance of turning out to be successful."[6]

In order to be an effective decision maker, managers must understand the context of the environment in which they are operating within, as well as the internal forces exerting influence over their employees and organization. This "knowledge base" includes information about the industry and its technology, company culture, policies and practices, available resources, and company goals and plans. There are seven steps in the rational process model:

- *Define the situation (problem).*
- *Describe and collect information needed to achieve the goal.*
- *Develop as many viable alternatives as possible.*
- *Develop agreement among those involved.*
- *Decide which alternative is optimal.*
- *Do what is indicated. Implement the decision.*
- *Determine whether the decision was a good one. Did the decision solve the problem?*

Rational decision making can help the decision makers to deal with difficult problems; "It is a well-defined step-by-step approach that required defining problems, identifying the weighing and decision criteria, listing out the various alternatives,deliberating the present and future consequences of each alternative, and rating each alternative on each criterion."[7]

Developing a Mission Statement

A mission statement is important because it addresses a basic human need for definition and direction. Deliberative mission statements provide direction and focus, strengthen unity among company employees, and serve to increase productivity.

> "In order to write good mission statements, we must first begin at the very center of our circle of influence, that center comprised of our most basic paradigms, the lens through which we see the world. Whatever is at the center of our life will be the source of our security, guidance, wisdom, and power."[8]

Does a company have to have a mission statement to be successful? In all likelihood if you were to ask this question to any business owner or manager you would get a definitive yes as well as a definitive no! However, a thoughtfully written mission statement spells out the reason a company is in business as well as the key values the organization is committed to. No matter how well written a mission statement its real value is derived from the purpose and direction it provides to every member of an organization. More than just a poster on the wall, a meaningful mission statement defines the purpose of the organization and the values and ethical principles that serve as the foundation for employee performance. A compelling mission statement can separate an organization from its competitors and assist in attracting the most capable employees, keep everyone moving toward a common goal, and ultimately drive performance.

Recommendations

The best-worded mission statements are simple and concise. They speak loudly and clearly, generate enthusiasm for the firm's core purpose, and elicit personal effort and dedication from everyone within your company. A well-crafted mission statement enables the organization, its managers and employees to have a big-picture perspective of "who we are, what we do, and where we are headed".

"Tesla's mission is to accelerate the world's transition to sustainable energy."

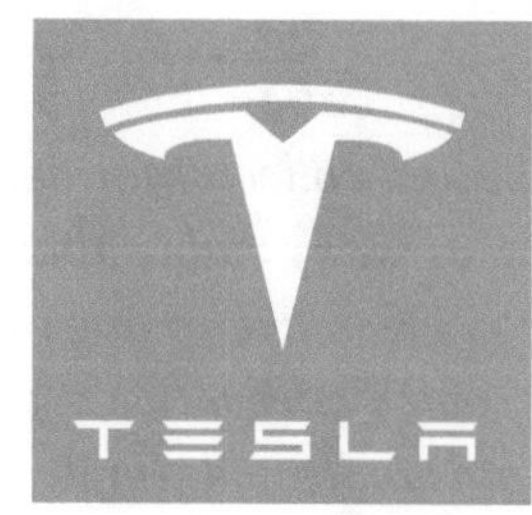

Types of Planning

Strategic Planning

Strategic planning is a systematic process wherein managers attempt to look into the future, create scenarios of the future based on current trends, and determine the most effective strategy for adjusting to the forces that will affect their organization. Strategic planning normally looks three to five years into the future and attempts to chart the best course of action based on the most dominant indicators of what the business environment will be like in those years.

Major indicators include shifting demographics, erratic economic cycles, ever-expanding government policies, and rapid advances in technology all influence strategy development. These indicators, if accurately anticipated, provide managers and their respective organizations with an understanding of the changes in: consumer lifestyles, fluctuations in the economy, and government policies that continue to influence the day-to-day operations of every business. Effective strategic planning helps managers formulate strategies so that their organizations can take full advantage of opportunities and whenever possible minimize threats.

Strategic planning requires top-level managers to make major decisions affecting the entire organization. It requires managers to develop a plan of action designed to positively affect the long-term performance of the company. A strategic plan is the output of the strategic planning process.

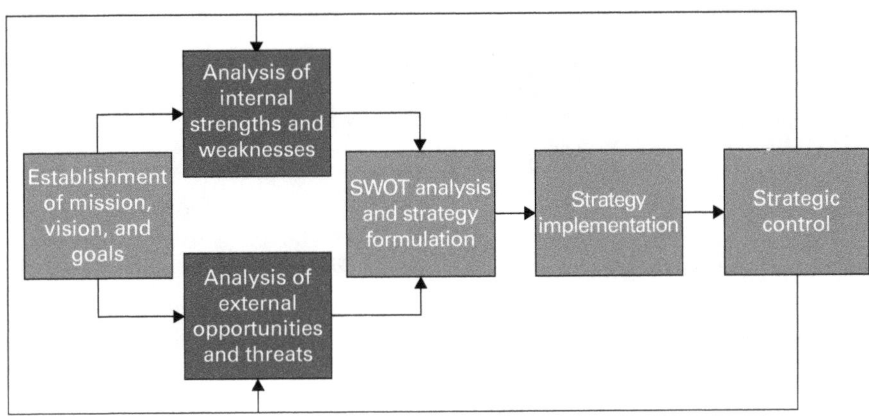

Source: Adapted from T. Bateman and S. Snell, M: Management, McGraw-Hill Irwin (2013) pp.99

At the strategic planning stage the company decides, among other important considerations, which markets to serve, what products or services to develop, sell and/or distribute, and what geographic regions the firm will compete.

Tactical Planning

Tactical planning, carried out by middle- and front-line managers, is short range planning typically covering a period of one to two years. Tactical planning typically encompasses the current operations within various departments within the organization. It is in essence the process of taking the strategic plan and breaking it down into specific, short-term actions and plans. Tactical plans are usually developed in the areas of production, marketing, human resources, finance, and facilities. It is the process of developing detailed, short-term plans, which address the following questions:

1. *What is to be done?*
2. *Who is to do it?*
3. *How is it to be done?*

Operational Planning

This type of short-term planning (typically daily, weekly, monthly, or quarterly) is more narrowly focused on the resources, processes, duration, time frame, quality control, and work standards that guide the implementation of the tactical plan. Frontline managers are responsible for adhering to the specific procedures and processes stipulated by middle management necessary to carry out the operational plan.

Contingency Planning

This type of planning requires managers to engage in a systematic process where they identify events or situations that could have an adverse affect on the organization.

> **Murphy's Law**
> Anything that can go wrong,
> Will go wrong.

This process requires managers to ask a series of "What if" questions in an attempt to develop a thoughtful and planned response to each scenario. The objective of contingency planning is not to identify and develop a plan for every possible contingency. Instead, a contingency plan will contain a series of strategies and/or action plans that allow the organization to anticipate, contend, diminish or even exploit a particular situation. The following questions are useful when developing contingency plans:

1. What events may occur that require a response?
2. What scenarios are most probable?
3. What is the worst-case scenario?
4. What event would cause the greatest disruption to the organization?

Organizing Function

The process of organizing involves the creation of the formal structure of the organization in which human and material resources are blended into a deliberate order so as to maximize organizational efficiency. The structure of an organization should be designed with the intent of creating a configuration that allows employees to effectively and efficiently accomplish the goals of the company.

> **"Structuring Work: The Art of Management"**
> "We don't hire the kind of people you can order around, like the foot soldiers in an army who charge from their foxholes without question when the sergeant yells. 'Let's go, boys!' We don't want drones who will simply follow directions ... We do want people who, once they buy into a decision and believe in what they are doing, will work like demons to produce something of the highest possible quality—whether a shirt, a catalog, a store display, or a computer program. How you get these highly individualistic people to align and work for a common cause is the art of management at Patagonia."[9] —Yvon Chouinard

Variables Affecting Organizational Structure

Technology

The type of technology that the firm utilizes to produce its products affects the design of the organization. The effective company uses technology and collaboration to focus its internal resources, reduce complexity of operations to gain benefits of speed, cost reduction, and access to new competencies.

Organization Size

As organizations downsize so too do the number of levels of management. Fewer levels of management, empowered workers, and fewer differences in responsibility allow for the increase in speed and decision making.

Tall vs. Flat Structures

Multiple layers of management and bureaucratic processes characterize tall, centralized, organizations. A centralized structure results in authority and decision-making limited to a small number of top-level managers. These bureaucratic processes create inefficiencies in communication and decision-making. Few layers of management characterize a flat, decentralized, structure with greater power delegated to lower-level employees. This shift to fewer management layers within an organization allows for a more rapid response to the competitive forces in the market as well as the constantly changing demands of the consumer.

Span of Control

This refers to the optimum number of subordinates that a manager can effectively supervise. There are three major variables that influence a manager's span of control: Capabilities of the Manager - Capabilities of Subordinates - Complexity of the Job

> "The commonly accepted definition of span of control is as follows: 'the number of subordinates directly reporting to a leader/manager.' For what it's worth, I really dislike the term and find it to be outdated at best, and destructive at worst. I prefer the more inclusive term constituency management. I want leaders to think span of influence and awareness, to shift thinking from rigid structures to lose collaborative networks, and to think open source not proprietary."[10]

Environmental Uncertainty

Rapidly changing environments require organizational designs that are flexible and capable of adapting to changes in a highly uncertain competitive environment.[11]

Bureaucratic Organizations

At the turn of the 20th century, because of the industrial revolution occurring in Germany, Max Weber developed the principles of bureaucracy[12], which were designed to ensure organizational efficiency. Weber believed that "rational authority" was more efficient because it was based on rules and procedures, a clear division of labor and distinct definitions of authority. Bureaucracy, as characterized by Weber, is based on the following principles:

- *A strict adherence to a "chain of command"*
- *Formal patterns of delegation*
- *Specific rules and regulations guiding employee actions/behavior*
- *Selection based on qualifications*
- *Departmentalization based on function*

- *Narrow span of management*
- *Tall organization*
- *Minimal communication between departments*

Levels of Management

Top Management is the highest level in the management pyramid. Individuals at this level are responsible for structuring work, controlling operations, budget development, obtaining funds and developing strategic plans. Managers at these levels have responsibilities for the entire organization involving multiple business activities. Top managers' have titles that include: CEO, CFO, CIO, and President.

Middle Management is responsible for translating the general goals and plans developed by top managers into specific tactical plans. Middle managers' job titles include: General Manager, Plant manager, and Regional manager.

Supervisory Management supervises line employees, not other managers, assigns work, evaluates daily performance, and supervises day to day operations. Although first-level managers typically do not set goals for the organization they have a very strong influence on the company as a result of their daily interaction with employees. These managers have job titles such as: Shift supervisor, Foreperson, Crew leader, Store manager.

Organization Chart

An organizational chart is a graphic depiction of the structure of an organization in terms of relationships among personnel and/or functional departments. An organizational chart represents lines of authority and responsibility and the lines that connect the shapes indicate relationships between the various positions within the organization. An organizational chart represents the formal structure of a business or company.

In a hierarchical organizational chart, the Chief Executive Officer is the top-level manager and underneath the chief executive officer are high-level managers or executives, and each succeeding level includes the subordinate employees of the line above. In traditional organizational charts, the shape is similar to a pyramid where solid lines depict a formal and direct relationship between positions. A dashed line indicates an advisory or indirect relationship between positions, while arrows indicate the flow of communication. In non-traditional organizations, where a more decentralized team structure or "boundaryless" structure is prevalent there are no line/vertical relationships or top-to-bottom lines of managerial authority. This type of organic structure creates a more flexible and responsive organization, which creates more involved and empowered employees.

Organization Models

A *Line Organization* is based on vertical relationships within the organization with authority flowing from the top down and employees reporting to a single manager. Line managers are granted formal line authority and power by the organization in order to direct and control the actions and work performance of line employees.

Advantages

- *Clearly defined lines of authority*
- *Easy to understand*
- *Every employee has only one supervisor*

Disadvantages

- *Inflexibility*
- *Poor communication*
- *Little support for line employees*
- *Decision making limited to top management*

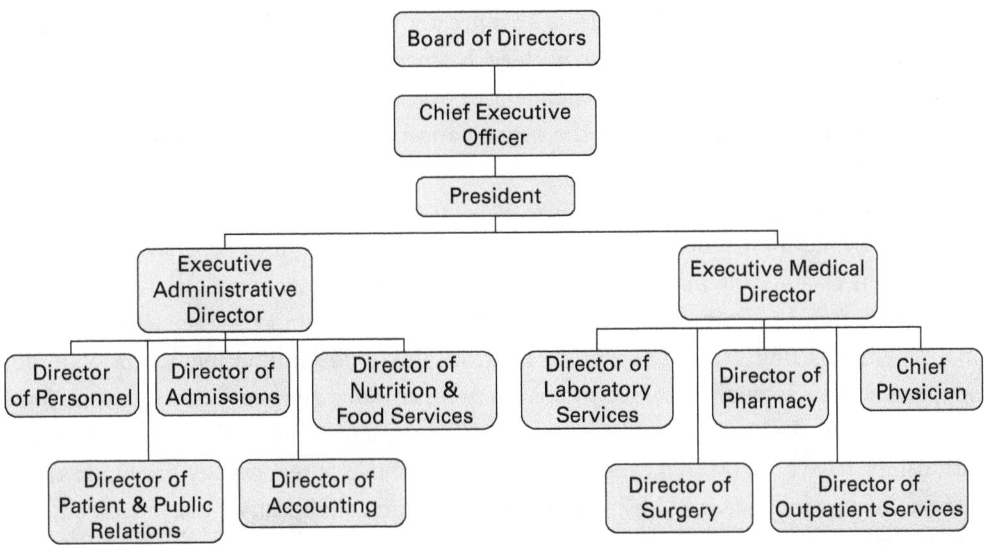

The *Line/Staff Structure* is unique from a line structure in that staff positions represent individuals (outside specialists) who serve in an advisory capacity and provide assistance and counsel to line managers while maintaining no formal line authority. Solid lines in an organization chart represent line positions while hyphenated lines represent staff positions.

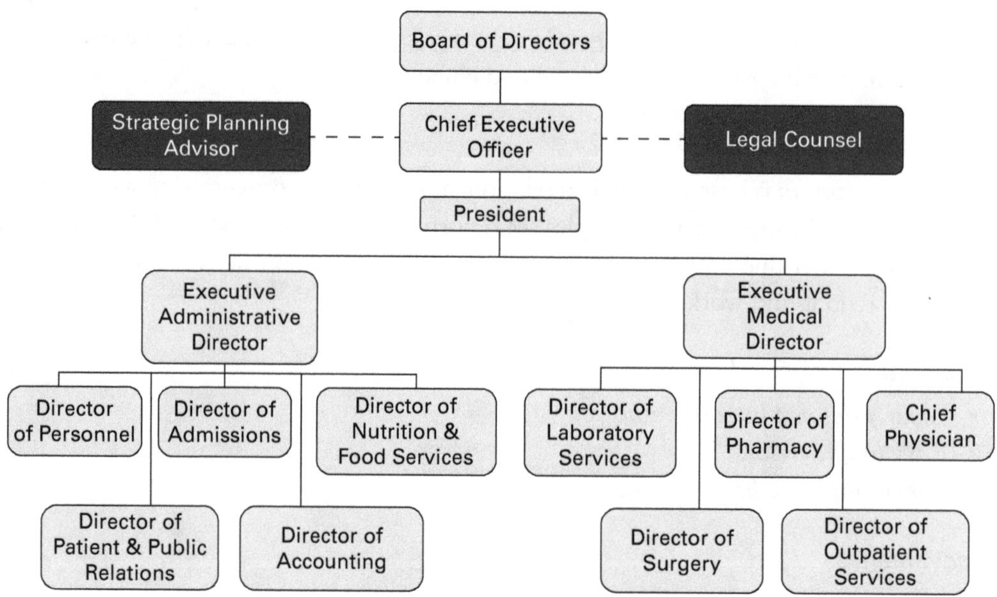

Adapting to Change

In virtually every organization, regardless of its size, the people and the functions they perform are not completely independent. To a greater or lesser degree, all parts of an organization have a reciprocal relationship with each other. In simple terms this means that the people in the organization are interdependent of one another and must be able to communicate, cooperate, and collaborate if the organization is to effectively utilize the resources of the firm.

Important developments in the last few decades of the twentieth century and the early part of the twenty-first century have focused on the nature of interdependence of people and functions within contemporary organizations. The resultant changes that have emerged involve the flattening of organizational structures, developing improved horizontal connections, de-emphasizing vertical reporting relationships, and eliminating layers of middle management. In a virtual sense, technology has contributed to even flatter organizational structures. With the creation and advancement of computer networks formal structural relationships have been blurred even further. The rapid rise of technology has made virtual organizations possible where (24/7) communication and collaborative, decentralized, decision-making are rapidly becoming the norm.

21st Century Transformation

"Organizational structure fulfills many functions—everyone in the organization knows who he or she reports to; how various repetitive/routine activities are to be discharged; who has what authority and responsibility; how personnel are grouped together (e.g., by departments or divisions); which individuals/groups have decision-making authority and which have primarily advisory functions (line versus staff functions); and what mechanisms are deployed primarily for reducing decision-making uncertainty, for ensuring differentiated or specialized responses to the operating environment, and for coordinating and integrating these differentiated or specialized responses. A well-designed structure that is compatible with strategy or is internally coherent and compatible with the organization's operating environment tends to contribute to superior organizational performance.

Certain kinds of structural changes, notably creating many self-contained, substantially autonomous units with stretch targets, extensive delegation of authority to lower level decision-makers, and de-layering (removal of some of the managerial levels to reduce the number of approving authorities for innovation) may increase the potential innovations of the organization."[13]

Restructuring

This process involves the redesign of an organization so that it can more effectively and efficiently service customers. It is a difficult process and requires managers to alter their thinking and develop new structures that break away from the traditional models advocated by Fayol, Weber and Taylor. Cross-functional structures represent a shift from highly specialized line structures to teams of individuals from various departments that go across traditional line relationships.

Inverted Organizations

The intention of this process is to turn the organization upside down with the contact people (empowered front-line workers) at the top and the top manager (chief executive officer) at the bottom. An inverted structure is intended to illustrate, both symbolically and structurally that management within the organization exists to support the efforts of non-managerial employees in all aspects of their job.

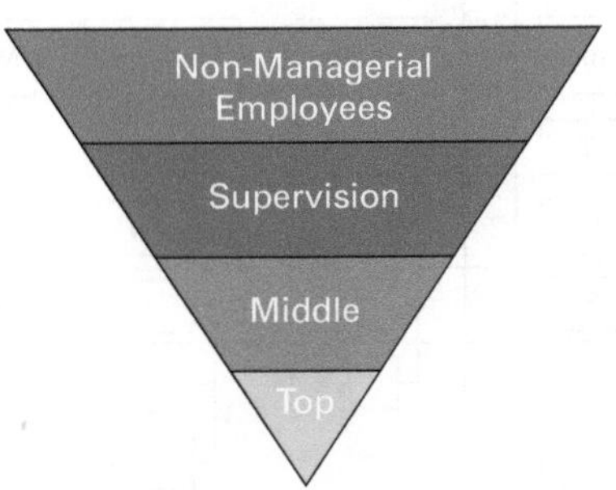

Cross-Functional Teams are comprised of employees from different departments who work on specific projects, such as developing new products or solving complex problems. Cross-functional teams represent a structural change within an organization and attempt to improve internal communication, coordination, and collaboration by bringing together people from different departments and areas of expertise. This will, in theory, allow the team members to see beyond their own limited point of view. These teams are; 1) empowered to make decisions on their own without seeking the approval of management; 2) often successful in reducing the barriers between functional departments; and 3) rely on technology to facilitate simultaneous intra-departmental work on various projects.

From Hierarchical Silos

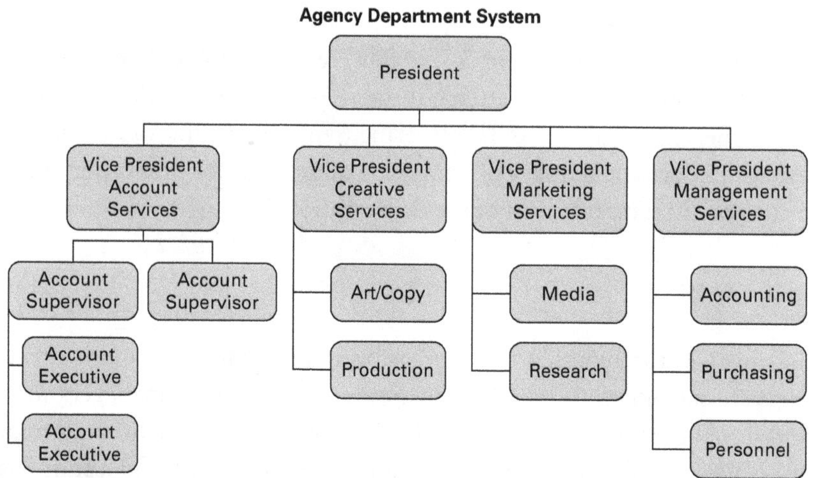

Lack of Communication
Individual Processes
Multiple Handoffs Less Efficient

To

Cross Functional Teams

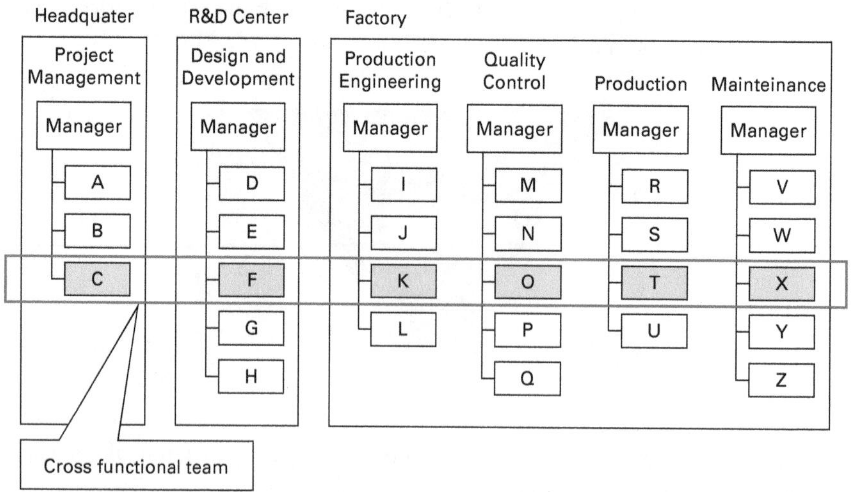

Open Channels of Communication
Greater Collaboration
Increased Efficiency & Result

Cross-functional teams also are characterized by the following limitations:

- Resistance to change (managers and employees).
- Uncertainty on the part of team members.
- Requires different skills from those used when working alone.
- Inappropriate team structure for the task.

Preconditions Necessary to Achieve Success

- *Proper membership (no unnecessary people)*
- *A clear vision and purpose*
- *The right connections (team members can reach others as well)*
- *Achievable, measurable results*
- *Understood and agreed-upon ground rules*
- *Intensive team building up front*

LEADING FUNCTION: EMPOWERING WORKERS

Leadership permeates every level of the organization and is the mechanism that directs and motivates employees to achieve organizational goals and objectives.

> **The courage of leadership is giving others a chance to succeed even though you bear the responsibility for getting things done.**
> • SIMON SINEK •

The one basic requirement of any leader is the willingness of others to follow. Building trust, providing timely information and feedback, training and developing employees to perform at the highest levels, and rewarding outstanding performance are the means by which leaders can empower members of their organization.

Styles of Leadership

Leadership style is the manner and approach of providing direction, implementing plans, and making decisions. Kurt Lewin (1939) led a group of researchers that identified three different styles of leadership.[14] The study revealed that leaders may choose to use all three leadership styles in their interactions with employees; however one of the three were normally dominant. Lewin and his fellow researchers identified three styles of leadership utilized when making decisions.

Leaders making decisions on their own without consulting others characterizes ***Autocratic Leadership***. This type of leader makes all the decisions, "calls all the shots", and fails to seek any input from subordinate employees. In addition, autocratic leaders provide specific directions of what needs to be done, who should perform the job, when it should be done, and how it should be done. There also exists a clear division between the leader and the followers. Researchers found that decision making was less creative under autocratic leadership and that it was far more difficult to move from an autocratic style to a democratic style than vice versa.

Participative (Democratic) Leadership attempts to involve subordinate employees in decision making. Participative leaders offer guidance to group members, but they also actively participate in the decision-making process allowing for input from all other group members. Participative leaders encourage group members to participate, but retain the final say over the decision-making process.

Laissez-Faire (Free-Rein) Leadership utilizes a minimal amount of supervision and provides subordinate employees the opportunity to make most decisions regarding how they will accomplish established objectives. While this style can be effective in situations where group members are highly qualified in an area of expertise, it can often lead to a lack of motivation as a result of poorly defined roles for individual employees.

Empowerment: Maximizing Employee Performance

> "In addition to self-awareness, imagination, and conscience, it is the fourth human endowment, independent will that really makes effective self management possible.… Empowerment comes from learning how to use this great endowment in the decisions we make every day" —*Steven Covey*

Empowerment provides employees with the authority and responsibility to respond quickly to customer needs and requests. Empowerment is a process wherein employees in an organization assume control over the performance of their jobs as a result of the transfer of power and authority to non-managerial personnel. This allows line employees to act on issues that they define as important. At the very core of empowerment is the transfer of power. Traditional management views power as a mechanism used to exert influence and control, often treating power as a commodity limited only to the purview of managers within the organization. Conceived in this way, power can be viewed as unchanging or unchangeable. However, power is dynamic and does not exist in isolation and as a result is constantly in a state of change. Power is created in relationships and empowerment is a process of changing the very nature of the relationship between manager and employee.

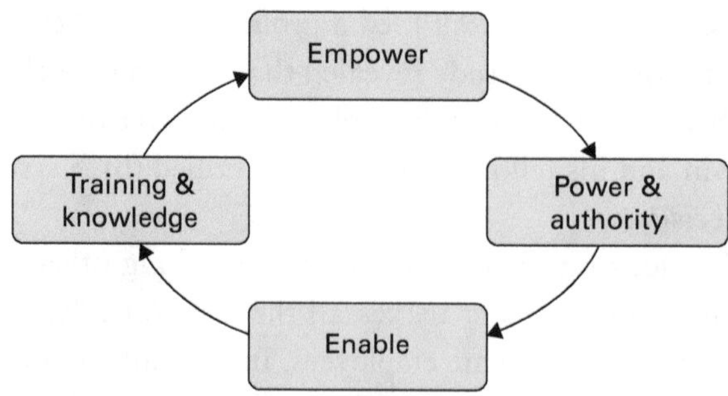

Enabling provides workers with the education and training they need to assume their new decision making powers. Absent the knowledge, skill, and training necessary to assume greater power employees will fail to produce the results necessary for the organization to prosper and grow.

> "As business schools parse the myriad elements of leadership, one thing has become clear: Leadership is an intensely personal business ... Leaders often follow such incredibly different paths and take such drastically different approaches that it's difficult to pinpoint the common traits that make them effective."[15]

Controlling Function

Controlling, although a separate management function, is directly related to planning. The controlling process ensures that plans are being implemented properly. Planning moves forward all the other management functions, and controlling reaches back and as such is both anticipatory and retrospective. Controlling is the final step in the functional chain of management activities and brings the functions of management full circle.

Control is the process through which standards of performance, for people and processes, are set, communicated, and applied. Effective control systems use mechanisms that monitor essential activities and when necessary initiate corrective action. The control process is continuous and cyclical which means that it occurs at regular intervals, on a regular basis, throughout the course of a year. The process attempts to anticipate problems and take preventive/corrective action. Controlling leads to the identification of new problems that in turn must to be addressed through a systematic process involving the following steps:

1. *Establish clear performance standards that are specific, attainable, and measurable.*
2. *Monitor and record actual performance.*
3. *Compare performance results to established plans and standards.*
4. *Communicate results and deviations with employees.*
5. *Take corrective action when performance deviates from established standards.*

MANAGING IN A CHANGING WORLD

The "art" of management continues to evolve as the world continues to change. Today managers must be prepared to adapt to a changing workplace and employee attitudes, earn the trust of stakeholders all while dealing with complex ethical issues. In addition managers must be capable of developing creative and competitive strategies while simultaneously attempting to anticipate the effects of economic and political uncertainties. Lastly, managers must learn and then incorporate the newest technologies into all aspects of the organization and its core operations.

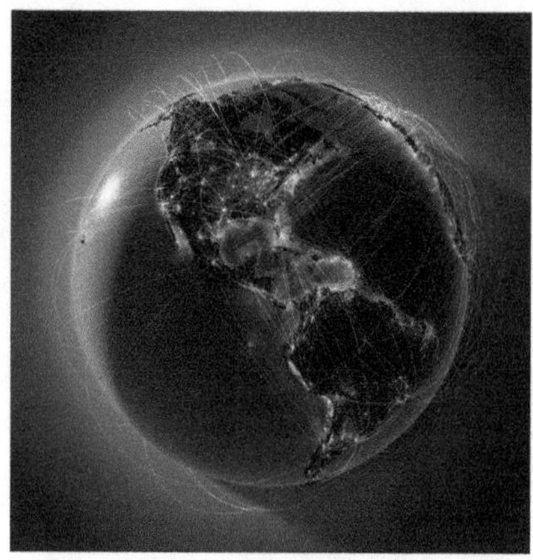

Managers, at every level in an organization, are going to have to learn how to manage in a constantly changing world where the only constant is change. The new reality is that how managers manage is changing and with this change a new paradigm for managing future organizations will be required. "The latest Gallup findings indicate that 70% of American workers are "not engaged" or "actively disengaged" and are emotionally disconnected from their workplaces and less likely to be productive. Currently, 52% of workers are not engaged, and worse, another 18% are actively disengaged in their work. Gallup estimates that these actively disengaged employees cost the U.S. between $450 billion to $550 billion each year in lost productivity."[16] The modern manager needs to get work done through engaged, self-managed, knowledge workers, who are no longer the "hired hands" of the industrial age. Not an easy task!

ENDNOTES

1. Lambert, Bob." Great-Quotes.com. Gledhill Enterprises, 2011. 16 December. 2011. <http://www.great-quotes.com/quote/1274730>

2. "Management Tools & Trends 2011." Bain & Company.13 Dec 2010 <http://www.bain.com/publications/articles/Management-tools-trends-2011.aspx>

3. Katz, Robert L. "Skills of an Effective Administrator." Harvard Business Review 52 (1974): 90-102

4. Goldman, Daniel, Richard Boyatzis, and Annie McKee. Primal Leadership: Learning to Lead with Emotional Intelligence. Boston: Harvard Business School Press, 2002.

5. Simon, Herbert A. The New Science of Management Decision. New York: Harper & Row, 1960.

6. Drucker, Peter. Management. New York: Collins, 2008.

7. Simon, Herbert, December 1978, *Rational Decision Making in Business Organizations.* Carnegie-Mellon University, Pittsburgh, Pennsylvania.

8. Covey, Stephen. " "Business Mission Statements." The Community. 2011 <https://www.stephencovey.com/mission-statements.php>

9. Chouinard, Yvon. Let My People Go Surfing: The Education of a Reluctant Businessman. New York, Penguin Books, 2006.

10. Myatt, Mike. "Span Of Control - 5 Things Every Leader Should Know." Forbes 5 Nov 2012. 24 Jul 2013 <http://www.forbes.com/sites/mikemyatt/2012/11/05/span-of-control-5-things-every-leader-should-know/>.

11. Nayar, Vineet. "Five Ways to Manage in Times of Uncertainty." CNBC 7 Mar.2012. 20 Apr. 2012 <http://www.cnbc.com/id/46643569/Five_Ways_To_Manage_in_Times_of_Uncertainty>

12. Weber, Max. General Economic History. London: Allen & Unwin, 1927.

13. Mir, Asif J. "21st Century Transformation." Organization Structure and Innovations 20 Apr. 2011. <http://asifjmir.wordpress.com/2011/04/20/organization-structure-and-innovations/>

14. Lewin, Kurt, Ronald Lippit and Ralph White. "Patterns of aggressive behavior in experimentally created social climates." Journal of Social Psychology 10 (1939): 271-301

15. Bisoux, Tricia. "What Makes Leaders Great." AACSB International: Biz Ed Magazine (2005): 40–45.

16. Gallup, State of the American Workplace. Gallup 2013. <http://www.gallup.com/services/176708/state-american-workplace.aspx>

SOURCES

1. Fig. 5.2: Copyright © 2016 Depositphotos/Zhuzhu.
2. Fig. 5.3: From: Robert Katz, Harvard Business Review. Copyright © 1974 by Harvard Business School Publishing.
3. Fig. 5.4: Source: https://commons.wikimedia.org/wiki/File:Generic_Strategy_Map.png.
4. Fig. 5.6: Copyright © 2016 Depositphotos/Ricochet69.
5. Fig. 5.7: Adapted from: Thomas Bateman and Scott Snell, M: Management, pp. 99. Copyright © 2013 by McGraw-Hill Education.
6. Fig. 5.13a: Copyright © S.s.kulkarni9090 (CC BY-SA 3.0) at https://commons.wikimedia.org/wiki/File:Departments_in_advertising_agencies.jpg.
7. Fig. 5.13b: Copyright © Bo-ci-an (CC by 3.0) at https://commons.wikimedia.org/wiki/File:APQP-CrossFunctionalTeam.png.
8. Fig. 5.16: Copyright © 2012 Depositphotos/Antartis.

Chapter 6

Motivation

Harnessing the Willing Participation of People

PROLOGUE

Our behavior each day is motivated by something. "*According to the oldest motivational theory on the books, organisms behave as they do because they are following a set of biologically pre-programmed instinctual urges. Like the birds and the bees, humans are enacting a set of behaviors hardwired into our neural circuitry. This theory is undoubtedly too simple to apply to humans, much less birds and bees. However, inner needs must certainly be part of the equation in understanding our behavior.*"[1] We may be motivated to avoid certain behaviors, such as speaking in public, by our fear and uncertainty. Or, we may be motivated to engage in challenging behaviors, like skydiving for the first time, in order to satisfy a need for excitement or to simply feel alive. As a student you may be motivated to "sleep in" rather than go to an early morning class. Maybe you are motivated to work extra hours so that you are able to spend some time away from school traveling with friends or family. You may even be excited about going to work because of a pending promotion within the company.

Motivation plays a central role in shaping individual behavior and the subsequent level of performance of every individual within their respective organizations. Motivation can be viewed from two distinct perspectives when applied to employee performance and behavior within a work setting. One perspective, based on the theories of Frederick Taylor in the early 1900s, is that workers do not typically work for intrinsic reasons, they instead work for extrinsic reasons and are motivated by economic incentives. The role of the manager, adhering to this perspective, is to trigger a change of behavior by offering some organizational incentive to an employee to work at a higher level of performance. The second perspective, often referred to as "process theory", is that an employee or individual seeks to satisfy some unique individual intrinsic desire or need in order to experience a sense of purpose, pride, accomplishment or fulfillment.

Regardless of one's perspective, motivation is often described as an individual's attitude that predisposes him/her to act in a specific goal-directed manner. Based on this definition

it is accurate to describe motivation as an internal state that ultimately determines and/or directs a person's behavior. At its most basic level motivation is the drive to satisfy the unique needs that come from being "hardwired" as a human being.

INTRINSIC VERSUS EXTRINSIC MOTIVATION

Managers within a work setting can attempt to influence, change, sustain, or modify employee behavior by using one of two, or a combination of the two, reward mechanisms.

Intrinsic Reward	Extrinsic Reward
Intrinsic motivation, deriving from within the person or from the activity itself, positively affects behavior, performance, and individual well being.	Extrinsically motivated behaviors are actions taken in response to some incentive that is externally administered. These incentives normally include some monetary benefit including, but not limited to, an increase in pay, material possessions, prestige, and positive evaluations from others. Financial, material, and social rewards qualify as *extrinsic rewards* because they come from the environment.
An employee who works to obtain *intrinsic rewards* derives pleasure from the task itself or experiences a sense of competence or self-determination. Intrinsic rewards are derived from personal feelings of self-esteem, self-satisfaction, and accomplishment and are intrinsic because they are self-granted.	Extrinsic rewards are always granted by someone else (manager, supervisor, etc.) in the organization and normally have an economic value attached.

In a world of continuous and inexorable change it is increasingly more important for managers to understand how to maximize the potential of a new generation of employees. For the millennials (born 1981–2001), entering the workforce today, they are motivated by both money and meaningful work. In addition, Millennials value greater autonomy, expanded creative freedom, long-term job security, pay raises, and upward mobility. One thing is clear, motivation continues to represent one of the most significant management challenges facing every organization. Change once again has become the only constant in a business environment experiencing a major shift in the demographic makeup of the workforce.

"Millennials have told us that businesses' greatest contribution was the financial benefit associated with job creation—but they see this as an outcome rather than a guiding principle of business conduct. So, to better understand their values, we asked Millennials, 'What are the most important values a business should follow if it is to have long-term success?' They responded that businesses should put employees first, and they should have a solid foundation of trust and integrity. Customer care and high-quality, reliable products also ranked relatively high in importance. Attention to the environment and social responsibility were also mentioned by a significant number of Millennials. It's noteworthy that few (5 percent) of those answering thought profit-focused values would ensure long-term success."[2]

WORK-LIFE BALANCE

The need of employees to maintain a work-life balance is reshaping the way in which we manage and motivate employees. Personal fulfillment, once commonly ignored or given very low priority at work, is now recognized as a critical issue when attempting to motivate employees. Management recognition of personal and family life continues to be one of the most important factors in creating greater employee loyalty and improved employee performance.

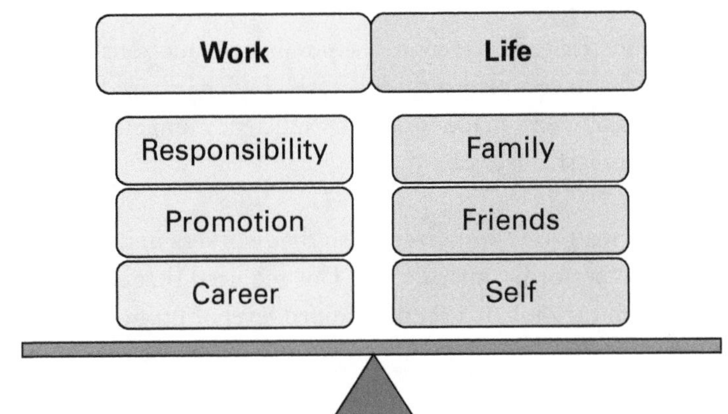

"We want Zappos to function more like a city and less like a top-down bureaucratic organization. Look at companies that existed 50 years ago in the Fortune 500 - most don't exist today. Companies tend to die and cities don't." As far as company restructures go, it's safe to say that it's a fairly controversial one. So, how will this change impact the health and wellness of the Zappos workforce? Rather than focus on work/life balance or work/life separation, I try to focus on work/life integration. When your co-workers also end up being your friends, and the work you do is also work you're passionate about, then it's not so much about work vs. life - it's just life."[3]

EARLY MANAGEMENT STUDIES

Scientific Management

Frederick Taylor is considered a controversial figure in the evolution of management history. His studies in the area of industrial engineering, particularly those involving time and motion studies, eventually resulted in dramatic improvements in employee productivity. Simultaneously, he is often credited with destroying the soul of the worker, of dehumanizing factories, making men nothing more than "cogs in the machinery" or inanimate objects.

The principles of scientific management relied on research and experimentation to determine the most efficient way to perform jobs. As a result jobs, applying the principles of Scientific Management, were highly specialized and standardized. Taylor was a proponent of removing anything that didn't add value and sought to determine the best practices possible. These principles and management techniques were the impetus for the development of assembly line methods and continue to be the basis in which manufacturing and production-oriented firms organize work within their organizations. Taylor's goal was to increase productivity by utilizing the following three key principles:

1. *Rules of Work (Conformity versus creativity)*
   The goal was to codify all methods of work into written rules and procedures.
2. *Time & Motion Studies*
   These studies were designed to reduce the number of "motions" workers needed to perform in order to complete a specific task. Taylor believed that breaking a job down into individual tasks made for greater efficiency and eliminated any useless motions needed to perform a job.
3. *Methods of Work*
   The goal was to create job specialization so that workers understood the specific tasks necessary to perform a specific job. This required that workers be thoroughly trained to perform each job at a predetermined level of proficiency.

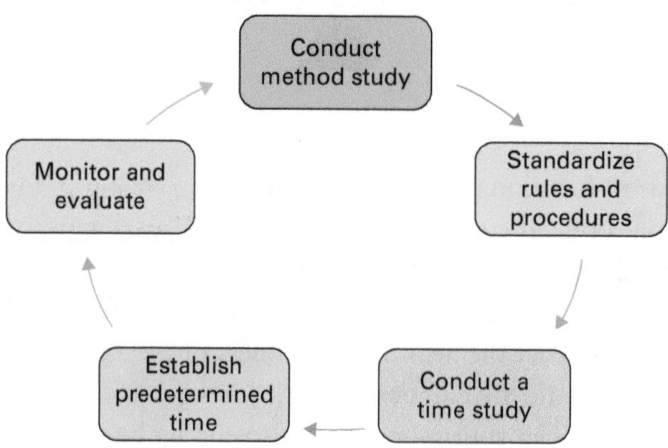

The principles of scientific management do not apply to today's "knowledge worker" and they are not consistent with current management trends designed to empower both employees and work teams. However, certain aspects of scientific management continue to be used by many organizations today.

"UPS knows how many times a driver reverses, how far away from their truck they are at any time, how many keystrokes are entered (reducing 1 keystroke, per driver, per day saves the company $100,000 per annum), the best route to take when delivering multiple parcels in a day (and whether the drivers deviate from that route), and how long it takes you to unlock a truck using a key, amongst other things. Using this data, UPS can optimise work design to maximise efficiency.

Taylor would no doubt have loved to work at UPS in 2014, with all of the data available to him—in fact, this particular brand of workforce analytics, with the new types of data and tools available today, represents a type of 'Neo-Taylorism'."[4]

Hawthorne Studies

The Western Electric Company at their Hawthorne plant from 1927–1932 carried out the Hawthorne studies. Initially the study was conducted to determine the best lighting to use within the plant in order to optimize productivity. Researchers from Western Electric and Harvard University led the Hawthorne studies. The studies were intended to examine the influence of environmental variables, specifically lighting, on a designated group of production workers. The groups of workers were divided into two subgroups: a test group, which would be exposed to environmental changes, and a control group who would work under normal, constant environmental conditions.

The researchers began by manipulating the lighting of the test group. When lighting for the test group was increased, their productivity increased—but the productivity of the control group increased, as well. This result was somewhat unexpected, since the lighting at the workstations of the control group had not been altered. The researchers then decreased the lighting at the test group's workstations. Surprisingly, both the test group and the control group continued to improve their productivity. There were no decreases in productivity until the light was reduced to the point where the workers could barely see.

The researchers concluded that light did not have a significant impact on the motivation of production workers.

These results were a major setback to the principles of scientific management, which held that employees were only motivated by individual economic interest. The Hawthorne studies drew attention to the social needs as an additional source of motivation. Taylor's emphasis on economic incentives was not wholly discredited, but economic incentives were now viewed as one factor—not the sole factor—to which employees responded. The resultant effect of the experiment was the identification of human and psychological factors that affected productivity. The factors identified were:

- *Social Group/Acceptance (Human factors)*
- *Participation in planning (Sense of involvement)*
- *Special atmosphere tied to additional pay (Piece rate system)*

Hawthorne Effect

This term was coined by Elton Mayo, Professor of Industrial Management, Harvard Business School, 1933, and refers to the tendency of people to behave differently when they are being studied. New assumptions resulted from the study and these new assumptions led to many theories about the human side of motivation. This study is often credited with the inception of the "Human Relations Movement" in management changing forever the manner in which employers attempted to manage and motivate their employees.

The Human Relations Movement in Management

As a result of the Hawthorne studies the established beliefs regarding the relationship between management behavior and employee/group behavior began to change. No longer were employees viewed as extensions of production machinery, or as often referred to as, "cogs in the machinery." Scholars in the field of management agreed that the Hawthorne studies impacted long held management views about the role of people in organizations. The studies revealed that an employee's feelings (needs) and adherence to group norms had a more profound effect on employee performance than did high degrees of specialization and standardized production processes as advocated by Frederick Taylor. The Hawthorne studies marked the beginning of the *Human Relations Movement* in management and established a new area of study known as organizational behavior. This new field of study now focused attention on the factors affecting the behavior of individuals and groups within the context of an organization as well as a new commitment to make management practices more humane. The human relations movement placed greater importance on employee satisfaction as a means of improving employee productivity and as a result changed the manner in which managers attempted to motivate their employees.

McGregor's Theory X and Theory Y

In 1960, Douglas McGregor wrote a book entitled *The Human Side of Enterprise*[5]. This book, which has become the basis for the modern view of people at work, formulated two sharply contrasting sets of assumptions about human nature. His Theory X assumptions were pessimistic and negative and, according to McGregor's interpretation, typical of how managers traditionally perceived employees.

Theory X Assumptions

- *Average person dislikes work.*
- *Average person must be forced, controlled, directed threatened, or coerced in order to put forth an effort and achieve organizational goals.*
- *Average person avoids responsibility, has little ambition, and wants security.*
- *Average person is primarily motivated by fear & money.*

Theory Y Assumptions

- *Average person likes work (as important as play).*
- *Average person naturally works toward goals.*
- *Average person seeks responsibility.*
- *Average person is capable of using imagination, creativity and cleverness.*
- *Average person's intellectual potential is only partially realized.*
- *Average person is motivated by a variety of rewards.*

It was McGregor's book, *The Human Side of Enterprise* that advanced the human relations movement in the field of management. In 1960, Theory X was adopted by a large percentage of managers and organizations. Many managers in 1960 thrived on the power and control they had over their employees, and their ability to coerce employees to do their bidding. The results of this management approach were almost always inferior to what could have been achieved with a more humanistic approach. It was almost impossible for managers in organizations in the 1960's to accept the fact that a Theory X approach to managing their employees was the source of their organizations declining performance and profits. Today it is hard to believe, that despite the passing of fifty years, there are still many Theory X managers and organizations around the world.

Theory Y managers and organizations understand that you achieve a higher level of commitment from human beings when you actually demonstrate through action and deed that you care about them. It is important that every individual within an organization know that they are appreciated and are an important part of the organization and its future success.

CONTENT THEORIES OF MOTIVATION

The content theories of motivation emphasize the needs, internal drive, that motivates specific behaviors in an attempt to fulfill the needs. The basic premise behind content theories is that if managers can identify the needs of their employees they can then design a reward system that will more effectively direct employee behavior and performance. Two major theories include:

- Maslow's Hierarchy of Needs
- Aldefer's ERG Model
- Herzberg's Two-Factor Theory

Maslow's Hierarchy

In 1943, psychologist Abraham Maslow published his now-famous Hierarchy of Needs[6] theory of motivation. Maslow proposed that motivation is a function of five basic needs. A *Need,* according to Maslow, is often defined as an internal state that drives individual behavior and makes certain outcomes or rewards attractive.

Individual Needs

Maslow asserted that every individual is motivated by his or her own unique needs and that their needs exist in a hierarchical order. Once a need is satisfied, its importance is diminished and the next higher need is activated, which is then satisfied, and the process continues up the hierarchy. Some needs involve a person's physical well-being, while others involve the individual's self-view and/or their interpersonal relationships. These five need categories were arranged in a hierarchy where needs emerge in a predictable "stair-step," ascending, fashion. Accordingly, when one's physiological needs are relatively satisfied, one's safety needs emerge, and so on up the need hierarchy, one step at a time. Once a need is satisfied, according to Maslow, it no longer is a motivator, and activates the next higher need in the hierarchy. This process continues until the need for self-actualization is activated.

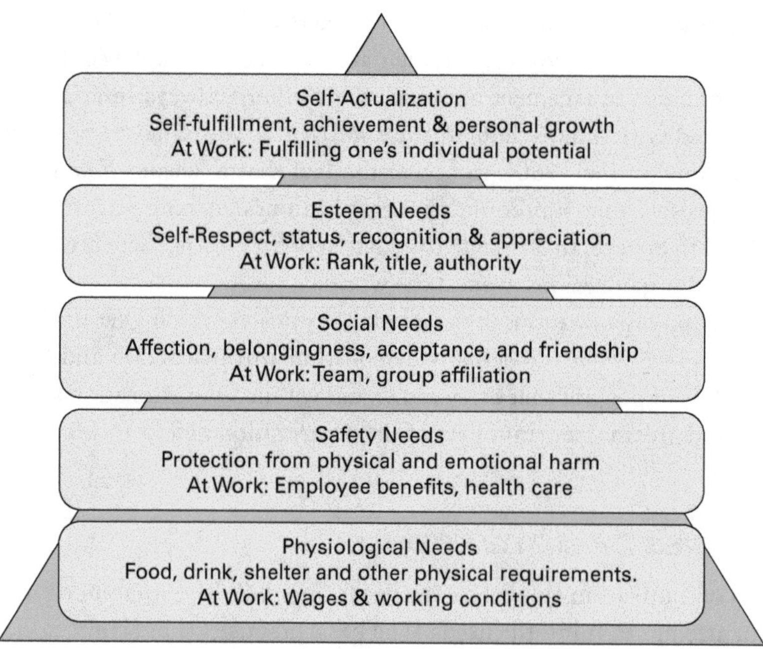

Alderfer's ERG Model

Clayton Alderfer's ERG Theory[7] is often considered more advanced than Maslow's theory because it focuses on the needs that influence an individual's behavior while at work. Alderfer believed that three sets of needs—existence, relatedness, and growth—could simultaneously motivate an individual to satisfy the needs at the same time. Even though the priority of these three needs vary from person to person, the theory does attempt to prioritize needs based on their tangibility. Existence needs are the most tangible and easiest to substantiate. Existence needs include all material and physiological factors including pay, benefits, food, water, air, clothing, etc. Relatedness needs are more difficult to verify and depend on the social relationships that the individual has with other people. Growth needs are the most difficult to verify because each individual will have their own unique set of objectives required to meet personal growth needs.

Alderfer also developed the ***frustration-regression principle*** asserting that if only two of the three needs are met the unmet need will cause frustration for the affected individual and as a consequence affect the other two requirements. For instance, if employees existence and relatedness needs are met, but opportunities for promotion and personal development are not being provided, employees will begin to depend heavily on relatedness. This could result in a workplace setting where employees engage in heavy gossip, speculation and undesirable personal relationships. The moment one need takes dominance over the others, the ERG Model begins to breakdown and the quality of the work environment begins to deteriorate.

From a management perspective this model requires managers to be cognizant of the fact that focusing on one need at a time will not improve employee motivation. The ERG Model requires managers to look beyond the traditional financial incentives to motivate people and instead recognize that all three needs must be considered and met simultaneously.

Herzberg's Two-Factor Theory

Frederick Herzberg, in his article published in the Harvard Business Review entitled, "One More Time: How Do You Motivate Employees," states that there are separate and distinct clusters of factors associated with job satisfaction and dissatisfaction.

> "Since separate factors need to be considered, depending on whether job satisfaction or job dissatisfaction is being examined, it follows that these two feelings are not opposites of each other. The opposite of job satisfaction is not job dissatisfaction but, rather, no job satisfaction; and similarly, the opposite of job dissatisfaction is not job satisfaction, but no job dissatisfaction.
>
> Two different needs of human beings are involved here. One set of needs can be thought of as stemming from humankind's animal nature. ... The other set of needs relates to that unique human characteristic, the ability to achieve and, through achievement, to experience psychological growth."[8]

Job dissatisfaction and satisfaction were more frequently associated with Hygiene Factors and Motivation Factors. Herzberg found job dissatisfaction to be associated primarily with ***Hygiene Factors;*** which are more closely associated with the "job context". The job context refers to the condition or environment in which the specific activities involved in the job take place. When met hygiene factors led to an absence of dissatisfaction. ***Motivation Factors*** were more closely aligned with the "job content," often associated with stimulating work, and when met created satisfaction.

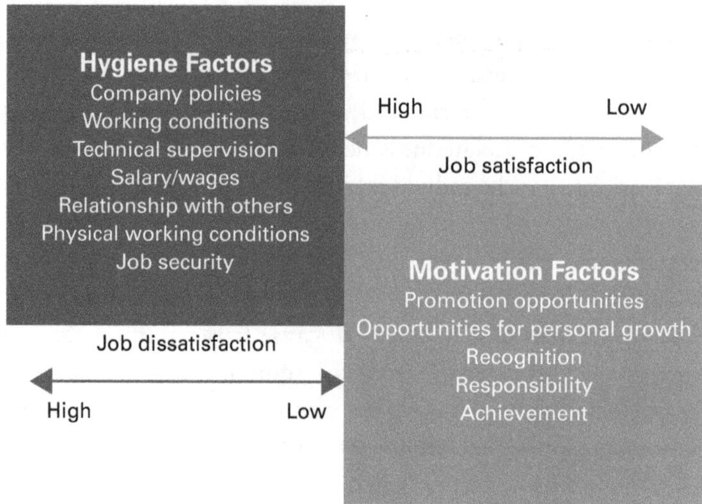

Job Enrichment

The basis for job enrichment was refined in 1975 by Hackman and Oldham[9] using what they called the ***Job Characteristics Model.*** This model assumes that if five core job characteristics are present, three critical psychological states of motivation, meaningfulness, responsibility, and knowledge of the results are produced resulting in positive outcomes as well as improved employee performance. Job enrichment is a motivational strategy used in designing jobs so that employees can satisfy their needs for growth, recognition, and responsibility.

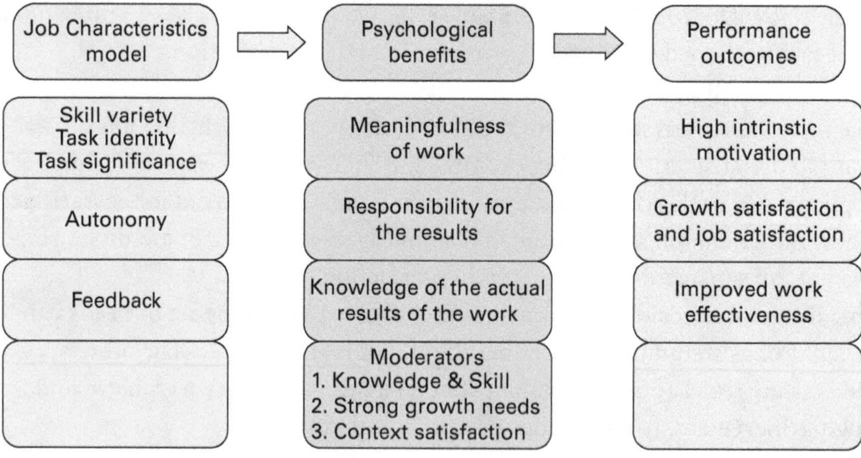

The fundamental principle is based on an expansion and scope of an employee's job by providing additional opportunities to perform a greater number of tasks, normally vertical in nature, that normally require a higher level of self-sufficiency. The goal of job enrichment is to give individual employees greater exposure to tasks normally reserved for individuals in higher positions within the organization. The ***five characteristics of work*** described by Hackman and Oldham are considered key factors affecting motivation and performance and the successful implementation of job enrichment.

Skill Variety	The degree to which the job requires a variety of different activities in carrying out the work, which involves the use of a number of an individual's skills and talents.
Task Identity	The degree to which the job requires completion of a "whole" and identifiable piece of work–that is, doing a job from beginning to end with a visible outcome.
Task Significance	The degree to which the job has a substantial impact on the lives or work of other people, whether in the immediate organization or in the external environment.
Autonomy	The degree to which the job provides substantial freedom, independence, and discretion to the individual in scheduling the work and in determining the procedures to be used in carrying it out.
Feedback	The degree to which carrying out the work activities, required by the job, results in the individual obtaining direct and clear information about the effectiveness of his or her performance.

PROCESS THEORIES OF MOTIVATION

The process theories of motivation concentrate on the specific behaviors that individuals engage in as they attempt to satisfy their needs and determine whether or not their choices of behavior were successful. Three major theories fall under this category:

- Expectancy Theory
- Equity Theory
- Goal Setting Theory

Expectancy Theory

Victor Vroom, Edward Lawler and Lyman Porter, as a result of their research, concluded that the relationship between people's behavior at work and their goals was not as simple as was first imagined by other scientists. Vroom realized that an individual's performance is influenced by a variety of factors including personality, skills, knowledge, experience and abilities.

Expectancy theory suggests that in spite of the fact that individuals may have different goals, they can be motivated if they believe that:

- There is a positive correlation between efforts and performance,
- Higher performance will result in a meaningful reward,
- The reward will satisfy an important need,
- The desire to satisfy the need is strong enough to make the effort worthwhile.

Expectancy theory holds that people are motivated to behave in ways that produce desired combinations of expected outcomes. Motivation, according to Victor Vroom, boils down to the decision of how much effort to exert in a specific task situation. Vroom defines motivation "as a process governing choices among alternative forms of voluntary activity."[10] In his view, behavior controlled the individual and was either motivated or was not motivated. The motivational force for a behavior, action, or task is a function of three distinct perceptions. These perceptions revolve around:

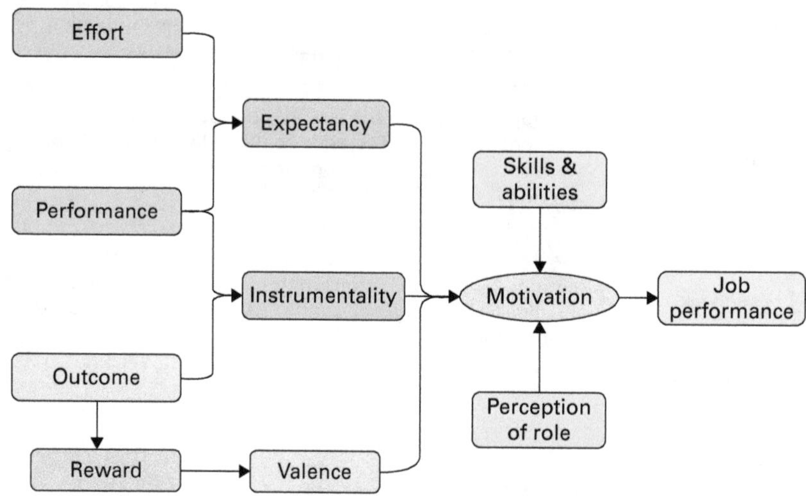

Expectancy, according to Vroom, represents an individual's belief regarding the likely probability that a particular behavior would be followed by a particular outcome. Expectancy is the belief that one's effort will result in the attainment of a desired performance goal.

$$E \rightarrow P$$

Instrumentality is a performance outcome perception. It represents a person's belief in the probability that a particular outcome is contingent (instrumental) on accomplishing a specific level of performance.

$$P \rightarrow O$$

Valence refers to the positive/reward or negative/punishment preference people place on outcomes. Valence mirrors our personal preferences and is ultimately determined by an individual's needs.

Equity Theory

Equity theory asserts that a major determinant of employee productivity and satisfaction arises from the degree of fairness or unfairness that an employee perceives in the workplace. Equity theory is built on the belief that employees become de-motivated, both in relation to their job and their employer, if they feel as though their inputs are greater than the outputs. John Stacey Adams formulated the principles of Equity Theory wherein he states that multiple subtle factors affect each individual's assessment and perception of their relationship with their work, and as a consequence their employer. According to the theory, every individual (employee) seeks a fair balance between what we put into our job (inputs) and what we get out of it (outputs). Inputs are normally associated with intangible contributions including, but not limited to, effort, loyalty, hard work, dedication, skill, determination, enthusiasm, trust, and personal sacrifice. Outputs are typically tangible rewards that include: pay, benefits, pensions, and bonuses. Outputs also include intangible rewards of recognition, praise, increased responsibility, training, advancement, and promotion. As a result of this process every individual (employee) forms perceptions of what constitutes a fair balance between inputs and outputs by comparing their own situation with other employees in the workplace. Based on the individual employees perception of "fairness" they will modify their behavior to coincide with the outputs received.

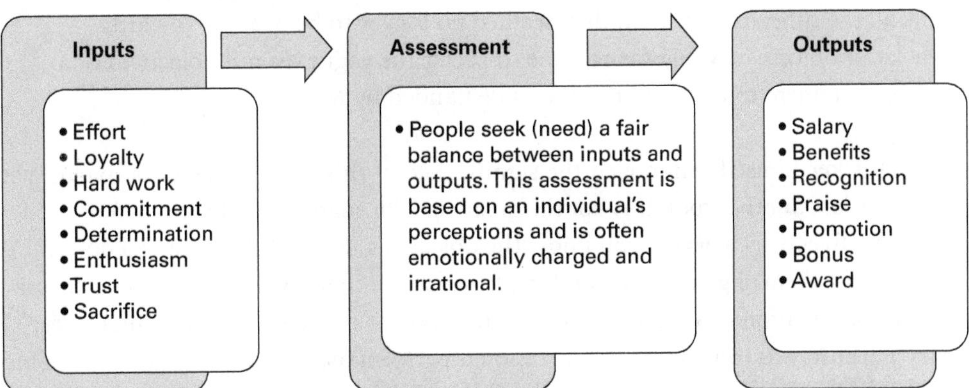

Goal Setting Theory

In the 1960's, Edwin Locke formulated the Goal setting theory of motivation. This theory stated that goal setting had a profound and direct impact on employee performance. It states that specific and challenging goals along with appropriate feedback contributed to higher and improved task performance. In an article entitled "Toward a Theory of Task Motivation and Incentives," Locke stated that clear goals and appropriate feedback would motivate employees. He also stated that when employees work towards a goal, it would serve as a major source of motivation resulting in improved employee performance. Locke's study also provided new insights between goals and performance. According to his study, specific and difficult goals produced better results compared to vague, randomly set or easy to do goals. His theory produced the following guiding principles:

- *Set specific goals*
- *The goals must be attainable*
- *The goals must be acceptable*
- *Seek out feedback*
- *The achievement of the goals is facilitated by organizational conditions.*

MANAGEMENT BY OBJECTIVES (MBO)

Management by Objectives was introduced by Peter Drucker in the 1950s and written about in his 1954 book, *The Practice of Management*.[11] It gained a great deal of attention and was widely adopted and utilized until the 1990s.

> "With the benefit of hindsight, it may seem obvious that managers must have somewhere to go before they set out on a journey. But Drucker pointed out that managers often lose sight of their objectives because of something he called "the activity trap." They get so involved in their current activities that they forget their original purpose. In some cases it may be that they become engrossed in this activity as a means of avoiding the uncomfortable truth about their organization's condition.
>
> One critic claimed that MBO encouraged organizations to tamper with their plans all the time, as and when they seemed no longer to be heading towards their latest objective. Many firms came to prefer the vague overall objectives of a mission statement to the firm, rigid ones demanded by MBO."[12]

Peter Drucker himself minimized the significance of this management approach, when he said: "It's just another tool. It is not the great cure for management inefficiency ... Management by Objectives works if you know the objectives, 90% of the time you don't."

MBO is "a system of goal setting and implementation that involves a cycle of discussion, review, and evaluation of objectives among all levels of management and employees." Its primary purpose was to increase organizational performance by aligning goals and objectives of employees and managers throughout the entire organization. Ideally this process was designed to provide employees with the opportunity to identify their objectives and the timelines for completion. It was developed to help employees motivate themselves.

There are six steps in the MBO process which involve:

1. *Goals are set by management with cooperation of subordinates.*
2. *Department objectives are set, including deadlines.*
3. *Individual objectives are set (managers and individual employee) in writing.*
4. *Communication occurs regarding progress toward objectives.*
5. *Results are evaluated.*
6. *Employees are rewarded for achieving goals.*

MOTIVATION: WHERE DOES IT END

In spite of the myriad of theories on motivation, a vast number of managers today often view motivation with a level of uncertainty mixed with cautious optimism. Twyla Dell writes, "The heart of motivation is to give people what they really want most from work. The more you are able to provide what they want, the more you should expect what you really want, namely: productivity, quality, and service."[13] The challenge, amidst a turbulent business environment and an ever-growing number of part-time and contingent workers, is to determine "what people really want." Based on the research, and the multitude of theories that have evolved from the research, it seems fair to conclude that for every individual what they want, and need, is a combination of two key variables. The first key variable will always be associated with earning enough money, an economic need, to support themselves and their family. The second key variable is likely to be based on a need to make a difference. "... today's employees are motivated to achieve more than ever simply by the opportunity to create impact ... Allow them to make a mark toward significance. Create the opportunity for their achievement to leave a long lasting legacy that rewards the organization they serve and for future generations to learn from."[14] The needs of each individual are in a constant state of flux and for managers this means that employee motivation is a constant, day-to-day, challenge that requires their empathy, patience, and dogged persistence to never give up.

"Motivation is a fire from within. If someone else tries to light that fire under you, chances are it will burn very briefly." —Stephen Covey

ENDNOTES

1. Whitbourne, Susan K., "Motivation: The Why's of Behavior." *Journal of Psychology, 29 Oct 2011.* <https://www.psychologytoday.com/blog/fulfillment-any-age/201110/motivation-the-why-s-behavior>

2. Deloitte. "The 2016 Deloitte Millennial Survey: Winning Over the Next Generation of Leaders". 2016. <http://www.deloitte.com/MillennialSurvey>

3. Groth, Aimee. "Holacracy at Zappos: It's either the future of management or a social experiment gone awry". Quartz, 2015. <https://qz.com/317918/holacracy-at-zappos-its-either-the-future-of-management-or-a-social-experiment-gone-awry/>

4. Hagan, Alex. "Frederick Taylor has been Reincarnated, and he now works for UPS". KIENCO, 5 May 2014. <http://www.kienco.com.au/blog/workforce-analytics-and-neotaylorism>

5. McGregor, Douglas. The Human Side of Enterprise. New York: McGraw-Hill, 1960.

6. Maslow, Abraham. Motivation and Personality. New York: Harper & Row, 1954.

7. C. Alderfer, Existence, Relatedness and Growth: Human Needs in Organizational Settings. Glencoe, IL, Free Press, 1972.

8. Herzberg, Frederick. "One More Time: How Do You Motivate Employees." Harvard Business Review (1968): 9

9. Hackman, J.R., and G.R. Oldham. Work Redesign. Reading, MA: Addison-Wesley, 1980.

10. Vroom, Victor. Work and Motivation. New York: John Wiley & Sons, 1964.

11. Drucker, Peter. The Practice of Management. New York: Harper & Row 1954

12. Hindle, Tim. The Economist Guide to Management Ideas and Gurus. London: Profile Books Ltd., 2008

13. Dell, Twyla. An Honest Day's Work: Motivating Employees to Give Their Best, Los Altos, CA/: Crisp Publications, Inc., 1988.

14. Glenn Llopis, "The Top 9 Things That Ultimately Motivate Employees to Achieve", Forbes 24 June 2012. <https://www.forbes.com/sites/glennllopis/2012/06/04/top-9-things-that-ultimately-motivate-employees-to-achieve/#4c9c7e96257e>

SOURCES

1. Fig. 6.4: Source: https://commons.wikimedia.org/wiki/File:Hawthorne,_Illinois_Works_of_the_Western_Electric_Company,_1925.jpg.

Chapter 7

Human Resource Management

Creating a Winning Team

PROLOGUE

People create organizations! Because of this reality every organization must attempt to create systems that accurately reflect the diversity and complexity of the people who comprise it. An organization cannot build an outstanding team of high performing professionals without a Human Resource Department providing the framework necessary to recruit, select, train, evaluate, compensate and retain prospective and current employees. The main focus of an HR department is to assist in the creation of sound policies and processes that enhance management's ability to keep a company staffed with new talent, operationally functional at every level within the organization, and compliant with the legal regulations as prescribed by law.

It is very likely that the very first formal interaction that a prospective employee has with an organization will be with the human resource department. Of all of the "resources" needed to develop and sustain a business none are more important than the people inside the company. The greatest source of a company's competitive advantage is the organization's employees, the people who actually breathe life into the organization.[1]

However, it is these very same people who represent the greatest expense within an organization, are the most difficult resource to manage, and are most affected by multiple legal statutes and regulations.

Human resource management encompasses every aspect of the employment process within a company from recruiting, hiring, training and development, performance evaluation, compensation, and when necessary, termination. Human resources, the people within every organization, need to be effectively managed, nurtured, and developed so that their unique skills and abilities can be effectively utilized by an organization.

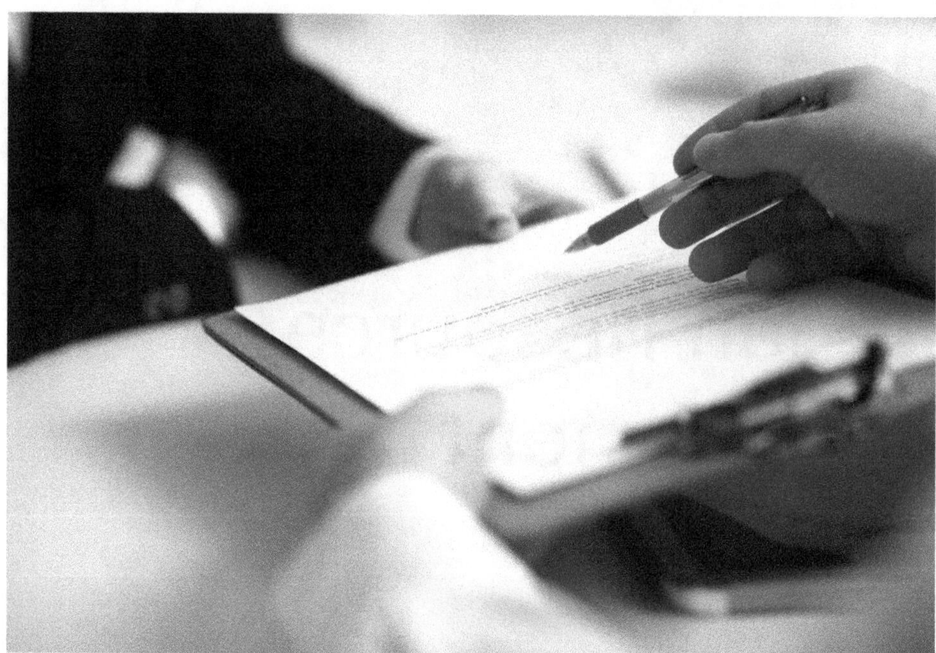

HUMAN RESOURCE PLANNING

Prior to beginning the planning process it is essential that the goals of the organization have been clearly defined because the Strategic Human Resource planning process is based on the overall goals of the organization. Strategic human resource planning is effective only to the extent that a company can accurately predict what events are likely to occur outside the company. Because the rapid pace of change in the workplace it has become increasingly difficult to predict what skills and therefore, what employees, will be needed in even the near future.

Managers, utilizing a strategic human resource planning process, attempt to ensure that the right person with the needed skills is in the right job at the right time. Some estimate that "well over $200 billion a year is spent worldwide in finding and hiring scarce, highly skilled talent, and in bringing new employees up to required skill levels through costly training programs."[2] The strategic HR planning process allows organizations to determine the staffing support they require to meet the goals of the company and most importantly the needs and demands of the customer. Under conditions of economic and environmental stability human resource planning focuses on meeting the short-term needs of the organization. However the planning process, today's dynamic business climate has changed the scope and focus of the strategic human resource planning process.

"Almost one-half of organizations reported that the biggest investment challenge facing organizations over the next 10 years is obtaining human capital and optimizing human capital investments."[3] Forward thinking managers now realize that in order to adequately address the new human resource challenges, they must develop innovative long-term and short-term strategies and solutions. As human resource managers develop more and more programs to serve the needs of their respective organizations, and influence the direction of their organizations, they face new and increased responsibilities and challenges.

Forecasting

HR Forecasting attempts to determine the supply and demand for various types of human resources, and to predict areas within the organization where there will be labor shortages or surpluses. The future of work continues to emerge as one of the biggest questions facing organizations over the next decade and beyond and as a result making the forecasting process even more complex. What influence will technology, computerization and artificial intelligence have on the future of work?

The real question is not so much about technology but instead about the manner in which people within organizations, human resources, will rely on, and be capable of using, the latest technology. The workforce of the future will continue to be affected by an aging workforce, expanding regulations and laws, rapidly changing trends among consumers, and the inevitable transition toward an automated workplace. The outcome of these changes will most definitely determine the future of work in the next decade.

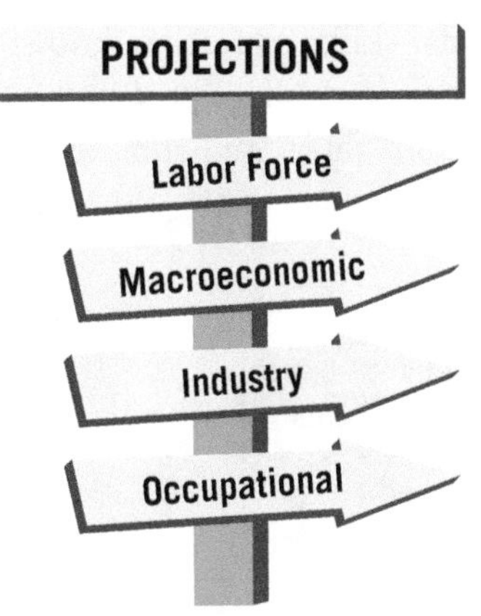

"The U.S. labor force is undergoing a gradual but significant change. Beginning in the latter part of the 20th century, three major demographic trends—slowing growth, aging, and increasing diversity—led to changes that have had a considerable impact on the profile of the labor force in the United States and are projected to affect the workforce in the foreseeable future. With the aging of the baby-boom generation, defined as persons born between 1946 and 1964, the older age cohorts are expected to make up a much larger share of the labor force."[4]

HR forecasting involves two specific tasks:

- Forecasting of the *internal supply*, includes an attempt to anticipate the number and type of employees who will be employed in the firm at some future date.
- Forecasting the *external supply*. Many factors influence labor supply, including demographic changes in the population, national and regional economics, education level of the work force, demand for specific employee skills, and government policies.

Once this forecast is complete the human resource planning process then engages in the following five-step process:

Step #1: Preparing a Human Resource Inventory

With the purpose of effectively assessing the skills and abilities of current employees managers begin by reviewing and then creating a database all of the pertinent

information about employees. This process is designed to insure that the labor force is technically up to date and has been thoroughly trained in order to efficiently carry out the specific duties and responsibilities of each job they perform within the organization. A typical inventory would likely include an assessment of the following information for each employee.

- Current Position
- Previous Position in Company
- Education (Licenses, Degrees)
- International Experience
- Prior Employment
- Language Skills
- Training
- Current and Prior Performance Appraisal Data

Step #2: Preparing a Job Analysis

Whereas the human resource inventory process focuses primarily on what specific skills and abilities current employees possess a job analysis involves a comprehensive study of what is done by employees in the organization who hold various job titles. For example, what does a college professor actually do? What are the minimal skills, education, knowledge and ability essential in order to carry out the responsibilities of a college professor? A job analysis is designed to answer these types of questions. A thoughtful and comprehensive analysis is then used to develop the following two important documents:

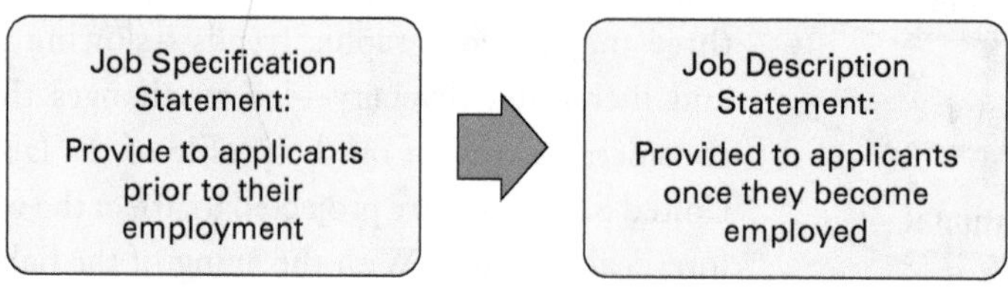
Job Specification Statement:
Provide to applicants prior to their employment
Job Description Statement:
Provided to applicants once they become employed

Job Specification Statement

This statement provides prospective candidates seeking employment with a written explanation of the minimum qualifications that they must possess in order to be considered as a viable candidate for a given job opening. This statement would include the following specific requirements:

- Educational qualifications
- Physical and other related attributes
- Physique and mental health
- Special attributes and abilities

Job Description Statement

A written summary of the job as an identifiable organizational unit and serves as the basis for establishing the duties, working conditions, tools, materials, and equipment related to the performance of a job. Preparing a thorough, complete job description is a critical first step in the selection process.

Step #3: Assessing Future Demand

This requires managers to become proactive in anticipating the human resource needs of the organization long before the need becomes apparent.

Step #4: Assessing Future Supply

HR managers must constantly assess the number and type of people who will be available for hiring in the future from the labor market at large.

Step #5: Establishing a strategic plan

This plan must address the following core HR activities:

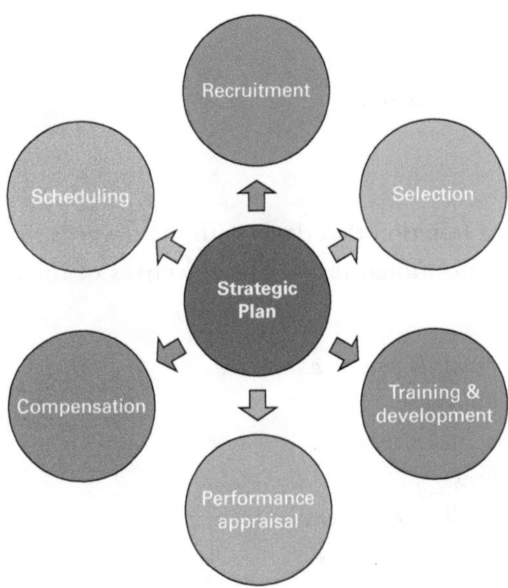

Recruitment

Recruiting is the set of activities an organization uses to attract job candidates who have the abilities and attitudes needed to help the organization achieve its objectives.

Selection

Reasonable criteria for the choice must be set prior to selection. A typical selection process would include the following six steps.

1. *Obtain complete application form.*
2. *Conduct initial and follow-up interviews.*
3. *Administer employment tests.*
4. *Background investigations.*
5. *Obtaining results from physical examinations.*
6. *Establishing trial period.*

Training & Development

Training is a form of education and involves all attempts to improve performance by increasing an employee's ability to perform through learning.

Performance Appraisal (Feedback)

Properly performed, performance evaluations can contribute to organizational objectives and employee development and satisfaction. There are six steps in the performance appraisals process:

1. *Establishing performance standards.*
2. *Communicating those standards.*
3. *Evaluating performance.*
4. *Discussing results with employees.*
5. *Taking corrective action.*
6. *Using results to make decision.*

Compensation

Compensation is the HRM function that deals with the rewards that employees receive in return for performing organizational tasks. The objectives of the compensation function are to:

1. *Create a system of rewards that is equitable*
2. *Attract potential employees*
3. *Provide productivity incentives*
4. *Keep valued employees*
5. *Provide employees with some financial security*

Scheduling

Workers' increasing need for flexibility has generated new innovations in scheduling. Such new innovations include job sharing, flextime, compressed workweeks, and working at home.

HUMAN RESOURCE MANAGEMENT: EMPLOYMENT LAW

In the United States *Employment Law*, or labor law, exists at both the state and federal levels. Employment law consists of a large body of laws, administrative rulings, and legal precedent that affect all areas of the employer/employee relationships.

> "Today, any employee who is not under a contract or a collective bargaining agreement is considered to be an at-will employee. This means that the employee may quit at any time for any reason or no reason at all, with no required notice to the employer. Similarly, an employer may fire an employee at any time, without notice, for almost any reason. The exception to the at-will rule is that an employer may not fire an employee for an illegal reason."[5]

Equal Employment Opportunity Commission

On July 2, 1964, the Civil Rights Act was passed. Among its many goals was the elimination of discrimination in the workplace through the creation of the Equal Employment Opportunity Commission (EEOC). The primary responsibility of the Equal Employment Opportunity Commission continues to be, whenever possible, the elimination of all forms of discrimination in the workplace. The agency's primary mission is to reverse the trend of discrimination in employment based on race, color, national origin, sex, religion, retaliation, age, gender, sexuality, genetics, and physical ability.

"The Equal Employment Opportunity Commission shall have authority to enforce the provisions of subsection (a) of this section through appropriate remedies, including reinstatement or hiring of employees with or without back pay, as will effectuate the policies of this section, and shall issue such rules, regulations, orders and instructions as it deems necessary and appropriate to carry out its responsibilities under this section. The Equal Employment Opportunity Commission shall -

(1) be responsible for the annual review and approval of a national and regional equal employment opportunity plan which each department and agency and each appropriate unit referred to in subsection (a) of this section shall submit in order to maintain an affirmative program of equal employment opportunity for all such employees and applicants for employment;

(2) be responsible for the review and evaluation of the operation of all agency equal employment opportunity programs, periodically obtaining and publishing (on at least a semiannual basis) progress reports from each such department, agency, or unit; and

(3) consult with and solicit the recommendations of interested individuals, groups, and organizations relating to equal employment opportunity."[6]

Major Forms of Legislation

The major topics included in any discussion of employment law include: employment discrimination, wages and compensation, workplace safety, work authorization for non U.S. citizens, and wrongful termination.

Each year, the Equal Employment Opportunity Commission releases a statistical breakdown of charges filed with the agency. For the 2015 Fiscal Year these were as follows:

The charge numbers show the following breakdowns by bases alleged:

- *Retaliation: 39,757 (44.5% of all charges filed)*
- *Race: 31,027 (34.7%)*
- *Disability: 26,968 (30.2%)*
- *Sex: 26,396 (29.5%)*
- *Age: 20,144 (22.5%)*
- *National Origin: 9,438 (10.6%)*
- *Religion: 3,502 (3.9%)*
- *Color: 2,833 (3.2%)*
- *Equal Pay Act: 973 (1.1%)*
- *Genetic Information Non-Discrimination Act: 257 (0.3%)*[7]

The major forms of legislation governing employee/employer include, but are not limited to, the following:

Title VII of the 1964 Civil Rights Act

A federal law that prohibits discrimination in hiring, promotion, compensation, training, or dismissal on the basis of race, color, religion, sex, or national origin (age was added later).

Civil Rights Act of 1991

The act allows for compensatory and punitive damages in intentional discrimination cases and allows for jury trials when such damages are sought. Before the CRA 1991, Title VII limited recoverable damages to equitable relief for back pay, lost benefits, and attorney's fees and costs. Under the provisions of the 1991 Act, parties could now obtain jury trials, and recover compensatory and punitive damages in Title VII and ADA lawsuits involving intentional discrimination. The Act placed statutory caps on the amount of damages that could be awarded for future financial losses, pain and suffering, and punitive damages, based on employer size. The maximum award of compensatory and punitive damages combined was set at $300,000 for the largest employers (more than 500 employees).

Pregnancy Discrimination Act (1978)

This act, which amended Title VII, was passed to protect pregnant women from employment discrimination. Employers must allow women to work until their pregnancy results in physical disability that interferes with their job performance and is the same level of disability that would cause workers with other medical problems to have to stop working. Employers must allow women to return to work after childbirth on the same basis as for other disabilities.

Family Medical Leave Act

The Family Medical Leave Act was signed into law in 1993 to balance needs of employers and employees in circumstances when employees must take extended medical leaves for serious medical conditions, including pregnancy, or to care for family members. The FMLA entitles eligible employees to take up to 12 workweeks of unpaid, job-protected leave in a 12-month period for specified family and medical reasons, or for any "qualifying exigency" arising out of the fact that a covered military member is on active duty, or has been notified of an impending call or order to active duty, in support of a contingency operation. The FMLA also allows eligible employees to take up to 26 workweeks of job-protected leave in a "single 12-month period" to care for a covered service member with a serious injury or illness.[8]

Americans with Disabilities Act of 1990 (ADA)

Prohibits employers from discriminating against qualified disabled individuals in hiring, advancement, or compensation, and requires them to adapt the workplace if necessary. "The ADA gives civil rights protections to individuals with disabilities that are like those provided to individuals on the basis of race, sex, national origin, and religion. It guarantees equal opportunity for individuals with disabilities in employment, public accommodations, transportation, State and local government services, and telecommunications."[9] Some of the key issues involving enforcement of this act involve:

- Who is covered—Qualified individuals with disabilities?
- How far does an employer have to go in order to provide reasonable accommodation?

Age Discrimination in Employment Act of 1967 (as amended in 1978)

The ADEA protects certain applicants and employees 40 years of age and older from discrimination on the basis of age in hiring, promotion, discharge, compensation, or terms, conditions or privileges of employment.[10]

Equal Pay Act of 1963

The Equal Pay Act requires that men and women in the same workplace be given equal pay for equal work. The jobs need not be identical, but they must be substantially equal. Job content (not job titles) determines whether jobs are substantially equal. All forms of pay are covered by this law, including salary, overtime pay, bonuses, stock options, profit sharing and bonus plans, life insurance, vacation and holiday pay, cleaning or gasoline allowances, hotel accommodations, reimbursement for travel expenses, and benefits. If there is an inequality in wages between men and women, employers may not reduce the wages of either sex to equalize their pay.[11]

INQUIRY AREA	ILLEGAL QUESTIONS	LEGAL QUESTIONS
National Origin	Are you a U.S citizen? Where were you or your parents born? What is your native tongue?	Are you authorized to work in the United States? What languages do you read/speak/write fluently?
Age	How old are you? When did you graduate? What is your date of birth?	Are you over the age of 18?
Marital/Family Status	What is your marital status? With whom do you live? Do you plan to have a family? If yes, when? How many kids do you have? What are your child care arrangements?	Would you be willing to relocate if necessary? Would you be able and willing to travel as needed for the job? Would you be able and willing to work overtime as necessary?
Affiliations	What clubs or social organizations do you belong to?	List any professional or trade groups or other organizations that you belong to that you consider relevant to your ability to perform this job?
Personal	How tall are you? How much do you weigh? (Not acceptable unless minimum standards are BFQ's)	Are you able to lift a 50 pound weight and carry it 100 yards, as this is part of the job?
Disabilities	Do you have any disabilities? Have you had any recent or past illnesses or operations? What was the date of your last physical exam? How's your family's health? Do you need accommodation to perform the job?	Are you able to perform the essential functions of this job? Can you demonstrate how you would perform the following job-related functions? As part of the hiring process, after a job offer has been made, you will be required to undergo a medical exam.
Arrest Record	Have you ever been arrested? If you've been in the military, were you honorably discharged?	Have you ever been convicted of ______? (The crime named should be reasonably related to the performance of the job in question.) In what branch of the armed forces did you serve? What type of training or education did you receive in the military?[12]

HRM: THE CHANGING LANDSCAPE

One of the primary functions of a human resource manager or human resource department is to ensure that the organization is aware of and compliant with all relevant legislation involving employment practices. Because legislation is continually changing each year the challenge of remaining informed is a difficult task. Legislation has made hiring, promoting, firing, and managing employee relations a more complex and dynamic process. It is important to remember that the whole purpose of HRM is to improve the work life of employees while at the same time ensuring that the goals of the organization are achieved. "Treating employees benevolently shouldn't be viewed as an added cost that cuts into profits, but as a powerful energizer that can grow the enterprise into something far greater than one leader could envision."[13] Finding and keeping the best talent available is a difficult task and requires human resource managers to be knowledgeable of the law when recruiting, selecting, developing, and maintaining employees as well as skillful in managing a complex and ever-changing, diverse workforce.

The human resource management function, if carried out effectively, can facilitate the successful execution of a company's business strategy and serve as the basis for its competitive advantage. To successfully manage the human resource activities within a company there must be an acute awareness of the law, a fact-based understanding of the demographic changes within the market, an intuitive understanding of the changing attitudes of the new generation of employees, and finally, it must be built on the premise that people are your greatest resource.

ENDNOTES

1. J. Slocum, D. Lei, and P. Butler, "Executing Business Strategies through Human Resource Management Practices," Organizational Dynamics, April-June 2014, pp 73–87.

2. Trilling, Bernie and Charles Fadel. *21st century skills: learning for life in our times,* Jossey-Bass, John Wiley & Sons, 2009.

3. "Challenges Facing Organizations and HR in the Next 10 Years SHRM Poll." Society for Human Resource Management. 2010. 11 May 2012. <http://www.shrm.org/Research/SurveyFindings/Articles/Pages/Challengesinnext10Yrs.aspx>

4. United States. Bureau of Labor Statistics. Labor force projections to 2018: older workers staying more active. Dec. 2010. 4 May 2012 <http://www.bls.gov/opub/mlr/2009/11/art3full.pdf>

5. Kubasek, N., et al. Dynamic Business Law: Summarized Cases. New York: McGraw-Hill Irwin, 2013.

6. United States. Dept. of Labor. Title VII Civil Rights Act 1964, as amended. Nov. 1991. 10 May 2012. <http://www.dol.gov/oasam/regs/statutes/2000e-16.htm>

7. United States, Equal Employment Opportunity Commission. "EEOC Releases Fiscal Year 2015. 11 Feb. 2016 <https://www.eeoc.gov/eeoc/newsroom/release/2-11-16.cfm>.

8. ibid

9. United States. Dept. of Education, Office for Civil Rights. Americans with Disabilities Act. 1990. 30 Jul. 2013 < http://www2.ed.gov/about/offices/list/ocr/docs/hq9805.html>.

10. United States. Dept. of Labor. Equal Employment Opportunity: Age Discrimination. 2013. 30 Jul. 2013 < http://www.dol.gov/dol/topic/discrimination/agedisc.htm>.

11. United States. Equal Employment Opportunity Commission. Equal Pay/Compensation Discrimination. 2013. 20 Jul. 2013 <http://www.eeoc.gov/laws/types/equalcompensation.cfm>.

12. "Federal Laws Prohibiting Job Discrimination Questions And Answers" U.S. Equal Employment Opportunity Commission, <http://www.eeoc.gov/facts/qanda.html>

13. Schultz, Howard, and Dori J. Yang. *Pour Your Heart into It: How Starbucks Built a Company One Cup at a Time.* New York, NY: Hyperion, 1997.

SOURCES

1. Fig. 7.1: Copyright © 2017 Depositphotos/Piratka20073.rambler.ru.
2. Fig. 7.5: Source: U.S. Equal Employment Opportunity Commission.

Chapter 8

Marketing

Understanding the Customer's Journey

PROLOGUE

Marketing affects virtually every decision you have made as a consumer. Either consciously or unconsciously your purchase decisions have been influenced by the marketing strategies of those companies attempting to sell you their products. However, as a result of the ubiquitous and endless amount of information available to consumers today the very nature of marketing itself is in a state of transformation. *"Eighty-one percent of shoppers conduct online research before they make a purchase. Sixty percent begin by using a search engine to find the products they want, and 61 percent will read product reviews before making any purchase."*[1] In the past, companies had more power to influence consumer purchase decisions. Sales people were trusted, and speaking to a company directly was a normal, logical step in the exchange process. This is no longer the case!

In the not too distant past entrepreneurs and managers focused their marketing efforts on three key variables:

- Understanding the customer,
- Knowing how, when, and where to market their product and by
- Building their brand.

These variables are now transforming into new dimensions that require marketers to utilize innovative marketing strategies that are based on:

- A comprehensive understanding of the client as an individual.
- An intuitive and precise understanding of the customer journey.
- The creation of an authentic brand that is reflected in the culture of the company.

Big data has transformed strategic decisions involving growth and competitive advantage because of the sheer volume and veracity of the data being produced. Big data, depending on the industry, encompasses information from multiple sources including consumer transactions, social media, enterprise content, and mobile devices. Marketers are now using big data to better understand individual customers, predict future behavior, create unique interactions and maximize the value of each interaction. Gone are the days where we just talk, in broad terms, about the nuances of age, gender, occupation, etc., that distinguish and segment consumers within the market. We now need to understand each customer, and their unique journey as a customer.

Journey Mapping Process

Here are the high level steps to create a Customer Journey Map.

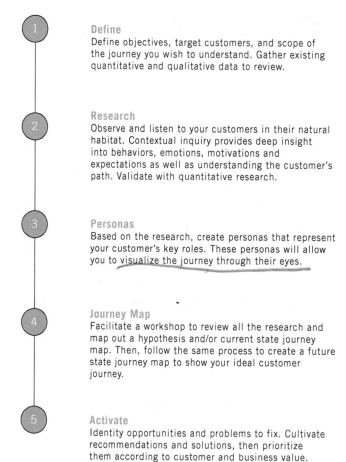

1 **Define**
Define objectives, target customers, and scope of the journey you wish to understand. Gather existing quantitative and qualitative data to review.

2 **Research**
Observe and listen to your customers in their natural habitat. Contextual inquiry provides deep insight into behaviors, emotions, motivations and expectations as well as understanding the customer's path. Validate with quantitative research.

3 **Personas**
Based on the research, create personas that represent your customer's key roles. These personas will allow you to visualize the journey through their eyes.

4 **Journey Map**
Facilitate a workshop to review all the research and map out a hypothesis and/or current state journey map. Then, follow the same process to create a future state journey map to show your ideal customer journey.

5 **Activate**
Identity opportunities and problems to fix. Cultivate recommendations and solutions, then prioritize them according to customer and business value. Create a roadmap and assign teams to projects. Measure your progress and watch your customer experience improve!

Understanding what market segment, and the unique dimensions of the customer's journey who comprise your target market, is foundational to the development of a successful marketing strategy. Companies that fail to continuously monitor and understand the needs of their customers, the strengths and weaknesses of their competitors, the changes in the external business environment, and continuously improve their value proposition will likely not survive or prosper in the rapidly changing marketplace.

HISTORY AND EVOLUTION OF MARKETING

Marketing from Ancient Greece to the modern 21st Century has been based on trade. Much of what we know about marketing today is rooted in the events that occurred during the Industrial Revolution where mass production and advancements in transportation and technology both required organizations to create more effective marketing strategies. The challenge during the Industrial Revolution, much like the challenges of the 21st Century, are exactly the same. How do we outsell the competition?

Production Orientation (1900s)

This approach focuses on the capabilities of the firm rather than on the needs of the market. During the early 1900s the demand for products exceeded the supply available creating a seller's market. The fundamental belief was that "A good product will sell itself" and that the primary focus of the firm was on producing goods based on their capabilities rather than on the needs of the market.

Sales Orientation (1920–1950)

As a result of mass production techniques the market changed with supply now exceeding the immediate demand for products. This created more of a buyer's market and as a result businesses were now compelled to engage in aggressive sales efforts in order to successfully sell their products. A sales orientation is based on the principle that consumers will buy more if a company utilizes more forceful sales and promotional techniques. Once again, just like the production orientation, the sales orientation fails to take into account the needs of the consumer. The most important lesson to be gleaned from an understanding of a sales orientation is that despite the nature and extent of your sales efforts a company cannot convince consumers to buy products that they do not need or want.

Marketing Orientation (1950s)

The nature of the marketplace completely shifted in the 1950's with the supply of products exceeding demand, thus creating a buyer's market. Consumers were no longer responsive to the "hard sell" tactics that were previously used to convince them to buy products that they did not need or want. Businesses began to understand that clever advertising and sales campaigns would no longer ensure the sale of their products or services. Instead, in order to be competitive, businesses were now required to examine the market, determine the needs of their customers, and then produce and market products to meet the specific needs and expectations of specific groups of consumers.

In today's business environment companies are required to build a culture and philosophy, based on the principles of the ***Marketing Concept,*** that embraces and implements a customer driven orientation into all facets of the organization. The goal of such an orientation is to deliver superior value and satisfaction in each and every customer interaction. This means that every individual within the organization is responsible for ensuring that customer's' needs, wants, and satisfaction are of foremost importance.

The Marketing Concept has three key components:

Customer Orientation*—Determine the needs of consumers, then produce and market products to meet their specific needs and expectations.*

Service Orientation*—Incorporate training of all employees in customer service for the purpose of creating superior customer satisfaction.*

Profit Orientation*—Market those goods/services that will earn profits ensuring the long-term survival and growth of the organization.*

"In a world where feature and price advantages can be quickly matched, if not bettered, by competitors from virtually anywhere in the world, a company's best source of sustainable competitive advantage may be the customer experience it delivers. Yet while many organizations understand and even embrace the concept of customer centricity, many fall short when it comes to executing customer-centric agendas in a way that delivers sustainable results.

The recipe for success is to consistently deliver a differentiated experience designed to satisfy the intentions and preferences of your target buyers—a feat that can only be accomplished with a deep understanding of the customer base and market; distinctive capabilities that enable a company to execute on the basis of customer insight; and the processes and systems to enable high performance."[2]

Customer Relationship Era (1990)

The concept of Customer Relationship Management (CRM) is an extension of the marketing concept. CRM involves learning as much as possible about customers and doing everything possible to satisfy, even delight, them with goods and services that exceed their expectations. CRM provides the means for companies to create a decisive competitive advantage necessary to increase market share and reduce operational costs while retaining existing customers. The relationship marketing era is based on the creation of a long-term, trusting, relationship with consumers in an attempt to foster customer loyalty and encourage repeat buying in the future.

"That's the thing traditional CRM systems don't account for well. Customer relationships aren't built on information, they're built on trust. And relationships are reciprocal ... When one party focuses too much on acquiring and leveraging information, trust can't help but be compromised, if not breached. The problem with traditional CRM is that it turns people into data and relationships into rules of engagement."[3]

MARKETING PROCESS: BUILDING YOUR MARKETING STRATEGY

The six step marketing process requires business owners and managers to critically analyze each phase of the process in order to ensure that the organization can create, communicate, deliver, and exchange product/service offerings that provide value and benefit to the consumer. Like most processes in business the marketing process is circular and as a result managers are continuously analyzing market data, seeking feedback from their target customer, refining their marketing mix, improving methods for building trust and loyalty, and evaluating and improving upon the customer's journey.

> "Companies have long emphasized touchpoints—the many critical moments when customers interact with the organization and its offerings on their way to purchase and after. But the narrow focus on maximizing satisfaction at those moments can create a distorted picture, suggesting that customers are happier with the company than they actually are. It also diverts attention from the bigger—and more important—picture: the customer's end-to-end journey.
>
> In our research and consulting on customer journeys, we've found that organizations able to skillfully manage the entire experience reap enormous rewards: enhanced customer satisfaction, reduced churn, increased revenue, and greater employee satisfaction. They also discover more-effective ways to collaborate across functions and levels, a process that delivers gains throughout the company."[4]

This process should be based on a clear understanding of the customer's journey as well as the basis for Customer Relationship Management (CRM) and the foundation for contemporary marketing strategy development.

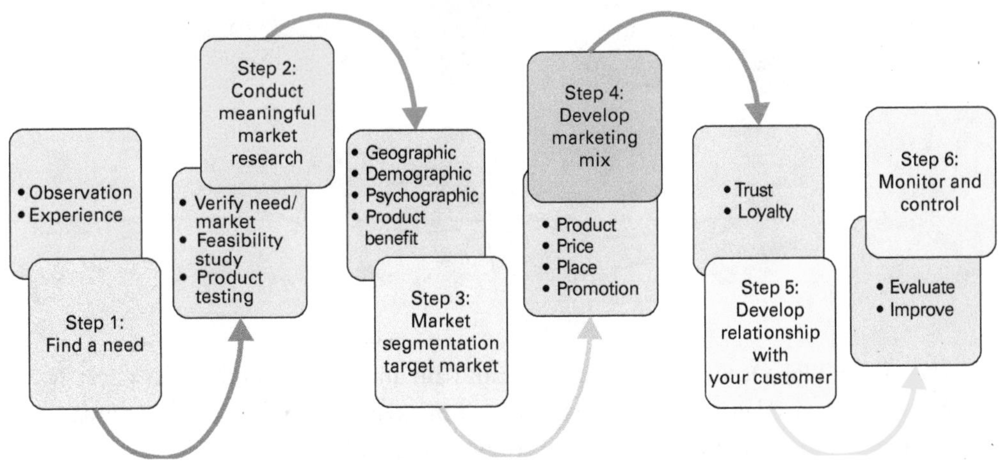

MARKETING ENVIRONMENTS

Prior to selecting a target market and developing the key elements of the marketing mix, it is essential to research, analyze, and understand the external forces influencing consumer purchase decisions.

Effective marketing relies on a continuous process of identifying existing customer needs and requirements and then anticipating future changes in the market. The marketing environment for most businesses, if not every business, constantly changes and with greater speed than ever before. The challenge facing marketing managers is, therefore, to remain informed of the forces driving change and then attempt to develop the appropriate strategies necessary to compete and win in the market.

This remains true for any company regardless of the industry, size, or market in which it operates. Five major forces shape the external, uncontrollable, marketing environment. In the short term, an organization and its management team must recognize that it is impossible to alter any of the macro-forces of the marketing environment. However, in the long term, organizations and their marketing teams must carefully consider the effects of the forces emanating from the external environment and then intelligently use this knowledge to make important decisions regarding the development of the most effective marketing mix. As an example, a manager may not be able to do anything in regard to the specific actions of a competitor in their market but nonetheless capable of developing marketing strategies that capitalize on the weaknesses of the competitor in order to gain market share.

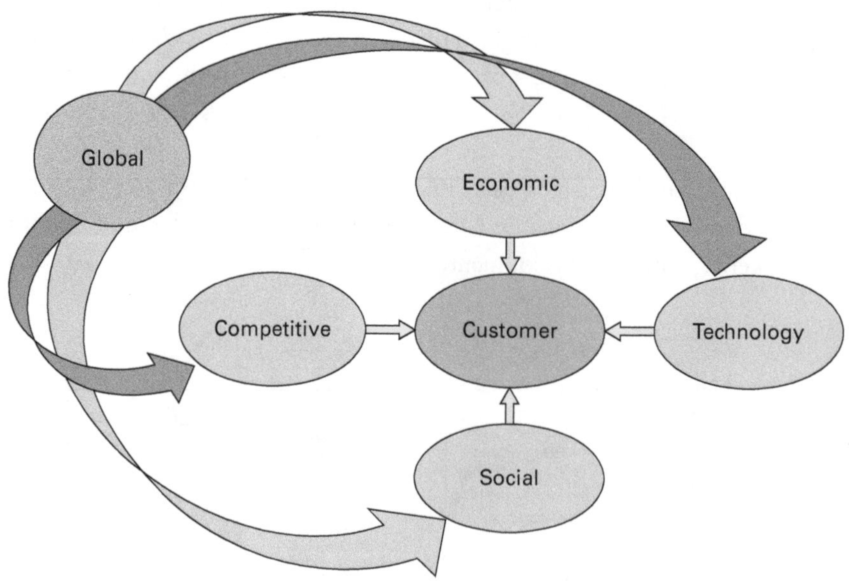

In their book Blue Ocean Strategies, W. Chan Kim and Renee Mauborgne assert that; "Blue oceans denote all the industries not in existence today—the unknown market space, untainted by competition. In blue oceans, demand is created rather than fought over. There is ample opportunity for growth that is both profitable and rapid. There are two ways to create blue oceans. In a few cases, companies can give rise to completely new industries, as eBay did with the online auction industry. But in most cases, a blue ocean is created from within a red ocean when a company alters the boundaries of an existing industry."[5]

It is often said, "knowledge is power" and when it comes to developing a winning marketing strategy it is incumbent upon the marketing manager to have the requisite insights and knowledge of the business environment in order to make both intelligent and informed decisions. Without such knowledge and insight any strategy is likely to fail.

Competitive Environment

In order to compete and develop the appropriate marketing strategies, the competitive environment must be defined and understood. Because of the dynamic nature of the competitive environment, marketers would be well advised to consider the following key questions:

1. Who are my primary competitors?
2. What is the nature of the competitive environment (e.g. monopolistic vs oligopoly)?
3. Are there similar or substitute products available?
4. Will competitive forces likely change?
5. What are the strengths and weaknesses of the competition relative to the current competitive forces?
6. Are there any new or emerging technologies?
7. Is it possible to establish and maintain a competitive advantage?
8. Is it possible to make the competition irrelevant?

Economic Environment

There are many economic factors that influence the development of a company's marketing strategy. Both internal and external economics play a huge role in the amount of marketing you can produce, your messaging, and the effect on the consumer and their patterns of consumption. Macro and micro economic factors must be analyzed to determine their impact on consumers. These factors include: the financial health of a region or country, supply and demand patterns, rate of inflation, GDP, unemployment, business cycles, exchange rates, trade agreements, tax rates, and consumer sentiment.

Technological Environment

Advancements in technology affect how marketers design, produce, price, distribute, promote, and track their products. In addition technology has forever changed the way that consumers access product information and purchase products. Consumers now have access to technology that allows them to design products, compare prices, read product reviews, and access technical information about any product at any time from any location.

2017's Top 10 Tech Trends for Marketers to Watch[6]

1. Smartphones Get Smarter
   Our smartphone habits have opened the door to more deeply comprehensive mobile marketing strategies.
2. Automation and Precision with Artificial Intelligence
   Marketers need to know what consumers value and their general preferences in order to effectively reach them. With the help of AI software, marketers can employ sophisticated, automated algorithms that tap more deeply into demographic and psychographic information.
3. Voice Your Needs
   Digital voice assistants – Siri, Alexa, Cortana, and so on – are able to answer questions, organize our schedules and perform simple tasks upon vocal command. Over the next few years, their capabilities and "skills" will grow to open a myriad of new marketing avenues.
4. New-flix
   As streaming video content increases in popularity, marketers are sure to bring their message via video. Companies are harnessing the potential of digital storytelling through video.
5. Internet of Things and Social Media Marketing
   One of the most well-known features of the internet is set to get a boost through Internet of Things technology: social media.
6. The Impact of Influence
   Marketing is all about influence, but influencer marketing adds a crucial step. Instead of a campaign that targets certain individuals (known as influencers) and entrusts them to spread the word to others via word-of-mouth marketing, thereby increasing a brand or product's visibility.
7. Think Systems – Not Singular Products
   The connective capability of mobile phones and devices has made it so one product is rarely the center of attention. With pressure points dispersed, individual tools are less important than systems with more durability.
8. Automation
   Marketing can be tedious. To effectively target an audience, you need to be thorough and consider all possible outlets. Using automation software, marketers can accomplish duties like sending emails and analytics easily.
9. Time for "Real-Time"
   Time is of the essence, especially if you're a marketer. You need to be aware of whether or not your campaign is effective, and you can't afford to wait weeks, or even days, to find out. With real-time data programs, marketers can receive information such as social media engagement across different regions.

10. The Power of Blockchain
Data is gravy to a marketer, and software might be the future of how data is handled. Software like Blockchain will allow for marketers to have full awareness in regards to the placement of their ads, this control could help increase trust between marketers and consumers through boosted transparency.

Social (Cultural) Environment

The social and cultural environment affects how and why people live and behave the way they do. "*Culture influences consumers' thoughts and behaviors. Research shows that culture operates primarily by setting boundaries for individual behaviors and by influencing the functioning of each institution as the family and mass media. Research also shows that people from different cultures consume differently primarily because of their differences in values and norms.*"[7] This ultimately affects consumer perceptions and buying behavior and eventually the economic, political, and legal environment.

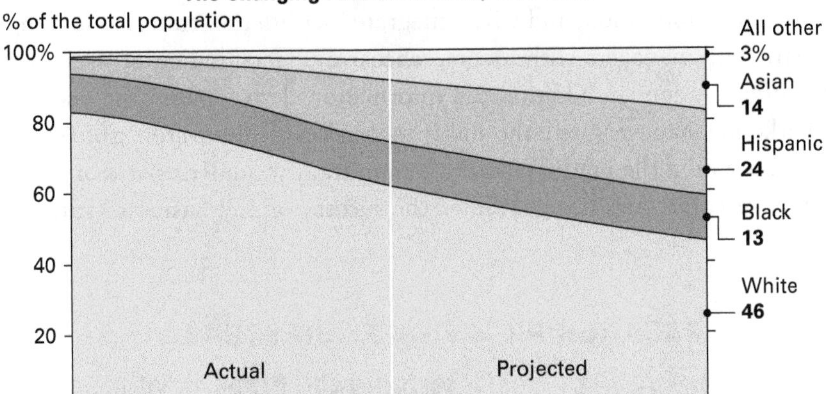

Note: Whites, blacks and Asians include only single-race non-Hispanics; Asians include Pacific Islanders. Hispanics can be of any race.
Source: Pew Research Center 2015 report, "Modern Immigration Wave Brings 59 Million to US, Driving Population Growth and Change Through 2065"
Pew Research Center

Global Environment

"*The global economic environment is changing rapidly. Globalization has led to astonishing increases in global trade. Trade currently represents 30 per cent of world gross domestic product (GDP) and is expected to grow to 50 per cent of world GDP by 2020. Greater participation in international trade is a prerequisite for economic growth and sustainable development in today's competitive world economy.*"[8] Increasing globalization not only affects large multi-national corporations that operate in markets around the world but it also impacts small to mid-sized companies who must now not only compete with companies "down the street" but also those companies from all around the world. Because of globalization there exists increased competition, new sources of raw materials, and cheaper manufacturing opportunities. Business owners and managers must now also take into account the changing global environment and understand how their respective businesses might likely be impacted by such variables as:

- *Market Trends*
- *Trade Agreements*
- *Legal & Regulatory Issues*
- *Shifting Economies*
- *Emerging Markets & Population Growth*
- *Competition*
- *Technology (access to consumers around the world)*

MARKETING RESEARCH

For entrepreneurs, business owners, and marketing managers marketing research is used to acquire critical knowledge of the competitive landscape. The research serves solely as a source of credible information, and when integrated within the strategic planning process, provides marketing managers with a comprehensive understanding of what is occurring outside the organization. In addition the information derived from the market research provides marketing managers with the ability to develop the innovative strategies necessary to compete and win in the marketplace. It is important to understand that simply engaging in market research does not guarantee the success of any business venture, product, or service.

MARKETING RESEARCH PROCESS: FOUR STEPS

Step 1: Define the Problem and Determine the Present Situation

This step requires marketers to conduct an in-depth analysis of the present situation resulting in a comprehensive understanding of the nature of the opportunities and threats that exist. In addition it is necessary during this step of the process to identify the type of data/information needed and the necessary methods required to collect the relevant data.

Step 2: Collect Relevant Data

There are two broad categories of data; Primary and Secondary Data. Primary data is data collected for the first time through personal experience, observation, or a formal process including, but not limited to, focus groups, surveys, questionnaires and interviews. Secondary data is often free and easily accessible from sources, such as trade associations, government agencies (Bureau of Labor Statistics, Census Bureau, Small Business Administration), industry publications, and academic journals. Although these sources are easily accessible and free they often do not provide the information necessary to solve the research needs of the firm. When additional information is needed researchers will often either use Secondary Data Providers or engage in the acquisition of primary data.

SECONDARY DATA SOURCES	PRIMARY DATA SOURCES
Includes all available existing sources of information.	*Includes all new data not previously published.*
Secondary data is information, which has been collected by other individuals or agencies for purposes other than those of our particular research study.	*The data is derived from first-hand sources by means of survey, observation, interview, questionnaire, or experimentation.*
Secondary data can be used to get a new perspective on a current study or to supplement or compare with other information.	***Focus Groups** are used to collect information about a specific product from a specific consumer or business segment of the market.*

Step 3: Analyze the Research Data

Once you've assembled all of the data (information) it is time to analyze the relevance of the data to your company. When doing this, it's important to look for trends as opposed to specific pieces of information. As you're analyzing your data look for patterns that either reaffirm or contradict your assumptions as it relates to the following:

- Market/Profit Potential
  A business is determined to be feasible if it can be shown that there is sufficient market demand - that is, that there exists an adequate number of customers in your geographic/target market who will purchase the necessary quantity of products/services needed to produce a profit.
- Competition
  Do a few large players dominate the market? Is it fragmented and/or comprised of numerous smaller players?
- Industry Trends
  What stage of the product life cycle is the industry? Is it a new industry? Mature industry? A mature industry may mean the market has been saturated, or that sales are no longer growing, and may even be falling.
- Capital Requirements
  What are total start-up costs needed in order to begin operations?

  What are the anticipated costs of land, plant and equipment? What are the day-to-day operating costs involved? This will provide an overview of the cash-flow requirements of the business.

Step 4: Choose the Best Strategy

An actionable marketing strategy develops realistic and practical ways to reach customers and encourage their future consumption of products or services and loyalty to a business. The most effective marketing strategy focuses on the opportunities that provide the greatest potential to increase sales and improve the company's competitive position by focusing on its core strengths. The interrelated elements of the marketing strategy are based on a clear understanding of the *Marketing Mix* and *Marketing Objectives.*

USING RESEARCH TO UNDERSTAND CONSUMER BEHAVIOR

Effective marketing research gets you close to the customer in an attempt to find out what they need and want. Consumer behavior involves the actions taken to obtain, consume, and dispose of products, including the decision processes that precede the actual purchase decision.

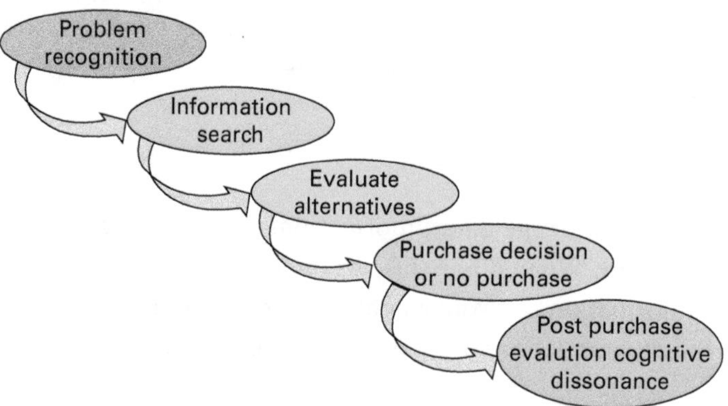

By studying people's purchasing behavior, market researchers can identify consumers' attitudes toward their products. This critical investigation into consumer behavior allows marketing managers to improve the effectiveness of the organization's marketing strategies that have been directed at specific target markets. Both personal and interpersonal factors influence consumer behavior and as a result marketers need to understand what motivates consumers, the customer journey, to buy certain goods and services.

Shifting Consumer Behavior

> "Today, bigger isn't always better, and ownership isn't equated with happiness. More and more consumers are finding joy in less, taking advantage of access-over-ownership service models and wealth is an increasingly outdated measure of success. These shifts are prompting global citizens to rethink what it means to live the good life, where "good" encompasses not just possessions, but also experiences and values."[9]

Ten Dimensions of Consumer Behavior[10]

Connected consumers are always on. For example, a large majority of those we surveyed check e-mail before going to bed at night.

Co-productive consumers are now a factor in the means of production. For example, they more frequently provide direct feedback to companies and help design products.

Social consumers interact with companies, institutions and each other through the Internet. For example, more than half report they increasingly use social media to interact with family members.

Individual consumers spend to express their particular personality and uniqueness: they want tailored offerings that will bring out who they really are.

Resourceful consumers work hard and spend thriftily to get ahead. They turn to new online platforms to buy used products, sell directly to other consumers, or participate in online auctions.

Disconnected consumers like to distance themselves from the constant presence of the digital world and are willing to spend to do so. They want products and services that help them leave the stresses of the world behind, ranging from scented candles to cruise vacations.

Experiential consumers want more than the digital world can offer. They seek the enjoyment of new and different experiences, from traveling to new places to attending live events.

Minimalist consumers purchase second-hand or reuse products. For example, they may prefer car-sharing services to outright possession, and tend to value access over ownership.

Conscientious consumers more frequently buy local, more often make what they need, and consider the environmental impact when deciding what to purchase. Also, they give away what they no longer need.

Communal consumers devote extensive time and money to causes with social impact—and they appreciate businesses that do the same.

Factors Influencing Consumer Behavior

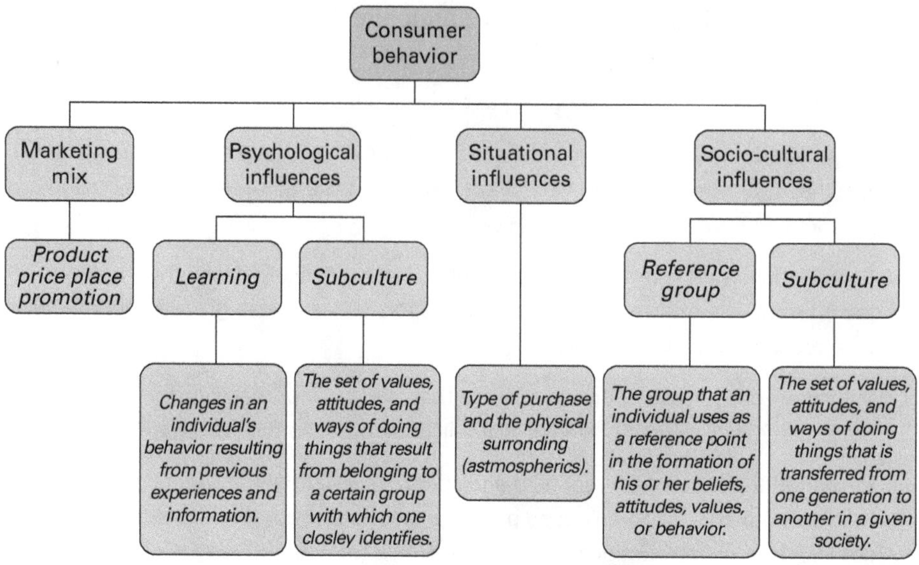

MARKET SEGMENTATION: YOU CAN NOT BE ALL THINGS TO ALL PEOPLE

Michael Porter proclaimed that the essence of "Strategy 101 is about choices: You can't be all things to all people." This means that the choice of your target market, how you have segmented the market, is a critical first step in the development of a marketing strategy. A ***market*** is comprised of people (B2C), or other businesses (B2B), which have the purchasing power, authority, and willingness to purchase the goods and services of the selling organization. This is a very important distinction to keep in mind when determining what segment of the market you will target. The "first" method of segmentation requires entrepreneurs and business managers to make decisions based on a very broad distinction of what market they will serve. Will the company target the "end-user" ***Consumer Market***, or will the company target those business intermediaries that comprise the ***Business-to-Business Market***?

Mass Marketing is based on the development of products that are designed to reach a large segment of diverse consumers. Mass marketing is based on the premise that "one-product-fits-all" and that there is no need to segment the market in order to meet the needs of the consumer. For those companies that intend to target a smaller *Niche* market the market segmentation process requires a more focused approach to dividing the total market into several, relatively similar, homogeneous groups. ***Target Marketing*** is the process wherein an organization decides which market segment(s) will be targeted, identifying the the unique needs of the consumers who comprise the market, and the development of an overall marketing strategy.

Relationship Marketing attempts to establish and maintain mutually beneficial exchange relationships with internal and external customers and stakeholders. Relationship marketing is an extension of customer relationship management and focuses on customer loyalty and long-term customer engagement. Its primary focus is on retaining existing consumers rather than attempting to create new consumers. This requires companies to move away from mass production to custom made goods that are designed to meet the unique needs and interests of the consumer while at the same time creating an emotional connection with the brand.

A ***Consumer Market (B2C)*** consists of end-user consumers. Market segmentation is used to divide consumers, based on a common set of characteristics or variables, into fairly homogeneous groups with similar needs and wants. Segmentation is simply the process of dividing a particular market into sections, which display similar characteristics or behavior.

There are a number of approaches to segmentation that allow an organization to divide their market into homogenous groups. These approaches include:

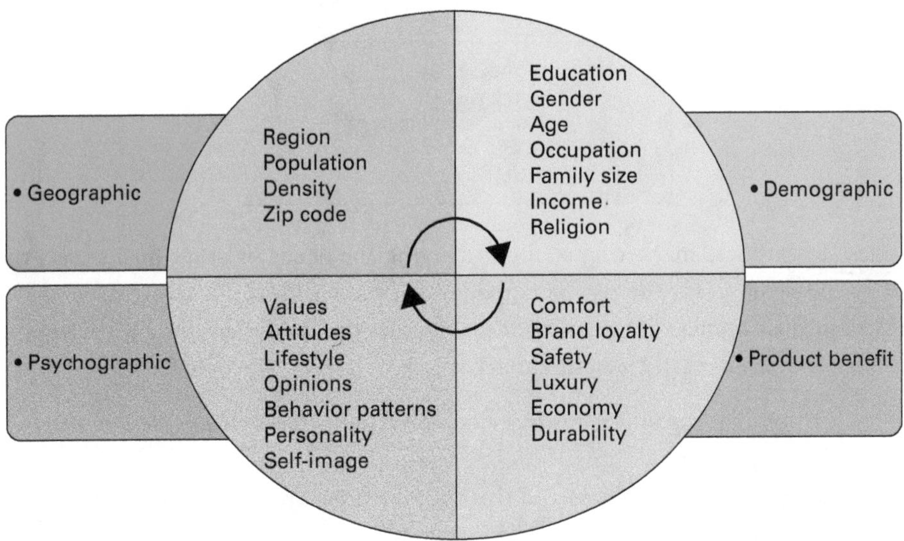

Geographic segmentation is based on location or region of a specific group of consumers. Marketers use geographic segmentation because consumers in different areas may display unique characteristics and behaviors that do not exist in other geographic regions. For example in beach communities (e.g. Santa Barbara) where there is a large group of consumers who surf, it is likely that marketers of surf related products would use this method of segmentation.

The word demographics, derived from the root word 'demography', is defined as the "study of the population." As a result, ***Demographic segmentation*** is used to divide the population into similar groups based on such variables of age, gender, income, occupation, marital status, and family life cycle amongst other variables.

Psychographic segmentation, sometimes referred to as behavioral segmentation, is a method of dividing markets on the basis of the values, attitudes and lifestyle (VALS) habits of customers. If Demographics describes "who" people are Psychographics explains "why" people buy. Successfully marketing any product requires a deep understanding of the customer's psychology, along with their needs, in order for the product to be successful.

Psychographic segmentation allows marketers to understand the motivational and unconscious drives of a specific target audience.

Product-benefit segmentation is based on the consumer's perception of value or benefit received from a good or service over alternative products. Due to the perceived value or benefit of a product marketers attempt to partition the market based on variables like quality, performance, reputation, service, brand name, or other benefits prospective consumers seek.

The ***Business-to-Business Market (B2B)*** is comprised of all individuals and organizations that purchase goods for the purpose of producing other goods and/or services.

Geographic
- Concentrated industries

Demographic
- Sales revenues
- Number of employees
- Number of buyers

Volume/End Use
- Heavy vs. light use
- Design specifications
- Design
- Price

Business-to-business marketing is about meeting the needs of other businesses, though ultimately the demand for the products made by these businesses is likely to be driven by consumers in their homes. There are four key factors that make business-to-business markets special and different to consumer markets:

- The decision-making unit is far more complex in business-to-business markets than in consumer markets
- Business-to-business products and their applications are more complex than consumer products
- Business-to-business marketers address a much smaller number of customers who are very much larger in their consumption of products than is the case in consumer markets
- Personal relationships are of critical importance in business-to-business markets.[11]

DEVELOPING A MARKETING STRATEGY/PLAN

Both for-profit and not-for-profit organizations need to develop a marketing strategy (plan) to effectively compete within the marketplace. A good marketing plan is essential to any business and in large part determines the likelihood of its success. A good marketing plan is the end product of your market research and is directed at a specific "target market." At a minimum the development of a marketing plan requires an understanding of the organizations:

- Target Market—Needs
- Product—Total Product Offer

- *Industry Patterns & Trends*
- *Product Life Cycles*
- *Competitive Environment & Primary Competition—Pricing Strategy*
- *Channels of Distribution*

Marketing Mix

Product—Product development involves decisions regarding packaging, brand name, trademark protection, warranties, and other key variables.

Price—Involves the creation of a pricing strategy designed to influence the consumer's perceptions of quality, value, and utility.

Place—Involves the physical distribution of goods, selection of appropriate channels, market coverage, and the number of intermediaries required to create time and place utility.

Promotion—Involves decisions about the nature of communication with the target customer and the appropriate mediums necessary to reach the customer. Promotion includes personal selling, advertising, public relations, and sales promotion.

Every company in every market must develop its own unique marketing mix. Whether it is successful or not successful is dependent upon the ability of the organization, and its management team, to create a unique strategy that appeals to specific consumer segments. When developing a marketing mix managers must make decisions that involve the following variables:

PRODUCT	PRICE	PLACE	PROMOTION
Function	List Price	Channel Members	Advertising
Appearance	Discounts	Market Coverage	Personal Selling
Quality	Allowances	Location	Public Relations
Packaging	Financing	Logistics	Sales Promotion
Branding	Lease Options	Utility	Message
Warranty	Break-Even		Media
Service/Support	Market Equilibrium		
Positioning			

In a general sense, the marketing mix, the four controllable variables within your business, allows companies to build and sell products or services that add value to their customers. Ultimately, consumers will buy products that they perceive are the best value for their money.

MARKETING'S TRANSFORMATION: PAY ATTENTION TO THE INDIVIDUAL

Marketing once again is in the midst of a major transformation. Although the basic concepts and functions of marketing remain the same, the methods used to engage the customer and create exchange have forever been altered by technology and the use of big data. In the recent past marketers typically focused their attention on understanding the needs of their target market, developing their marketing mix, and building product/brand preference. However, with the advent of big data, described as data from digital sources, marketers now have access to large volumes of information about individual consumers. This information, big data, allows marketers to more accurately predict the behavior of individual consumers, which in turn allows for the creation of a marketing mix that is designed to maximize each and every customer interaction. Marketers can no longer sit back and engage in endless market research in a veiled attempt to understand markets or market segments of consumers. Instead, it has now become essential to understand the needs of individual consumers, using big data, in order to add greater value to every consumer interaction, regardless of where it occurs. "Every enterprise needs to fully understand big data—what it is to them, what is does for them, what it means to them—and the potential of data-driven marketing, starting today."[12]

ENDNOTES

1. Morrison, Kimberlee. *81% of Shoppers Conduct Online Research Before Buying [Infographic] MineWhat.com compiled data to provide insight into what motivates shoppers.* <http://www.adweek.com/digital/what-national-geographic-did-to-earn-3-million-snapchat-discover-subscribers-in-just-3-months/>

2. Driggs, Woody. "Serving Up Customer Delight." CRM.com Apr. 2008. 12 May 2012. <http://www.destinationcrm.com/Articles/Columns-Departments/The-Tipping-Point/Serving-Up-Customer-Delight—46872.aspx>.

3. McKee, Steve. "How Social Media is Changing CRM." Bloomberg Businessweek 8 Jun 2012. 3 Aug 2013 < http://www.businessweek.com/articles/2012-06-08/how-social-media-is-changing-crm>.

4. Alex Rawson, Ewan Duncan, and Conor Jones, "The Truth About Customer Experience." Harvard Business Review, Aug 18, 2014. <https://hbr.org/2013/09/the-truth-about-customer-experience>

5. Kim, W. Chan and Renee and Renee Mauborgne. *Blue Ocean Strategy: How to Create Uncontested Market Space and Make Competition Irrelevant.* Harvard Business School Publishing Corporation, 2015.

6. Kotz, Beth. "2017's Top 10 Tech Trends for Marketers to Watch". piesync. 1 May 2017. <http://blog.piesync.com/tech-trends-marketers/>.

7. de Mooji, Marieke. *Consumer Behavior and Culture: Consequences for Global Marketing and Advertising, 2nd.* Sage 2011.

8. "ESCAP Trade Facilitation Framework." United Nations ESCAP. 2003. United Nations. 27 Mar. 2012 < http://www.unescap.org/tid/publication/t&ipub2327_part1.pdf>

9. Connelly, Sheryl. "Looking Further with Ford: 2017 trends." *Mediaford.com.* <https://media.ford.com/content/dam/fordmedia/North%20America/US/2016/12/7/2017-Looking%20-Further-with-Ford-Trend-Report.pdf>

10. "Energizing Global Growth: Understanding the Changing Consumer." Accenture. 2013. 8 Aug 2013 <http://www.accenture.com/SiteCollectionDocuments/us-en/landing-pages/energizing-global-growth/Energizing-Global-Growth-Final.pdf>.

11. Hague, Paul et al. "B2B Marketing: Four Factors that Make Business-To-Business Special" B2B International.com <http://www.b2binternational.com/library/whitepapers/whitepapers04.php>

12. Lisa Arthur, "What Is Big Data." Forbes August 15, 2013. <https://www.forbes.com/sites/lisaarthur/2013/08/15/what-is-big-data/#70cc1cc85c85>

SOURCES

1. Fig. 8.1: Adapted from: Tandemseven, https://www.slideshare.net/TandemSeven/journeymapinfographic-v52.

2. Fig. 8.2: Source: https://commons.wikimedia.org/wiki/File:Business_Feedback_Loop_PNG_version.png.

3. Adapted from: Beth Kotz, "2017's Top 10 Tech Trends for Marketers to Watch," Piesync.com. Copyright © 2017 by PieSync.

4. Fig. 8.5: Source: http://www.pewresearch.org/fact-tank/2016/03/31/10-demographic-trends-that-are-shaping-the-u-s-and-the-world/. Copyright © 2015 by Pew Research Center.

5. Fig. 8.9: Source: Accenture, Energizing Global Growth: Understanding the Changing Consumer Dimensions of Behavior Change and Case Studies. Copyright © 2013 by Accenture.

Chapter 9

Product Development

What Pain Are You Solving?

PROLOGUE

For most businesses, new product development has become the single most important factor driving the success, or failure, of the firm. The increased emphasis on product development has spurred a surge of new products in the marketplace and based on the latest statistics 35%[1] of new consumer products are destined to fail. For a company to successfully bring new products to the market, they must simultaneously meet three critical objectives: maximize the benefit to the customer, minimize the time it takes to get the product to the market, and provide a compelling reason for consumers to buy from you instead of your competition.

As the result of a market that is in constant flux it is essential for managers and their respective organizations to continuously develop new products that remain relevant, viable and profitable. *"Ideas, in a sense, are overrated. Of course, you need good ones, but at this point in our supersaturated culture, precious few are so novel that nobody else has ever thought of them before. It's really about where you take the idea, and how committed you are to solving the endless problems that come up in the execution."*[2] However numerous factors can cause new products to fail. One of the most common causes of new product failure is a lack of preparation necessary to successfully launch the product. It is not unusual for companies to direct all of their attention to the design and manufacturing of a new product only to neglect the needs of the consumer, the availability of competing products, and their underlying value proposition.

An important question every entrepreneur and/or marketing manager must ask himself/herself when developing new products is: why do so many new products fail? Obviously new product failure is not the result of a single mistake but the result of numerous errors in the process of product development. As is often the case entrepreneurs and/or marketing managers become so enamored with their new product ideas that they fail to engage in meaningful research in order to confirm their assumptions about the product and the market. Companies who fail to do their research and more importantly ignore the dynamic forces of the market are likely to become a statistical footnote in the new product failure rates.

Products will regularly fail because the pricing strategy or distribution channels are flawed. Sometimes the promotional strategy fails to effectively engage the target customer or adequately communicate the value proposition of the product. Whatever the reason, it is important to understand that new product development requires more than just a "gut feeling" as the rationale for developing a new product. Instead new product development requires research that is both thoughtful and comprehensive as well as a marketing strategy that has been designed to meet the needs of the target customer while at the same time carving out a unique competitive advantage. Ultimately market research should answer the most fundamental questions confronting any new product: "Who will buy the product? and Why will they buy our product?"

Successful product development is the result of an integrated process that relies on credible research and an intuitive understanding of the opportunities and threats within the market.

PRODUCT: THE "FIRST P" OF THE MARKETING MIX

If you think about any product you have ever purchased you probably opted to buy the product because of the manner in which marketers had bundled its unique attributes. As a consequence a product is often described as a bundle of physical, service, or symbolic attributes designed to satisfy consumer needs. The term product applies to all of the following categories:

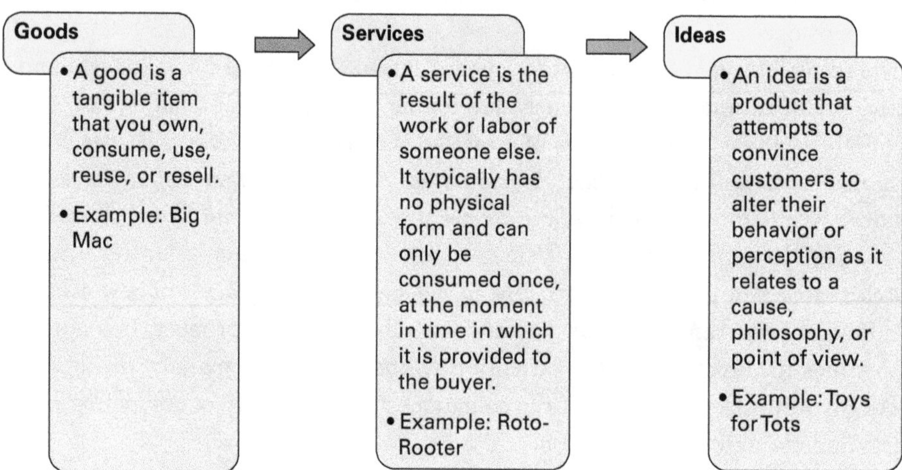

Goods
• A good is a tangible item that you own, consume, use, reuse, or resell.
• Example: Big Mac
Services
• A service is the result of the work or labor of someone else. It typically has no physical form and can only be consumed once, at the moment in time in which it is provided to the buyer.
• Example: Roto-Rooter
Ideas
• An idea is a product that attempts to convince customers to alter their behavior or perception as it relates to a cause, philosophy, or point of view.
• Example: Toys for Tots

NEW PRODUCT DEVELOPMENT PROCESS: SIX STEPS

Identifying and developing new-product ideas, and effective strategies to market them, is often the key to a firm's success and long-term survival. But this isn't easy. Because introducing new products on a consistent basis is important to the future success of any organization, the new-product development process requires significant time, effort, and talent—and still the risks and costs are high. To create successful new products, companies must: understand their customers, markets, competitors, and most importantly develop products that deliver superior value to customers. The new product development process is comprised of the following six steps:

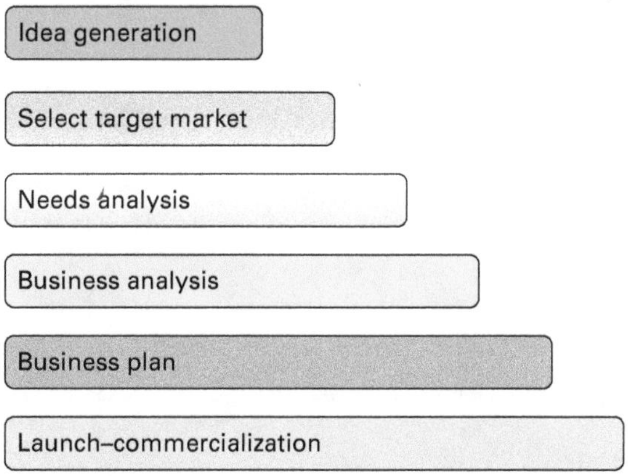

Idea generation

Select target market

Needs analysis

Business analysis

Business plan

Launch–commercialization

Step #1: Idea Generation ... The Process of Discovery!

New ideas can come from a company's own internal sources, customers, sales or production staff. External sources are also a valuable source of new ideas and include; focus groups, competitors, distributors and suppliers, trade associations, advertising agencies, or government agencies.

> "Steve Jobs was always an experimenter and a doer. Although some of Apple's products, such as the Newton, the Lisa, and Apple TV, might be considered failures, he bounced back numerous times and introduced dazzlingly exceptional products that have and still are dominating the market. He is a superb example of an experimenter who sometimes failed in the marketplace, but learned from his mistakes and achieved subsequent success."[3]

The purpose of the idea generation phase is to use previously acquired knowledge, personal experiences, and new knowledge and then transform that information into some new product or service that can be applied to a new situation or problem. Often the hardest part of generating new product ideas is knowing where and how to begin looking for idea. Some methods for generating new ideas include:

- *Brainstorming*
- *Experience*
- *Frustrations*
- *Observations*
- *Need deficiency*

Step #2: Select Target Market … Who Will Buy Your Product?

Once an idea for a new product is conceived the most logical next step is to ask; who will buy it? The second step of the new product development process is designed to determine what segment of the market should be targeted? Who is the specific target customer for the new product? Establishing a specific target market allows marketers to more effectively screen new product ideas based on an explicit understanding of the needs and wants of the market. This understanding should eventually lead to a product and marketing mix that will provide the firm with a sustainable competitive advantage.

Reformat layout of information and picture below

- Target Market
  - B2C – End User
  - B2B – Marketing Intermediary
- Segmentation of Market
  - Geographic
  - Demographic
  - Psychographic
  - Product Benefit
  - Volume
- What is a Market?
  - Consumers or clients who have:
    - Capacity to buy—Purchasing Power
    - Authority to Buy—Ability
    - Willingness to Buy

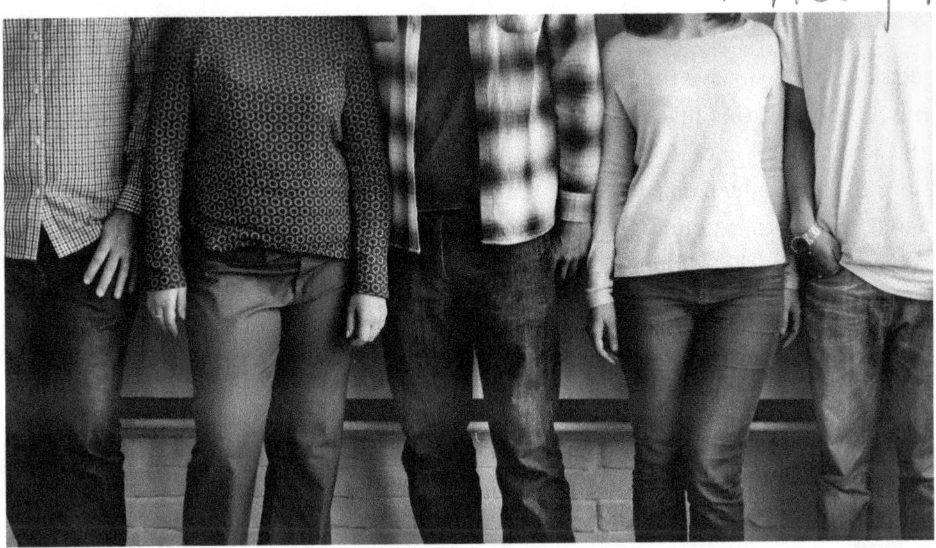

Step #3: Needs Analysis: Customer Validation

Companies must determine whether or not a new product has the potential to succeed or fail. Making this decision requires knowledge and insight derived from experience and credible research. The most fundamental question that must be addressed is: Does a need for the product exist in the market? In order to intelligently answer this important question marketers conduct market research using two sources of data:

- *Primary Data "Bottom Up"*
    - Observation
    - Interview
    - Survey
    - Questionnaire
    - Concept Testing
- *Secondary Data "Top Down"*
    - Census
    - Trade Association
    - Industry Publication
    - Small Business Administration

To effectively determine the needs within the market businesses need up-to-date information. The information derived from market research should provide a clear understanding of consumer needs, current and future market demand, scope and nature of the competition, and major demographic shifts in the population. Because businesses operate in a dynamic environment market research is essential in order to keep abreast of the changes in technology, consumer tastes, number of competitors, and economic conditions.

Step #4: Business Analysis

Product ideas that survive the preceding steps now face further quantitative and financial scrutiny. Normally, this involves questions about the design and engineering of the product, the actual creation of a prototype, concept testing wherein you solicit initial consumer reactions to the product, size of the potential market, potential sales, growth projections, estimated costs, profit potential and scalability. Key questions that must be addressed at this stage of the process include:

- What are the capital requirements?
- What are the one time startup costs?
- What are the ongoing operating expenses?
- Is the product scalable?
- What is a realistic return on investment (ROI)?

Step #5: Business Plan

For most new entrepreneurs, developing and writing a business plan is often a very formidable task. However, the very process of writing a business plan is often more important than the plan itself. A business plan is an essential tool necessary to create a viable business. The plan allows the entrepreneur to pull together all of the elements of the entrepreneur's vision and serves as a blueprint for how the business will operate.

Although there are a variety of opinions regarding what constitutes a good business plan it is fair to say that at a minimum a business plan should include the following key components:

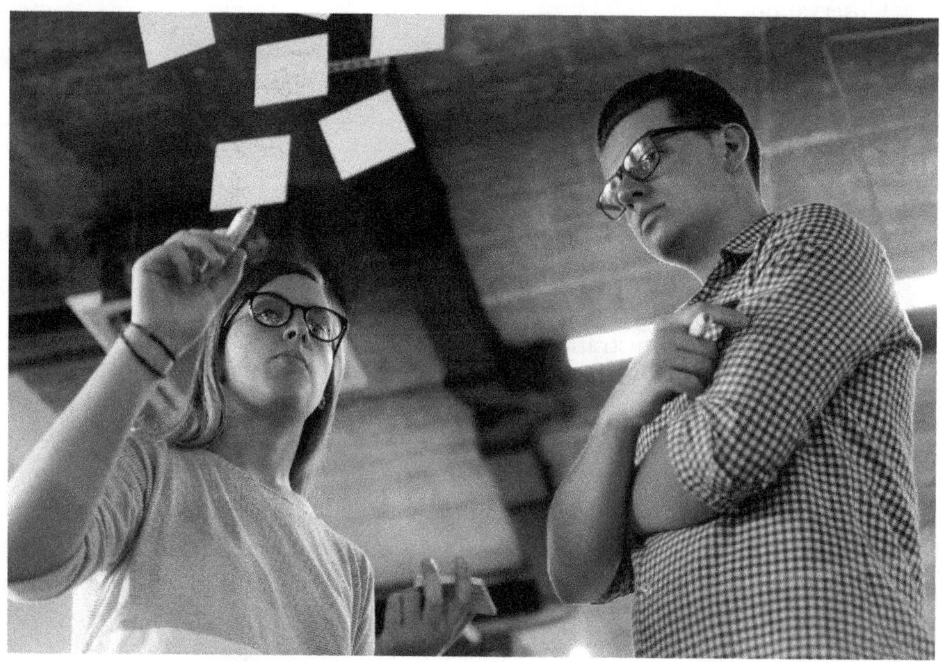

- Executive Summary
- Description of Product or Service
  - *Describe what you are selling. Focus on customer benefits.*
- Market Analysis
  - *You need to know your market, customer needs, where they are, and how to reach them.*
- Goals and Strategies
  - *Your plan should address two fundamental questions:*
    - *Where do we want to go as an organization?*
    - *How do we get there?*
- Management Team
  - *Education, relevant experience, and specialized skills.*
- Financial Plan
  - *Include balance sheet, income statement, sales projections, cash flow, break-even analysis, major assumptions, and business ratios.*

Step #6: Launch—Commercialization

Following development and testing of the product, it is time to launch and commercially produce the product. The key questions at this step of the process are:

- When: Timing of the launch?
- Where: In what geographic region will the product launch?
- Who: What market segment will initially be targeted?

It is at this point; if you have written a credible business plan that has addressed these three key questions, that you now ready to implement your plan.

PRODUCT DIFFERENTIATION: WHAT MAKES YOU REMARKABLE?

Product differentiation involves the modification of a product in an attempt to make it more attractive to a specific target market as well as distinguish it from competitors' products. The changes made to modify a product can range from subtle to substantive changes in packaging, processes, advertising, size, shape, color, ingredients, or location.

In order to successfully differentiate their products companies need to shift their strategy from competing solely based on price to competing on non-price factors such as product characteristics, distribution strategy, or promotional variables. A company's product differentiation strategy is determined by how the product is positioned in the market. ***Product positioning*** requires marketers to develop a specific marketing strategy that influences the perception of the product based on a wide variety of factors, including, but not limited to, brand name, packaging, quality, and price.

The purpose of engaging in product differentiation is to establish a position in the market such that potential customers will view your product as remarkable. "*Your market demands two things: Remarkable goods and services. Stories worth sharing. Things worth talking about. Something they would miss if you were gone. Because they have options, more than ever before.*"[4]

In order to position a product within the market a marketing manager will develop a unique ***total product offer*** that consists of everything that is used to influence the perceptions of the customer and/or their evaluation of the product prior to making a purchase decision. A total product is comprised of a value package normally consisting of the following:

Physical product	Product image
Product features	Packaging
Quality	Reputation
Brand name	Warranty
Customer service	Accessibility for purchase
Atmospherics speed of delivery	Price

PRODUCT POSITIONING: CONSUMER VERSUS INDUSTRIAL GOODS

When companies attempt to position their products within the market their primary goal is to influence the consumer's perception of a product's value relative to that of the competition. ***Product positioning*** is a deliberate attempt to create a unique and consistent customer perception about a firm's product(s) and image. A product or service may be positioned on the basis of an attitude, benefit, use or application, price, and/or level of quality. It targets a product for a specific market segment(s) and can be positioned in many different ways. To position a product marketers will utilize the three other elements of the marketing mix; price, place, and promotion to shape the consumers perception of the product and as a result determine its classification.

Consumer Goods and Services

The "end-user" consumer purchases consumer goods from retail stores that are intended for their own personal, family, or household use. Sometimes the same product can be classified as a business or consumer product as a result of its intended use. Examples would include cameras, power tools, light bulbs, and batteries. Consumer products are grouped into four subcategories on the basis of how they are positioned in the market and the consumer's buying habits.

Convenience Goods & Services

A convenience product is a relatively inexpensive product that is purchased frequently, immediately, and with little effort. Convenience goods are often divided into two subcategories: staple and impulse items. ***Staple*** convenience goods are basic items that consumers plan to buy before they enter a store, and include milk, bread, and toilet paper. ***Impulse*** items are other convenience goods that are purchased without prior planning, such as candy bars, soft drinks, and magazines. Location, brand name, and distribution are critical factors affecting the successful marketing of these goods and services.

Shopping Goods & Services

A shopping product is generally more expensive than a convenience product and is not as widely distributed. These goods usually have a higher value than convenience goods, are bought infrequently, and have a longer life span. Consumers for these products invest a significant amount of time comparing several similar brands based on such factors of price, quality, brand name, style and color. All of these factors are key issues in the consumer decision process and in the end determine whether a consumer will buy the product. Televisions, computers, clothing, automobiles, and furniture are all examples of shopping goods.

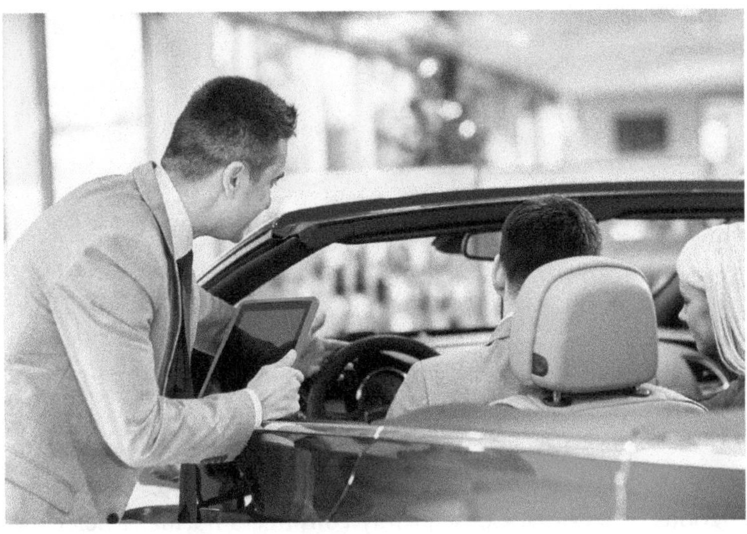

Specialty Goods & Services

Marketers of specialty products attempt to establish a perception of exclusivity, quality, and status. As a result consumers develop a strong preference for these products and conclude that there is no reasonable substitute for the product. Consumers of specialty goods tend to be highly selective and willing to put forth a special effort to buy the product. The distribution and availability of specialty goods is limited to only a few outlets within a geographic region. In addition, brand name, price, quality, promotion, and packaging are key features utilized to create the perception of style and class. Examples of specialty goods might include automobiles (Bentley), jewelry (Cartier), perfume (Paco Rabanne), and watches (Vacheron Constantin).

Unsought Goods & Services

Most consumers are unaware, have limited knowledge, or little interest in purchasing these types of goods or services. Consequently consumers normally defer the purchase of unsought goods unless there exists some crisis or adversity that requires their purchase. Examples of unsought goods might include products or services like life insurance, in-home health care, or coffins.

The distinction between convenience, shopping, specialty, and unsought goods is not always easy to define. The classification of each consumer product is based on consumers' buying habits as well as the positioning of the product in the market. Consequently an item like shampoo might be classified as a convenience good (Prell) and at the same time classified as a shopping good (Suave). The classification, or more specifically the positioning, of a company's products serves as the basis for determining the marketing strategies needed to successfully communicate the value proposition of your product with your target market and ultimately capture market share within the marketplace.

Industrial Goods & Services

Industrial goods and services are products that companies purchase for use in the operation of the company, for production of other products, which are then sold in a business-to-business market. As opposed to consumer goods, which are directly sold to the end user, industrial goods are categorized as per their uses. Some are used directly in the production of the products for resale, and some are used indirectly.

Industrial goods are also referred to as capital items in the balance sheets of the company because of their durability and the fact that their cost is equalized over a period of many years. However, some industrial goods are readily used up and are accounted for as an expense in a company's income statement.

Industrial goods are divided into the following seven subcategories.

- *Installations*
  From an accounting perspective these products are considered capital items because they require large sums of money to acquire and possess a longer life span. Examples of installations would include such products as: conveyor systems, robotics equipment, specialized tools, or fixed structures like a building.
- *Accessory Equipment*
  These are capital items that are less expensive, less durable than installations, and are indirectly involved in the production process. Examples would include: hand tools, computers, calculators, compressors, and forklifts.
- *Component Parts*
  Expense items that includes parts and materials used in the production of other products. These products are typically sold to marketing intermediaries. Examples might include: diodes, resistors, switches, knobs, transistors, batteries, windshields, and gaskets.
- *Raw Materials*
  Expense items, comprised of natural resources and materials used to create other products and are typically sold to intermediaries. Raw materials must undergo some type of adaptation or transformation prior to their use in the manufacturing of different kinds of goods and services.
- *Supplies*
  These are typically considered expense items, not part of a final product, and are used primarily to support a company's daily operations. Supplies include computer paper, ink cartridges, light bulbs, cleaning supplies, staples and post-it-notes.
- *Service*
  Includes any maintenance or repair.

Production Materials

Those materials used directly in the production of a product. Molds, heating and cooling chambers, spot welders, mechanical lathes, and even machines used to automate the packing process are examples of production materials.

PRODUCT LIFE CYCLE

This is a theoretical four-stage model depicting the transitory process of a product or product class over a period of time. A product's life cycle can be divided into distinct stages that are characterized by changes in revenue and sales over a period of time. The life cycle concept can apply to a specific brand (Apple) or to a specific category of products (cell phones) and is used by business owners and managers as a diagnostic tool to determine the nature of their marketing strategy as it relates to the dynamics of the market. The duration of any product brand or category may be as short as a few months for a fad item or take place over an extended period of time such as gasoline-powered automobiles.

Product Life Cycle: Building Brand Awareness and Loyalty

At each stage of the product life cycle marketers will attempt to build and then measure brand loyalty from three different perspectives:

1. Brand recognition
2. Brand preference
3. Brand insistence

These three perspectives are the result of consumer preferences that have been influenced by the marketing strategies of the firm, for a particular brand at a particular point in time in the product life cycle.

The typical product life cycle (PLC) has four stages
- Introduction
- Growth
- Maturity
- Decline

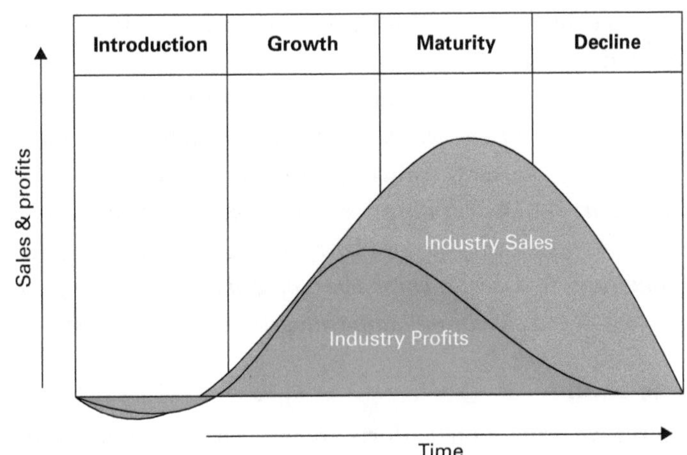

Introductory Stage

- Full-scale launch of a new product requiring heavy promotion designed to create primary demand.
- Marketing costs at this stage are normally very high.
- Primary Promotional Objectives → Product Awareness & Brand Recognition
  Informational advertising is utilized to explain the availability, use, and benefits of the product.
- Sales are in short supply and increase slowly.
- Little to No Profit
- Limited Competition
- Marketing Strategy

  Product— *One or few products, relatively undifferentiated*

  Price— *Normally high in an effort to recover development costs. In some case a penetration pricing strategy is utilized in an attempt to capture market share.*

  Placement— *Often times the strategy is selective and scattered as the company attempts to implement the optimal distribution plan.*

Promotion— *The overall goal is to build product/brand awareness and provide incentives (samples, coupons) to attract early adopters as well as resellers of the product.*

Growth Stage

- Continue heavy promotional efforts.
- Primary Objective → Product Acceptance and Brand Preference Persuasive advertising designed to create demand.
- Rapidly increasing sales.
- Profits rise very rapidly.
- Increasing competition with many new competitors as well as large companies who acquire smaller firms.
- Begin seeking new users and attracting early adopters of the product(s).
- Marketing Strategy

  Product— *A new emphasis is placed on product features, packaging, and quality.*

  Price— *Price remains unchanged if customer demand remains high; or, if necessary, reduced to attract additional customers.*

  Placement— *Distribution becomes more intensive in an attempt to provide greater utility to a wider range of consumers/resellers.*

  Promotion— *Greater emphasis is placed on promotion, with an emphasis on aggressive brand name advertising, in an attempt to build brand preference.*

Maturity Stage

- Aggressive promotional efforts are utilized to maintain market share.
- Primary Objective → Product/Brand Insistence
- Sales are increasing but at a much slower rate—flattening out
- Profits continue to fall with prices in decline
- Decreasing competition
- Marketing Strategy

  Product— *Stylistic, rather than functional, modifications are made to the product as well as new features added as a means of differentiating the product from the "look-a-like" products that are now available in the market.*

  Price— *Price reductions are implemented in response to increased competition.*

  Placement— *New channels are created and additional incentives are offered to resellers.*

  Promotion— *Multiple forms of promotion are used to differentiate the product and build (reinforce) brand loyalty.*

Decline Stage

- Little to no money spent on promotion.
- Sales continue to decline
- Profits flat/negative
- Continued decrease in competition
- Selling price continues to decline, with fewer buyers of the product.

Product— *Products are reduced and/or de-marketed while others are modified in an attempt to extend the life cycle of the product.*
Price— *Prices are reduced in an effort to liquidate discontinued inventory.*
Placement— *Channels that are no longer profitable are eliminated.*
Promotion— *Expenditures are kept to a minimum. Impersonal forms of promotion are normally utilized with the goal of maintaining brand image.*

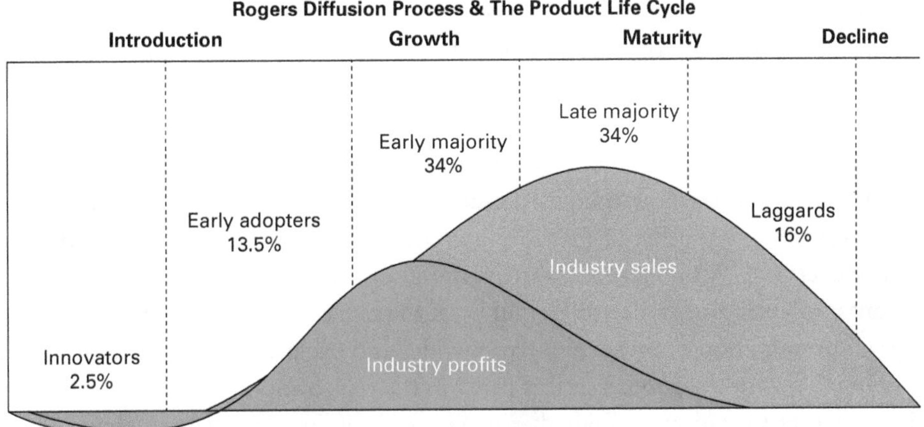

"Diffusion research considers time as a variable to a much greater degree than do other fields of communication study. Time is involved in diffusion in (a) the innovation-decision process, the mental process through which an individual passes from first knowledge of a new idea, to adoption and confirmation of the innovation; (b) innovativeness, the degree to which an individual is relatively earlier in adopting new ideas than other members of a system; and (c) an innovation's rate of adoption, the relative speed with which an innovation is adopted by members of a system."[5]

Diffusion theory attempts to explain the conditions that increase or decrease the likelihood that an innovation, a new idea, product or practice, will be adopted by members of a given culture. In the above reference image of multi-step diffusion, the opinion leader, called innovators and early adopters, exerts significant influence on the behavior of individual consumer and their purchase decision. Diffusion research centers on the conditions that increase or decrease the likelihood that members of a given culture will adopt a new idea, product, or practice. Diffusion is the "process by which an innovation is communicated through certain channels over a period of time among the members of a social system." An innovation is "an idea, practice, or object that is perceived to be new by an individual or other unit of adoption."[6]

BRANDING

Companies actively engage in product branding for numerous reasons but in all likelihood the most basic reason is to distinguish their product from all other products. The overall 'branding' of a company or product is generally considered successful when the general public recognizes the name, logo, symbol, or design features that identify the company and its products. The most important benefit of branding is that consumers are more likely to remember your business. A strong brand, brand name and trademark help to keep the product in the mind of your potential customers.

In order to assure that your brand is legally protected it is important to register your brand, brand name, trademark, or any other form of intellectual property through the United States Patent and Trademark Office.

"A trademark is a brand name. A trademark or service mark includes any word, name, symbol, device, or any combination, used or intended to be used to identify and distinguish the goods/services of one seller or provider from those of others, and to indicate the source of the goods/services. Although federal registration of a mark is not mandatory, it has several advantages, including notice to the public of the registrant's claim of ownership of the mark, legal presumption of ownership nationwide, and exclusive right to use the mark on or in connection with the goods/services listed in the registration.

It is important to understand whether you should file for a trademark/service mark, a patent, and/or a copyright. While all are types of intellectual property, each protects something very specific."[7]

Brand

A brand is represented in the name, symbol, or design or some combination that identifies the product(s) of the seller and distinguishes them from the competition. Examples would include: United States Marine Corp and General Electric.

Brand Name

This is a word, letter, or group of words or letters included in a name to identify and distinguish it from the competition. The brand name is the part of the brand that can be vocalized. This can include a name, symbol, design, or combination thereof to identify the products of one firm to that of the competition. Examples would include: Google, YouTube, Facebook, Hurley, and Starbucks.

Trademark

A trademark is a brand that has been given legal protection. Trademark protection includes the name, design, logo, slogan, packaging elements, and product features such as color and shape. Examples would include: NBC Peacock and Nike Swoosh.

STAGES OF BRAND LOYALTY

Brand Awareness

Refers to how quickly or easily a brand name comes to mind when a product category is mentioned. Brand awareness is an important way of promoting products where few factors differentiate one product from its competitor's products. In the soft drink industry very little separates a generic soda from a brand-name soda in terms of taste. However, consumers are very aware of the brands Pepsi and Coca Cola and this brand awareness translates into higher sales, market share, and profit.

Brand Equity

Brand equity refers to the intangible value that a company establishes as a result of its successful marketing efforts to establish a strong brand. It is the combination of factors that consumers associate with a particular brand name. Companies can build brand equity for their products by creating some distinctive, value-added, qualities that result in a personal commitment to and demand for a particular brand. Making products that are memorable, recognizable and superior in quality and reliability all contribute to positive brand equity.

Brand Loyalty

Brand loyalty refers to the degree to which consumers are satisfied and committed to further purchases of a specific brand-name product. Consumers demonstrate their brand loyalty by consistently purchasing the same brand product each time they seek to make a purchase of a particular product or service category.

PRICE DETERMINATION

Pricing is one of the most significant marketing mix components because price is the only marketing mix variable that actually generates revenues. Creating a pricing strategy is not a simple process of attempting to recover the costs associated with selling a product. Instead, it is a complex process with numerous implications for the manufacturer, marketing intermediaries, and the end-user consumer. Creating an effective pricing strategy is of great importance because it affects sales revenue and the behavior of the target market. The entire process of establishing a pricing strategy must be viewed from two distinct perspectives; first, the point of view of the company and its strategies, and second, from the viewpoint of the consumer. However, it is important to recognize that there are other, external influences on price beyond the firm's need to recover the costs of selling a product.

Economic theory assumes that the price of a product will be based on achieving profit maximization. Since it is very difficult to anticipate the number of products that will be purchased at a certain price, a *cost-plus* approach is typically utilized to determine price. However, there are three other critical factors that should be taken into account prior to establishing a price for a specific product.

1. *Pricing Objectives*
2. *Pricing Strategies*
3. *Break-Even Point*

Pricing Objectives

When establishing a price for a product it is essential to first determine the pricing objectives the company will pursue. Like any aspect of business when establishing pricing objectives it is important to insure that they are specific, attainable, timely and measurable. The following is a list of unique pricing objectives illustrating the importance of determining what it is you are attempting to accomplish prior to setting a price for any product.

- *Target return on investment (profit).*
- *Market Share (increase)*
- *Creating and/or maintaining an image.*
- *Increasing sales.*
- *Furthering social objectives.*
- *Volume*
- *Status Quo (meeting the competition*

Pricing Strategies

Without a sensible pricing strategy a company will likely fail to realize its revenue goals and ultimately maximize its profits. A company's prices need to accurately reflect the value of the company's product, as compared to the competition, and reflect what the market, specifically your target market, is willing (able) to pay for your product. With this in mind it is important to consider these key variables when developing a pricing strategy.

- Fixed & Variable Costs
- Buyers Price Sensitivity
- Actions of the Competition
- Stage in the Product Life Cycle
- Demands of Large Clients
- Quality of the Product

There are two broad strategies that a company can utilize when establishing their pricing strategy. A ***Skimming Strategy*** sometimes referred to as a *Market-Skimming* strategy is based on initially setting the prices high so as to "skim" revenue from the "early adopters" in the market. Companies will employ this type of strategy when their product has a perceived as having some unique attributes. This strategy works best when:

- *Quality and image support the higher price.*
- *Enough buyers want the product at that price.*
- *Cost of producing a small volume cannot be high.*
- *Competitors should not be able to enter the market easily.*

The second strategy is a ***Penetration Strategy***, or *Market Penetration strategy*, wherein the price is set at a low initial price in order to penetrate the market quickly, capture a large share of the market, and deter new competitors from entering into the market. A penetration strategy produces a lower profit margin for every unit sold and as a result requires a higher volume of sales in order reach break even. This strategy works best when:

- *The market is highly price sensitive*
- *Production and distribution costs fall as sales volume increases.*
- *Low price minimizes the number of competitors.*

Break-Even Analysis

"Break-even analysis determines the level of sales that generates neither profits nor losses and hence causes the for to 'break even'. Break-even analysis also permits management to see the effects on the level of profits of (1) fluctuation in sales, (2) fluctuations in costs, and (3) changes in fixed costs relative to variable costs. Break-even analysis is based on the following three mathematical relationships: the relationship between (1) output and total revenues (sales), (2) output and variable costs of production, and (3) output and fixed costs of production."[8]

Managers use this type of analysis to determine the relationship between sales and costs. A break-even analysis allows managers to determine what sales volume must be achieved before the company "breaks even," where total costs are equal to total revenue. Understanding the point at which a company can begin earning a profit is an important insight that enhances the planning process in any organization. The following represents the formula for calculating break-even in quantities/units:

$$\text{Break Even Point (In Units)} = \frac{\text{Total Fixed Costs}}{\text{Selling Price} - \text{Variable Cost/Unit}\ (\text{Contribution Margin})}$$

$$\text{Break Even Point (In Units)} = \frac{162{,}750}{21.00 - 14.36} = \frac{162{,}750}{6.64} \approx 24{,}511 \text{ units}$$

Sample Problem:

The restaurant that you own has the following fixed and variable costs.
Fixed costs are estimated at $162,750 per year
Variable cost per meal is estimated at $14.36
These meals would be sold for an average of $21.00 each.

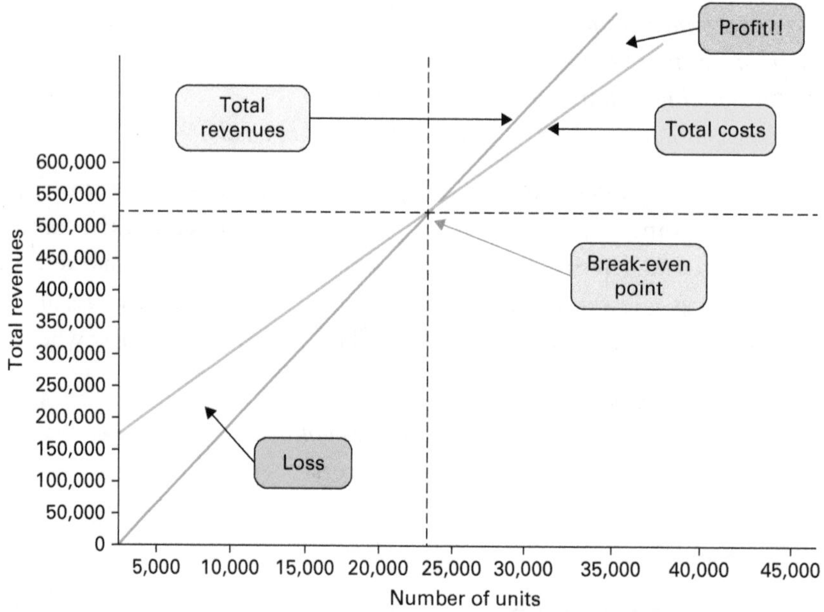

IMAGINATION: THE KEY TO NEW PRODUCT DEVELOPMENT

"I think we're way too focused on creativity. It's misguided. We should be focused on imagination ... The real key is being able to imagine a new world. Once I imagine something new, then answering how to get from here to there involves steps of creativity. So I can be creative in solving today's problems, but if I can't imagine something new, then I'm stuck in the current situation ..."[9]

Marketing, and more specifically product development, is an essential function in any business. Successful product development results in getting the right product at the right price, promoted in the right medium, and making it available in the right place. In order for managers and entrepreneurs to successfully develop new products, based on consumers' needs and wants, requires a new way of thinking, a new paradigm. No longer can you proclaim what is impossible. Instead it is incumbent upon every person within every organization to imagine what is possible. To be limited by what you perceive as impossible is as John Seely says "to be stuck in the current situation."

In a future filled with new technologies the product development process will require individuals who possess a disposition and attitude that transforms constraints into opportunities, engage in constant inquiry and embrace change. Lastly, and maybe most importantly, the future requires individuals who use the gift of imagination to see possibilities where others only see walls of impossibility. It is now your time!!

ENDNOTES

1. Crawford, C. Merle (1987) "New Product Failure Rates: A Reprise" *Research Management* 30 4, p. 20–24
2. Lindgren, Hugo. "Be Wrong As Fast as You Can." New York Times 4 Jan 2013. 10 Aug 2013 <http://www.nytimes.com/2013/01/06/magazine/be-wrong-as-fast-as-you-can.html?pagewanted=all&_r=0>.
3. Sanders, G. Lawrence. *Developing New Products and Services, v1.0.* FlatWorld Knowledge. New York: 2012
4. Martinuzzi, Bruna. "*Seth Godin on Effective (and Ineffective) Marketing Tactics for Small Businesses*", American Express: Open Forum. 12 Aug 2016. <https://www.americanexpress.com/us/small-business/openforum/articles/seth-godin-interview-marketing/>
5. Rogers, Everett M. Diffusions of Innovations. New York: Simon & Schuster, 2003.
6. ibid
7. United States. United States Patent and Trademark Office. Trademark Basics. 2013 < http://www.uspto.gov/trademarks/basics/index.jsp>.
8. Mayo, Herbert B., *Basic Finance: An Introduction to Financial Institutions, Investments and Management.* Ohio: South-Western: Cengage Learning 2012.
9. Wladawsky-Berger, Irving, "Imagination, Creativity and Related Subjects". USC Annenberg Innovation Lab. 28 Jan 2014. <http://archive.annenberglab.com/blogs/iberger/2014/01/imagination-creativity-and-related-subjects"

SOURCES

10. Fig. 9.15: Source: https://commons.wikimedia.org/wiki/File:YouTube_Logo_2017.svg.
11. Fig. 9.16: Source: https://commons.wikimedia.org/wiki/File:Logo_NIKE.svg.

break even

Chapter 10

Distribution

Getting the Right Products to the Right Place at the Right Time

PROLOGUE

"Place," or distribution, is normally thought to be the least essential component of the '4Ps' of marketing. Marketing consultants and academics tend to focus their attention and research on the more significant aspects of marketing like promotion and product development rather than on the mundane aspects of logistics and distribution. Big mistake! Distribution (place) is a critical area of marketing management and an essential component of a firm's marketing mix.

Most companies spend an enormous amount of time and money to develop and market a great product. Far too often what gets short changed in this process is how your distribution strategy will ultimately facilitate the exchange process. Engaging the consumer in the exchange process requires the effective distribution, or placement, of products in the channel of distribution. Marketing managers, in order to get the product to the consumer or client must address the following key questions:

1. How do I ensure time and place utility if my target market is not near a retailer that is selling the product?
2. What strategy is important to compete with a product that is available through a much more vibrant distribution system?
3. Who are the key players in the distribution channel and how do we capitalize on their functional strengths to meet the needs of our customers?

Due to the rapid changes in technology and delivery systems managing distribution channels has become a cornerstone of a company's marketing strategy and even its competitive advantage. Think Amazon! "*With the amount of traffic Amazon attracts, third-party merchants and manufacturers want to get their products on Amazon. Amazon has cultivated a huge marketplace with third-party merchants and presents it all seamlessly to its visitors. Many customers don't even know that about half the items sold on Amazon.com come from third-party merchants and are simply fulfilled by Amazon."*[1] Although industries and individual firms differ in their distribution strategies it is safe to say that in today's business environment organizations must endeavour to keep inventory levels at a minimum, while meeting consumer demand whenever possible in order to reduce costs.

Because producers/manufacturers typically do not sell their products directly to the end-user consumer they utilize vertical networks to get their products to their intended client (B2B) or consumer (B2C). The specific structure of these vertical channels of distribution is, to a large extent, dependent upon three key variables:

- The nature of the product.
- The firm's intended target market.
- The level of market coverage required.

Nonetheless in a typical channel of distribution there are various intermediaries who perform a variety of critical functions that include: buying, selling, transporting, storing, grading, financing, risk taking, and providing market information. It is as a result of various marketing intermediaries performing these essential functions that manufacturers, wholesalers, and retailers create time and place utility for their products. These intermediaries form what is commonly referred to as a channel of distribution and create and facilitate the creation of time, place, service, information and possession utility. In the absence of an effective distribution system it would be nearly impossible to meet the needs of the consumer and ultimately transfer ownership through the exchange process.

It should be obvious that distribution is crucial to the success of any business, regardless of its size, and is an integral part of a company's marketing mix. The main objective of any distribution strategy is based on how to successfully carry out the following three critical tasks: getting the right products, to the right place, at the right time.

DISTRIBUTION: TWO MAJOR COMPONENTS

Channels of Distribution: Consumer Products

A channel of distribution represents a series of relationships between marketing intermediaries who join together to transport and store goods in their path from producer to consumer. The channel members, or marketing intermediaries, add value to products at each stage in the distribution channel by providing utility to other channel members. Form, time, place, ownership, information and/or service utility is based on the ability of each channel member to efficiently perform the essential functions within the distribution channel. The goal of any distribution channel is to create efficiencies in delivering the product to the consumer.

Manufacturer
Wholesaler
Retailer
Consumer

"Channel structures can assume a variety of forms. In the extreme case of Boeing aircraft or commercial satellites, the product is made by the manufacturer and sent directly to the customer's preferred delivery site. The manufacturer, may, however, involve a broker or agent who handles negotiations but does not take physical possession of the property. When deals take on a smaller magnitude, however, it may be appropriate to involve the retailer—but no other intermediary. For example, automobiles, small planes, and yachts are frequently sold by the manufacturer to a dealer who then sends directly to the customer. It does not make sense to deliver these bulky products to a wholesaler only to move them again. On the other hand, it would not make sense for a California customer to fly to Detroit, buy a car there, and then drive it home."[2]

Physical Distribution

This refers to the actual movement of goods and services from the producer to the user. The various components of physical distribution include transportation, warehousing, materials handling, inventory control, and order processing. Typically physical distribution involves various modes of transportation to create time and place utility.

- Railroad
- Truck
- Ships
- Pipeline
- Airplane

"Distribution's stock is rising within the supply chain. C-level executives are starting to view distribution as a frontline business strategy—and rightly so.

Managing a modern-day supply chain is complex. To succeed, supply chain executives target distribution as a key differentiator to reduce costs, improve service, and build brands. If positioned correctly and given proper attention, distribution will accelerate business performance."[3]

TWO MAJOR CATEGORIES OF MARKETING INTERMEDIARIES WHOLESALERS

Wholesale firms are essential to the economy. They buy large lots of goods, usually from manufacturers, and sell them in smaller quantities to businesses, governments, other wholesalers, or institutional customers. They simplify product, payment, and information flows by acting as an intermediary between the manufacturer and the final customer. They also provide storage services for manufacturers and retailers who are unable to store or warehouse products until they are required to meet consumer demand.

Wholesale firms provide businesses a nearby source of goods made by many different manufacturers; they provide manufacturers with a manageable number of customers, while allowing their products to reach a large number of users; and they allow manufacturers, businesses, institutions, and governments to devote minimal time and resources to transactions by taking on some sales and marketing functions—such as customer service, sales contact, order processing, and technical support—that manufacturers otherwise would have to perform.

Retailers

In a distribution channel the retailer performs many critical activities that benefit both channel intermediaries and the end-user consumer. Retailers are those companies that sell goods or services to the end-user consumer for their own personal use and perform numerous critical distribution activities that include:

- Collecting information about customers in the store.
- Sales Promotion: Co-Op Advertising
- Advising manufacturers on necessary product design changes.
- Offer smaller volume of goods for consumers to buy.
- Offer a wide variety of products in a single store location for consumers.
- Absorb risk by taking title (ownership) of the products and assuming the costs associated with maintaining adequate inventory levels.
- Storing and warehousing inventory.
- Financing
- Record and provide feedback to wholesalers and manufacturers

Five Major Methods That Retailers Compete

***Price**—Price competition is becoming more intense as a result of the internet where the virtual endless array of products at reduced/discounted prices is readily available.*

***Service**—This can be accomplished through customer relations/service, delivery, installations, or any other "value-added" activity.*

***Location**—The location of a company is critical in providing time and place utility for the consumer.*

Selection*—The product mix is directly related to the needs and wants of the target audience. Smaller firms have found it necessary to offer a wider selection of products with fewer product categories.*

Entertainment*—The "atmospherics", or physical environment, are controllable characteristics of a retail space designed to entice a customer to enter the store and make a purchase. Atmospherics can include the store's layout, noise level, temperature, lighting and decorations.*

RETAIL DISTRIBUTION STRATEGY

When creating a retail distribution strategy it is important to keep in mind the degree of market coverage you want to achieve. A sound distribution strategy takes into account the positioning of the product; convenience, shopping, specialty, and unsought good, as well as the needs of the target market. In addition, a retail distribution strategy must take into account the commonly used retail axiom of "location, location, location." What this means is that a retail distribution strategy should be designed to support the overall goals of the organization, meet the needs of the target audience, work in concert with the other elements of the marketing mix, provide the utility required to efficiently bring the product to the consumer, and most importantly adapt to unprecedented change and disruption. *"If Moore's law continues to hold true, it tells us that the exponential changes now being observed in technology will likely continue to drive related changes in the retail marketplace. What challenges retailers face today only heralds the beginning of more disruption and a greater retail evolution ahead."*[4]

There are three distinct distribution strategies that retailers can use to make available their products to their target customer:

- Intensive Distribution
- Selective Distribution
- Exclusive Distribution

Intensive Distribution

Typically used for convenience products this type of distribution provides for saturation coverage of the market by putting products into as many retail outlets as possible.

This strategy works best for products that consumers use on a regular (daily) basis and often need to replace. The purpose of this type of strategy is to place the product in multiple locations so that consumers come across the product frequently, making it easy for them to remember and buy the product.

Selective Distribution

Often used for the distribution of shopping products this strategy is designed to limit the number of retail outlets in a particular geographic region. Selective distribution means that retail locations are carefully screened and only a few stores, in a particular geographic region, are permitted to carry certain product lines. This strategy enhances the ability of the retailer to charge full price as well as enhance their image.

Exclusive Distribution

This strategy creates a legally binding distribution agreement wherein one retail store or chain of stores is allowed a to market and sell a specific product or product line within a specific geographic region. This strategy allows for the creation of an "exclusive" image of the product, the retailer, and the manufacturer. An exclusive distribution strategy is based on the premise that a company (Cartier) is interested in marketing "quality, not quantity."

VERTICAL MARKETING CHANNEL SYSTEM

"A conventional distribution channel consists of one or more independent producers, wholesalers, and retailers. Each is a separate business seeking to maximize its own profits, perhaps even at the expense of the system as a whole. No channel member has much control over the other members, and no formal means exists for assigning roles and resolving channel conflict. In contrast, a vertical marketing system (VMS) consists of producers, wholesalers, and retailers acting as a unified system. One channel member owns the others, has contracts with them, or wields so much power that they must all cooperate. The VMS can be dominated by the producer, the wholesaler, or the retailer."[5]

A vertical marketing system is comprised of the same company or business who owns the production, wholesale and retail portions of a distribution channel. VMS is often defined as a planned channel system designed to reduce the costs associated with the production and delivery of a product to the market. There are three types of vertical marketing systems.

Level of Control Over Channel Members

Corporate VMS	• Common ownership over all members of the distribution channel and/or the supply chain.
Contractual VMS	• Channel members establish contractual agreements in order to have specific distribution functions (transporting, storing, financing, etc.). Performed by various intermediaries in the channel of distribution. The creation of a contract allows channel members to establish a formal structure for the distribution of products without having to make large capital investments in the infrastructure of their respective companies.
Administered VMS	• A dominant member of the distribution channel assumes a leadership role as a "channel captain." A channel captain is frequently the most powerful member of the channel of distribution, and often the one that decides the specifications for distributing goods. The channal captain is sometimes the manufacturer but in the case of a chain store it is most likely the retailer (Costco).

"Senior managers of most of the companies involved in moving goods or services from suppliers to end users would agree: Their distribution channels are outdated and unwieldy, serving neither customers nor channel partners as well as they should. In a few cases, distribution channels are streamlined and satisfying for all participants. In some cases, technology has improved things dramatically. But in most scenarios, distribution channels, taken as a whole, seem more like a repository of lost opportunities than an effective delivery system that appropriately serves and rewards all participants. Powerful channel members routinely impose their will, weaker participants suffer along because they see no way out, and customers … ? Despite much talk of customer-focused companies, customers are often ignored when it comes to distribution."[6]

UTILITY: THE ROLE OF THE INTERMEDIARIES

Intermediaries help create exchange through the creation of utility. An intermediary creates greater accessibility to the consumer and reduces the number of contacts between the consumer and the various intermediaries.

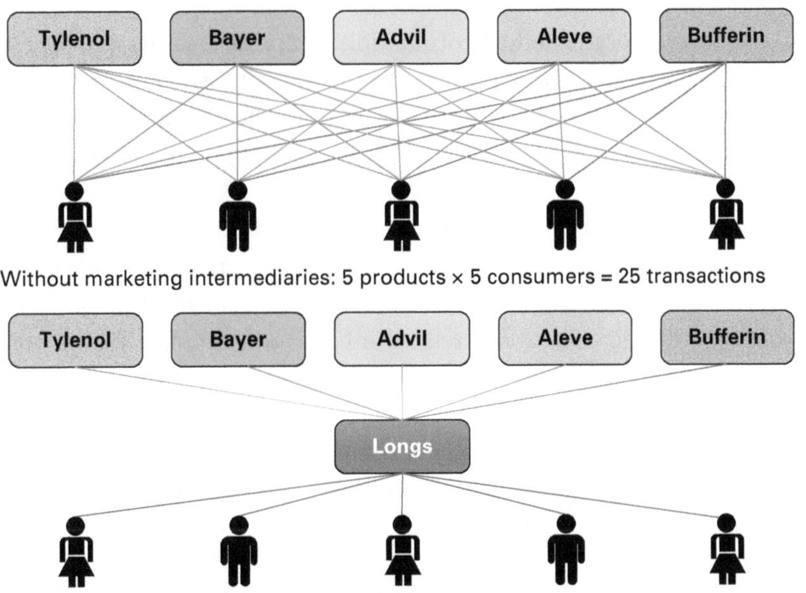

Utility is often referred to as the "want satisfying ability" of a good or service. In economic terms, utility is the value that is added to goods and services by marketing intermediaries as a result of the critical activities they perform to make products more useful and accessible to consumers.

	TYPES OF UTILITY
Form Utility	The transformation of raw materials into useful products.
Time Utility	Making the product available when the customer wants to buy them.
Place Utility	Making the product available in a convenient location, where the customer wants to buy the product.
Possession Utility	Occurs when there is transference of ownership (title) from the seller to the buyer.
Information Utility	Intermediaries create a two-way flow of information between marketing participants.
Service Utility	Those services provided during and after the sale and usage of the product.

SUPPLY CHAIN MANAGEMENT

The concept of Supply Chain Management, or SCM, is based on the fundamental principle that essentially every product that reaches the consumer, or business client, is the result of the collective and collaborative efforts of multiple organizations. In spite of the fact that supply chains have existed for a long time, most organizations continue to fail to understand and manage the entire chain of activities that, in the end, allow them to efficiently deliver products to the final customer. When the supply chain is ignored or mismanaged the resultant effect is an ineffective supply chain with rising costs at each stage of distribution.

Supply chain management (SCM) involves the oversight of materials, information, and finances as they move in a process from supplier to manufacturer to wholesaler to retailer and finally to the consumer. The process involves the movement of raw materials, parts, work in progress, finished goods, and related information through all the organizations involved in the supply chain and the coordination and integration of these flows both within and among companies. Supply chain management attempts to optimize the shipment of goods and services from supplier to customer by reducing manufacturing time, minimizing inventory requirements, and streamlining order fulfillment and processing.

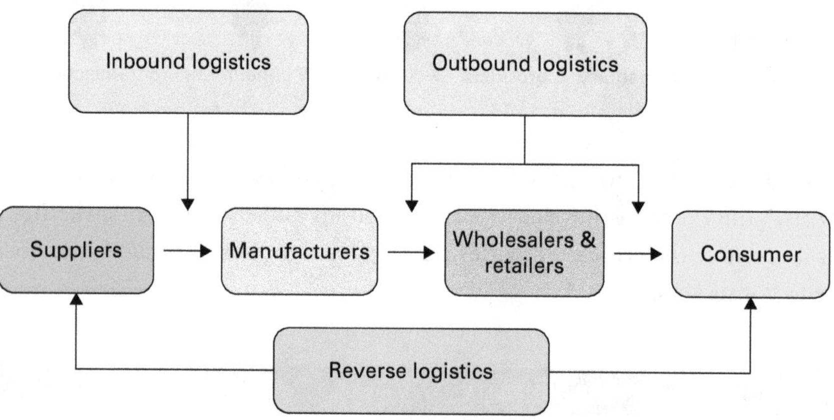

Enhancing Sustainability Through Your Reverse Supply Chain

"While many companies are coming up with promising solutions for the sustainability conundrum, from green fleet vehicles to installing lighting systems that conserve electricity, many of these ideas are cost-intensive, and as technology changes, will have to continue to adapt. Taking a deeper look at how your organization is addressing sustainability in every area of your operation, will provide your management team with insight on how to better implement changes that can adapt with technology cycles. As a retailer, utilizing a streamlined process that shifts returned and overstock inventory into online marketplaces, rather than disposing of them in traditional ways, will provide you with a self-sustaining, green process that will easily adapt through technology shifts. Over the next several years, consumers and businesses alike will only continue to rely more on online resources to purchase goods and assets. In taking the steps to incorporate smart reverse logistics now, your organization will gain an enhanced sustainability initiative that will continue to magnify positive environmental impact and value in the future."[7]

SUPPLY CHAIN MANAGEMENT FUNCTIONS

The following are the basic components that comprise supply chain management:

Inbound Logistics	This process brings raw materials, packaging, other goods and services, and information from suppliers to producers.
Factory Processes	Involves the changing of raw materials and parts and other inputs into outputs. (Transformation Process).
Materials Handling	The movement of goods within a warehouse, factory, or store.
Outbound Logistics	Manages the flow of finished products and information to business buyers and consumers. This has become one of the biggest problems for new online retailers.
Reverse Logistics	This process involves all of the activities required for the efficient reuse of products and materials. It is designed to move previously-shipped goods from the consumer back to the manufacturer due to repair, service, credit or recycling.

DISTRIBUTION: CREATING A PRESENCE IN THE MARKET

As a student your success is in part dependent on your ability to attend class each day, arrive to class on time, and submit (deliver) your work on the required due date. If you fail to meet these expectations in your college class you will likely experience, just like any business, a lack of success and bitter disappointment. I hope that this analogy provides you with a greater understanding and appreciation of the importance of distribution and its relevance to the creation of a winning marketing strategy that facilitates the timely delivery of products to the consumer in a manner that adds utility and value to their lives.

Even though distribution may not be the most glamorous element of the marketing mix, it should be apparent that the placement and/or distribution of a product is a critical component of a company's marketing mix. In a global economy where marketers from all around the world are attempting to establish and maintain some competitive edge in the market, distribution is often overlooked as a means of establishing a unique competitive advantage. In a survey conducted by Hitachi Consulting, spanning nine European countries, "The survey found that a little over half of the respondents (55%) do not regard their business's supply chain as a fundamental source of business value and competitive advantage and almost a third (29%) see it as purely an operational function ... Almost half (45%) of respondents did not believe that their organization's supply chain would deliver increased profitability and 46% did not believe that their organization's supply chain would deliver a reduced working capital requirement."[8] Cathy Johnson, vice president at Hitachi Consulting, comments on the findings: "A supply chain that doesn't support the overarching business strategy, and which doesn't deliver competitive edge—and which isn't going to deliver a material change in performance over the next five years—is clearly not a desirable asset."[9] Creating a presence in the market, managing the supply chain, providing world-class customer service, and integrating technology into the distribution process can be the difference between those companies that succeed and those that fail. The goal for every company in the new global economy should be to distribute products around the world as efficiently as possible and distribution is fundamental to achieving this goal.

ENDNOTES

1. Levy, Adam. "Nobody talks about Amazon's true competitive advantage". Business Insider, 29 Nov 2016 <http://www.businessinsider.com/amazons-competitive-advantage-over-walmart-and-target-2016-11>
2. Channels of Distribution. Lars Perner, 2008. Marshall School of Business, University of Southern California. <http://www.consumerpsychologist.com/distribution.html>.
3. Hollmeyer, Louie. "Distribution Takes Center Stage". InBoundLogistics Jan 2005 <http://www.inboundlogistics.com/cms/article/distribution-takes-center-stage/>.
4. Lobaugh, Kasey and Jacob Brunn-Jensen. "Deloitte Retail Volatility Index: How 100 years of conventional wisdom is being disrupted". Deloitte, 2016. <https://www2.deloitte.com/us/en/pages/consumer-business/articles/beyond-trends-retail-volatility-index.html>
5. Kotler, Philip T. and Gary Armstrong. *Principles of Marketing*, 16th. Pearson 2014.
6. Rangan, V. Kasturi. "The Promise of Channel Stewardship." HBS Working Knowledge (2006). 25 Apr. 2012 <http://hbswk.hbs.edu/item/5375.html>
7. Angrick, Bill. "Enhancing Sustainability Through Your Reverse Supply Chain" Reverse Logistics. Edition 50. <http://rlmagazine.com/edition50p12.php>
8. Hitachi Consulting ,"The Supply Chain Disconnect: 80% of Managers Don't See Supply Chain as Business Strategy Enabler" PR Newswire, 2013 Dec 11.
9. Ibid

SOURCES

1. Fig. 10.2: Copyright © 2011 Depositphotos/Digitalgenetics.
2. Fig. 10.4: Copyright © 2013 Depositphotos/Radub85.
3. Fig. 10.5: Copyright © Stu Pendousmat (CC BY-SA 3.0) at https://commons.wikimedia.org/wiki/File:CostcoMoncton.JPG.
4. Fig. 10.6: Copyright © 2018 Depositphotos/Pio3.

Chapter 11

Promotion

Find Your Story

PROLOGUE

Promotion is the process wherein businesses attempt to communicate with their target audience in an effort to precipitate the exchange process. At its most basic level promotion is designed to inform, persuade, or remind consumers of the need to buy a specific product. The key ingredient to successful promotion is rooted in the ability of a business to succinctly state what is unique, or useful, about their product and the benefits derived from its purchase. It is designed to tell a story.

Companies have always attempted to use promotion to build a brand identity, communicate changes in longstanding products, or introduce new products or services to their customers. In the past businesses would primarily use mass mediated advertisements to communicate with their consumers in an attempt to influence future purchase decisions and behavior. However, because of technology, social media and all of the various forms of communication, our lives and how we interact with one another has changed in profound ways we never would have imagined only a few short years ago. Digital technology is arguably the most significant change in how businesses market and promote their products to the consumer. With 24/7 customer engagement via social media the process of engaging the customer is now only a click away.

Despite the availability of digital technology the challenge of communicating and influencing a large and diverse consumer market continues to remain a significant challenge due to the fact that every person interprets commercial messages differently. In order to overcome this challenge businesses must develop messages that fit the media utilized, appeal to the unique attributes of the target audience, reinforce the perceptual value of the product, and explicitly define the promotional objectives of the company. Businesses and their marketing managers have at their disposal four major methods of promotion: Advertising, Personal Selling, Sales Promotion and Public Relations. Taken together these comprise the promotional mix.

STORIES: THE PUREST FORM OF COMMUNICATION

"Stories are the most primitive and purest form of communication. The most enduring and galvanizing ideas and values of our civilization are embedded in our stories ... Smart, future-oriented companies use this ancient impulse in new ways, by telling us stories that people can watch on YouTube and share on Facebook.

TOMS

One for One

When you have a memorable story about who you are and what your mission is, your success no longer depends on how experienced you are or how many degrees you have or who you know. A good story transcends boundaries, breaks barriers, and opens doors. It is a key not only to starting a business but also clarifying your own personal identity and choices.

It's important to know your audience. At its center, your story is a specific idea or product or expertise that you're offering. You can't be all things to all people and still maintain your credibility and integrity. Make sure your story is crafted to appeal to the people you really want to become your supporters and that it draws from your core strength."[1] —Blake Mycoskie

INTEGRATED MARKETING COMMUNICATION

Ideally the four elements of a company's promotional mix should be integrated regardless of the objectives of the promotion utilized. Integrated Marketing Communication (IMC) is based on the development of a coordinated promotional message that effectively communicates a company's ***Unique Selling Proposition*** (USP).

"Before you can begin to sell your product or service to anyone else, you have to sell yourself on it. This is especially important when your product or service is similar to those around you. Very few businesses are one-of-a-kind. Just look around you: How many clothing retailers, hardware stores, air conditioning installers and electricians are truly unique? The key to effective selling in this situation is what advertising and marketing professionals call a "unique selling proposition" (USP). Unless you can pinpoint what makes your business unique in a world of homogeneous competitors, you cannot target your sales efforts successfully."[2]

Unique selling proposition

Fed Ex...
"When It absolutely, positively has to be there overnight."

DeBeers...
"A Diamond is Forever."

Target...
"Expect More. Pay Less."

Nyquil...
"The nighttime, coughing, aching, sniffing, stuffy head, fever, so you can rest medicine."

In order to develop an integrated, coordinated message, or USP, a company must:

- Identify their Target Market 
- Define their Promotional Objectives
- Determine their Promotional Budget
- Develop a Unifying Message that will:
  - Build Brand Equity
  - Provide Product Information
  - Manage Demand & Sales
  - Differentiate Products
  - Influence Perceptions, Attitudes, & Buyer Behavior (USP)
- Develop and Implement an Integrated Marketing Communication Plan
  - Develop all promotional activities, budgets, schedules, media
- Evaluate Effectiveness
  - Did the firm accomplish its stated objectives?

Emerging Methods of Integrated Marketing Communication

Content Marketing

Content marketing is about storytelling and humans from every culture, in every country in the world, have told stories for as long as they could speak. For every business it has become necessary to provide potential customers with relevant and useful content, stories, in order to help them solve their unique needs. Customers want valuable information, more specifically content, rather than impersonal advertising when making purchase decisions. "*Content marketing is a strategic marketing approach focused on creating and distributing valuable, relevant, and consistent content to attract and retain a clearly-defined audience—and, ultimately, to drive profitable customer action.*"[3]

Content marketing means creating and sharing free content to attract and convert prospects into customers, and customers into repeat buyers. It is essential to understand your target market and subsequently what interests and concerns them, what information and answers they're seeking—and build content with them in mind. Content which clearly demonstrates you understand their needs, wants, and issues will resonate and win you loyalty points, while inspiring, educating, entertaining or providing useful and insightful content will keep people interested and coming back for more.

The content a company shares is closely related to what they intend to sell through content that is designed to build a personal relationship with people so that they know, like , and trust you enough to do business with you. Content marketing uses blogs, podcasts, video, and social media sites as a vehicle for enhancing exposure and sharing compelling word-of-mouth stories about your products or brand.

Social Media Marketing

The Internet has led to dramatic changes in the marketing environment requiring marketers to rethink almost every aspect of their marketing mix. The World Wide Web continues to evolve with 3.5 billion plus Internet users worldwide providing consumers with easy access to information and an unlimited selection of products. Consumers now have the power to control what and how much information is received as well as what information and content gets disseminated.

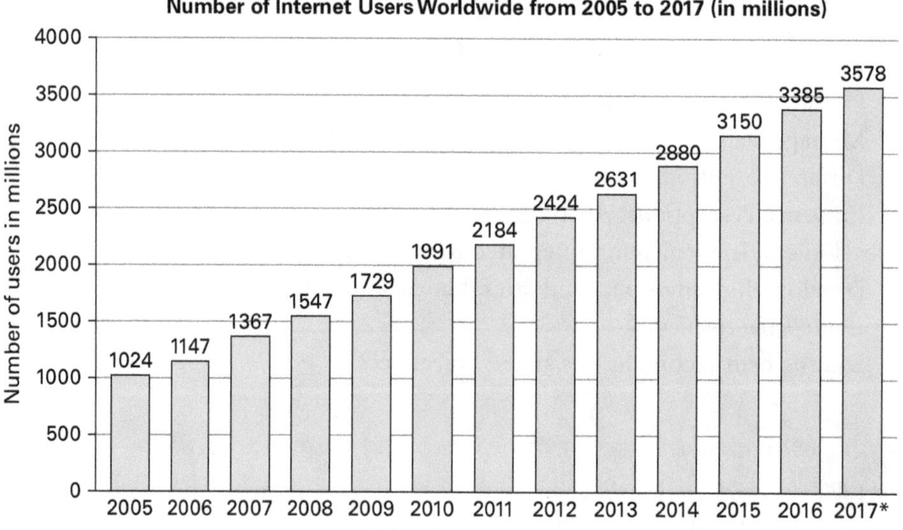

The Internet has also increased the ability of businesses to target customers more effectively through the Net and offers them an interactive medium allowing for a two-way communication flow. Consumers now control when and which messages and content they are exposed to and more importantly can now provide their own unique content. Unlike other media, social media is a communications medium, allowing companies to more effectively, and in real time, create awareness, disseminate information, shape consumers attitudes, and position and brand their products.

This form of interactive marketing communications *"allows consumers to learn from and teach others about a brand, as well as express their commitment to a brand and observe the brand loyalty of others.*"[4] Companies like Twitter, Tumblr, Facebook, Youtube, Reddit, Linkedin and others have changed the way that businesses market themselves and their products. Understanding how to use this new media is critical to the success of any business as it attempts to break through the noise and effectively engage and communicate with their customers.

Viral Marketing

Viral marketing has generated a lot of excitement recently and according to Jonah Berger there are six key drivers of effective viral marketing. They are "*Social Currency (e.g., sharing things that make people look good), Triggers (acknowledging that we talk about things that are top-of-mind), Emotion, Public (imitating what we see others do), Practical Value (news people can use) and Stories (information passed along under the guise of idle chitchat).*"[5] Viral Marketing has become an essential component of any integrated marketing communication strategy and it is intended to create consumer curiosity and desire in order to generate the demand for a company's products or services.

Viral marketing includes paying customers to say positive things on the Internet or setting up multiple selling schemes whereby consumers get commissions. Viral marketing is a technique that induces websites or users to share a marketing message to other sites or users, creating a domino effect wherein the message expands exponentially increasing visibility and influence. "*Getting your brand noticed via social media grows more difficult with each passing day. Users upload 100 hours of video to YouTube every 60 seconds and share more than 4.75 billion pieces of content on Facebook every 24 hours. Add to that 500 million new tweets per day, and the chances of breaking through to a wider audience can seem virtually nonexistent.*"[6] People who engage in word of mouth (WOM) promotion through viral marketing often receive SWAG that can include free tickets, shirts, and other merchandise.

Blogs

Short for web log, it is an online journal or diary that looks like a webpage but is easier to create and update by posting text, photos, videos, or links. Blog publishing companies like Blogger allow companies and individuals to post a journal entry, without any character limit, on any subject. Whether it's a blog where moms share their daily adventures in parenting, a food blog, travel blog, or a business providing updates to its products or services, blogs have new content added several times a week. The blog "owner" has the ability and freedom to express his/her opinions, share information, or engage in a discussion about one or more topics.

Microblogs

Twitter is the most well known social networking and microblogging service in the market today. It enables its users to send and read messages known as tweets, which consist of text-based posts of up to 140 characters displayed on the author's profile page and delivered to the author's subscribers who are known as followers.

SOCIAL MEDIA: A NEW DIGITAL STRATEGY

> "As a central feature of their digital strategy, companies made huge bets on what is often called branded content. The thinking went like this: Social media would allow your company to leapfrog traditional media and forge relationships directly with customers. If you told them great stories and connected with them in real time, your brand would become a hub for a community of consumers. Businesses have invested billions pursuing this vision. Yet few brands have generated meaningful consumer interest online. In fact, social media seems to have made brands less significant. What has gone wrong?
>
> To solve this puzzle, we need to remember that brands succeed when they break through in culture. And branding is a set of techniques designed to generate cultural relevance. Digital technologies have not only created potent new social networks but also dramatically altered how culture works. Digital crowds now serve as very effective and prolific innovators of culture—a phenomenon I call crowdculture. Crowdculture changes the rules of branding—which techniques work and which do not. If we understand crowdculture, then, we can figure out why branded-content strategies have fallen flat—and what alternative branding methods are empowered by social media."[7]

PROMOTIONAL MIX

A combination of personal selling and non-personal selling activities designed to communicate multiple promotional messages to a specific target audience.

Developing a Promotional Mix: Key Factors

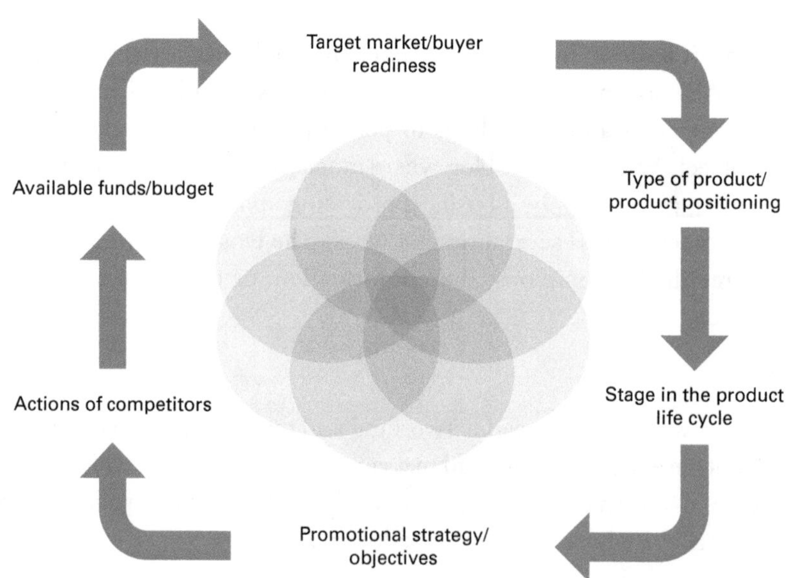

Target Market/Buyer Readiness

The ultimate goal of any form of promotion is to convince the firm's target customer to buy a particular product. The success of any promotional effort is based, in part, on an understanding of the readiness of your target customer to take action. Buyer readiness and behavior is based on the consumer's willingness, authority, and capacity to buy. Like the other P's of the marketing mix, the promotional mix is most effective when it is based on a comprehensive understanding of the target customer and their unique needs and behaviors. Consumer behavior and readiness can often be influenced through an understanding an intelligent application of the AIDA model.

Type of Product & Product Positioning

Promotional applications vary between consumer and industrial markets. Consumer goods (convenience, shopping, specialty, and unsought) normally utilize (in the following order) the following forms of promotion: advertising, sales promotion, personal selling and public relations. On the other hand, Industrial goods (installations, accessory equipment, component parts, etc.) will normally utilize (in the following order) personal selling, sales promotion, advertising and public relations. Understanding your intended target market, how you will position your product, and what methods of promotion will be most effective is essential to the determination of the optimal promotional mix.

Stage in the Product Life Cycle

In each stage of the product life cycle the methods of promotion used will vary. Prior to determining the nature of the promotional mix it is of critically important to determine at what stage of the life cycle your product or industry are in. Understanding the dynamics of each stage of the life cycle allows you to determine the most appropriate promotional mix in order for you to most effectively communicate with your target market and achieve your promotional objectives.

Promotional Strategy/Objectives

Developing an effective promotional strategy requires more than just a casual awareness of the methods of promotion. Promotion, like most business activities, is an ongoing process that requires a significant amount of information, knowledge, and planning. A promotional strategy is nothing more than a plan of action. The effectiveness of your strategy depends on more than how much money you have available or are willing to spend. An effective promotional strategy is the result of your plan and the consistency with which you carry it out. The following are two broad promotional strategies each used to reach a distinct industrial and consumer market:

> *Push Strategy—The producer uses advertising, personal selling, sales promotion, and all other promotional tools to convince wholesalers and retailers to sell their merchandise.*

Pull Strategy—Heavy advertising and sales promotion are directed toward end-users consumers so that they will seek out and request certain products from retailers.

Actions of Competitors

Your competition is vying for the same customers and their actions will vary based on the nature of the competitive environment (monopolistic vs. oligopolistic, etc.), the positioning of their products (consumer good vs. industrial good), the region of the country/world in which they operate, the nature of their competitive advantage (mass distribution, brand name, etc.), and the overall objectives of the company.

To develop a winning promotional strategy you must first begin by explaining the general nature of competition, how are their products positioned in the market, do they have a strong brand name presence in the market, how effective is their current promotional mix? The key when thinking about your competition is to understand what makes the customer choose one product or service over another.

Available Funds/Budget

There is no real practical rule of thumb for determining the amount of money a company should budget and/or spend on its promotional activities. The obvious key variable determining the extent of your promotional efforts is the available funds that can be budgeted to advertising, sales staff, sales promotion and public relations. Every company has financial limitations which directly affect the nature and scope of its promotional activities. Nonetheless, most experts suggest that "*New companies: For companies that have been in business for one to five years, we suggest using 12 to 20 percent of your gross revenue or projected revenue on marketing. (Companies less than a year old, tend to need to ramp up before spending marketing dollars.) Established companies: For those companies that have been in business more than five years and have some market share/brand equity, we suggest allocating between 6 and 12 percent of your gross revenue or projected revenue.*"[8]

AIDA MODEL

The first formal advertising model, AIDA, is based on a hierarchy of effects involving four stages of communication results: awareness, comprehension, conviction, and action. The model contended that it is possible to pick the appropriate stage in the communication process and use it to define promotional (advertising) objectives.[9]

Effective promotion is often based on understanding the purchase decision of the consumer based on the stages of the AIDA Model.[10] According to this model, the most important role of an advertisement is to attract consumers. The hierarchy of effects explains how advertising affects the consumer buying process and asserts that consumers move through a logical step by step process when exposed to advertisements and that a purchase will only be made when all steps in the hierarchy of effects have been completed. The AIDA model asserts that consumer Awareness leads to greater Interest, which in turn leads to Desire, and eventually leads to the consumer taking Action.

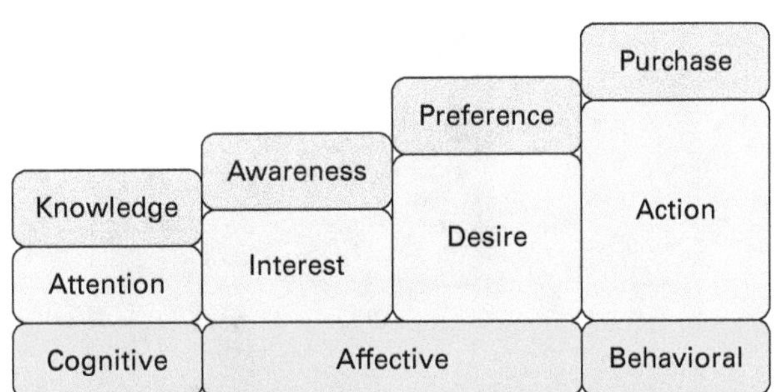

Consumers actually have three types of responses to promotional messages. The first is a *Cognitive* response based on how the consumer thinks about the product and the need to purchase the product. The second response is an *Affective* response and is an emotionally charged response that appeals to hoe the consumer feels about the product. The final response is *Behavioral (Conative)* wherein the consumer actually engages in some action that results in the purchase of a product. In making a purchase decision, consumers go through each of the AIDA steps to some degree, but the steps may not always follow the AIDA order. Using this model as the basis for formulating a promotional mix will improve the ability of a company to engage its target audience and ultimately design promotional activities that effectively influence the consumer's purchase decisions.

FOUR KEY ELEMENTS OF THE PROMOTIONAL MIX

Advertising

This is a paid, non-personal process wherein a business or nonprofit organization sponsors the production and dissemination of information through various mediums that are normally directed at a large and diverse number of potential buyers. These mediums include television, radio, newspaper, magazine, flyers, billboards, transit and digital (mobile phones). There are various types of advertisements utilized by organizations to achieve different goals as well as reach different market segments. Each type of advertising engages in promotional efforts that are designed to elicit a unique response from the market/consumer.

Institutional Advertising

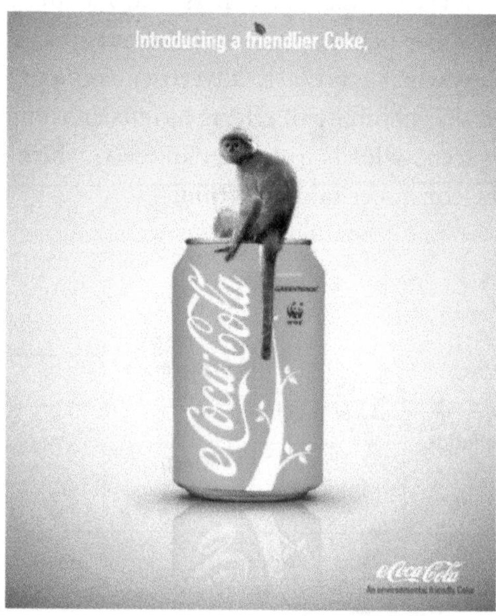

Advertising whose primary purpose is to promote the image of a corporation rather than the sale of a product or service, also called corporate advertising. This advertising is used to create public awareness of a corporation, improve its reputation, image, and relations with the various stakeholder groups in the marketplace. This form of advertising includes not only end-user consumers and distributors, but also suppliers, shareholders, employees, and the general public. Institutional advertising focuses on the enhancement of the name, prestige, and goodwill of a company.

In the example on the preceding page, Coca Cola, promotes environmental awareness, showing their concern for the environment rather than attempting to promote the sale of their products.

Advocacy Advertising

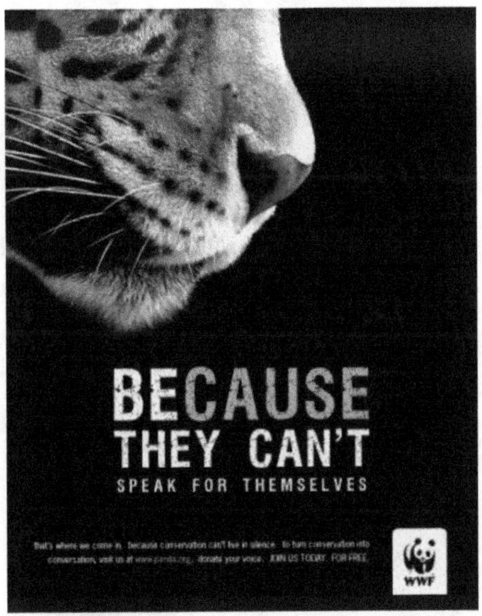

Sometimes referred to as "cause" advertising, these types of advertisements are designed to promote a specific point of view, a position on a contemporary issue, or raise awareness of an important social issue. The advertising can target current legislation, political issues, and other issues, which are deemed of interest to the public. Normally these advertisements promote a political view, social cause, or point of view regarding a controversial issue or other social issue of public importance in a manner that supports the interests of the sponsors.

In the example above, the World Wildlife Fund promotes the interest of the organization and does not promote a product or service.

Comparison Advertising

Comparison ads are typically used to promote shopping goods and make direct comparisons between the sponsor company's products and the leading competitor's products. Comparison advertising is often considered to be the most forceful and persuasive form of advertising because the advertiser is singling out a specific competitor. This type of advertising can be effective for a start-up or low-share brands because of its ability to associate itself with an established brand, causing consumers to believe the two brands/products are similar, stimulate comparison-shopping, and facilitate brand differentiation. This allows the advertiser to create "brand equity" between their product and the market leader.

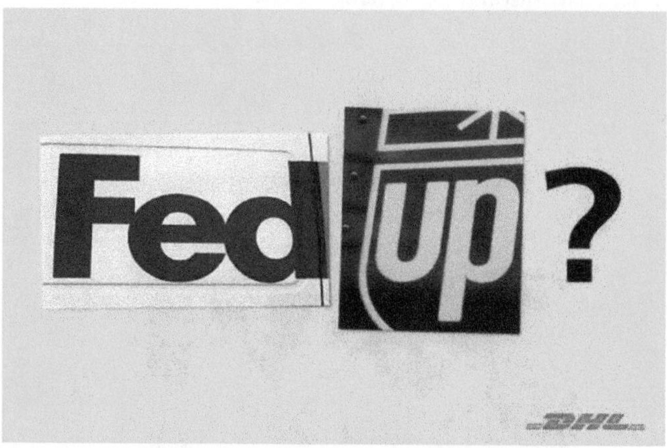

In the above example, DHS, makes vague references to FedEx and UPS, in an attempt to associate itself with the leading established brands, causing consumers to believe they are similar.

Product Advertising

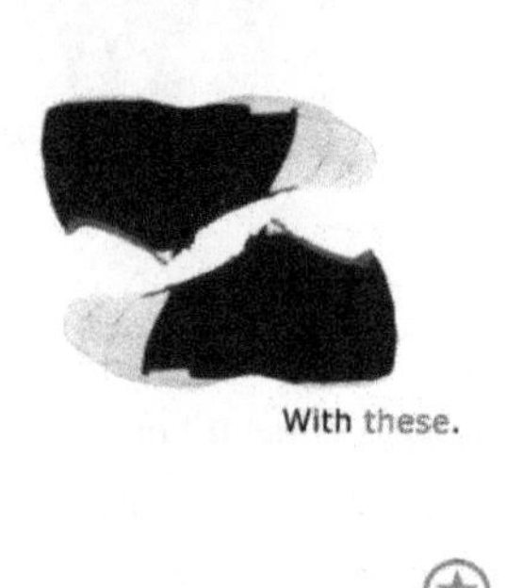

These types of ads can be directed at either consumer or industrial buyers. These ads promote a specific good or service and are designed to create interest in the product, maintain product awareness, explain how the product is used, describe the benefits derived from its use, or reinforce brand loyalty.

In the above example, Converse is attempting to promote a specific product/model, the "Converse Wade".

Sales Promotion

This form of promotion involves the use of discounts, sales, contests, coupons, samples, demonstrations, etc. to stimulate demand. Sales promotion can be directed to either the end-user consumer, sales staff within the organization, or channel members. This is usually a short-term process used in conjunction with other promotional activities specifically designed to increase sales of specific products during a limited time span.

Included in sales promotion is ***direct marketing.*** This form or promotion communicates directly with the target customer in an attempt to prompt a response or transaction. Because of the Internet and new technologies direct marketing activities have changed significantly in the last two decades. Companies can now engage their customers via e-mail, handheld devices, and cell phones. Marketers can also access customer databases to identify and track consumer purchases, offer personal incentives via loyalty programs and credit card rewards programs. These databases have enabled marketers to more precisely focus their promotional efforts in order to provide consumers with greater convenience and access to any product, as well as information about competing products, and the ability to self select what incentives best meet their unique needs.

Sales promotion activities are designed to supplement personal selling, advertising, and public relations by stimulating interest and enthusiasm for the product(s). Customary sales promotion activities involve:

- *Trade Shows*
- *Cooperative Advertising*
- *Price Reductions*
- *Contests*
- *Coupons*
- *Rebates*
- *Samples*
- *Displays (Point-Of-Purchase)*

Marketers who employ sales promotion as a key component in their promotional strategy should be aware of how the climate for these types of promotions is changing. Many consumers in today's market are conditioned to expect a promotion every time they make, or are considering, a purchase. With consumers being inundated on a daily basis with a wide variety of promotional incentives customer loyalty no longer serves as the primary promotional strategy but instead increasing sales via discounts and other financial incentives. For marketers the challenge is to balance the advantages of short-term promotional incentives versus the potential erosion of consumer loyalty to their brand. Any effective sales promotion campaign requires managers to be aware of consumer buying behavior as well as the nature and extent of the competition. It is also important to understand the specific objectives the firm is attempting to accomplish when using sales promotion.

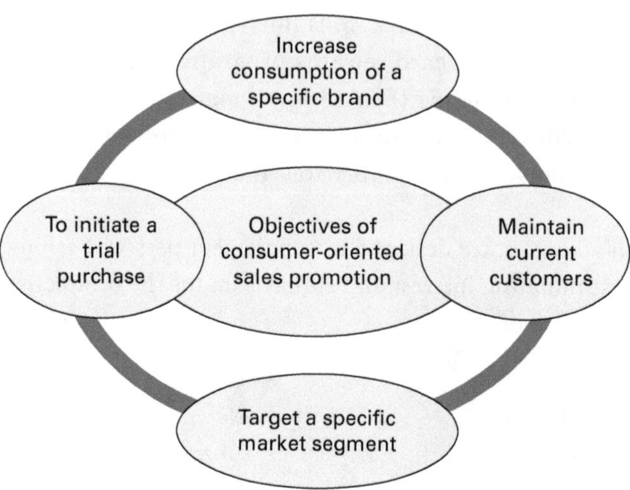

Public Relations

This is the element of the promotional mix that attempts to evaluate public attitudes, identify issues of public concern, and execute strategies that increase public understanding and acceptance by various stakeholders such as: *Customers, Employees, Vendors, Stockholders, and the Government.* The goal of public relations is to either maintain or improve the public image of the company in order to influence the decision process (vote, donation, or purchase). "As a management function, public relations encompasses all of the following:

- Anticipating, analyzing and interpreting public opinion, attitudes and issues that might impact, for good or ill, the operations and plans of the organization.
- Counseling management at all levels in the organization with regard to policy decisions, courses of action and communication, taking into account their public ramifications and the organization's social or citizenship responsibilities.
- Researching, conducting and evaluating, on a continuing basis, programs of action and communication to achieve the informed public understanding necessary to the success of an organization's aims. These may include marketing; financial; fund raising; employee, community or government relations; and other programs.
- Planning and implementing the organization's efforts to influence or change public policy. Setting objectives, planning, budgeting, recruiting and training staff,

developing facilities — in short, managing the resources needed to perform all of the above."[11]

Personal Selling

"Sales? Bleech. To the smart set, sales is an endeavor that requires little intellectual throw weight—a task for slick glad-handers who skate through life on a shoeshine and a smile. To others it's the province of dodgy characters doing slippery things—a realm where trickery and deceit get the speaking parts while honesty and fairness watch mutely from the rafters. Still others view it as the white-collar equivalent of cleaning toilets—necessary perhaps, but unpleasant and even a bit unclean. I'm convinced we've gotten it wrong."[12]

This interpersonal process involves a face-to-face interaction between an agent of the company selling the product, salesperson, and the consumer/client. The process involves the following seven steps:

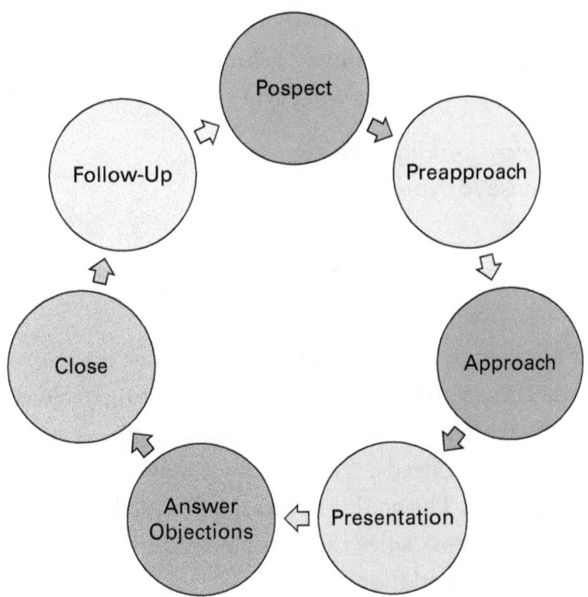

Prospect and Qualify

Success is often determined by your ability to:

- *Collect relevant information of your target customer*
- *Accurately assess customer needs*

The *Preapproach* is a key component to the selling process. As such, you need to know as much about your company, store, and its inventory. You need to understand the features and benefits of your products and its availability. You need this information before the customer ever walks through the door or calls on the phone.

The *Approach* is often the most important part of your sales presentation. This is the stage in the selling process where you are selling yourself to the customer. You must establish rapport and open up the flow of information between you and your customer. Your approach includes how you "greet" the customer and your attempts to establish a dialogue and rapport with the customer.

The *Presentation* is your first chance to make a good impression. Customers make positive purchase decisions because they perceive or realize some value or benefit from the purchase of the product. All customers want to know is, "What's in it for me?" This is where a successful salesperson can display their ability by illustrating a product's features or explaining the product's benefits.

To deal with negative comments (objections), you must recognize that usually the customer is asking for more information or reassurance. It is also important to remember that resistance occurs when the customer doesn't understand the benefits of the merchandise. Therefore, it is your job to *Answer Objections* and make certain that the customer fully understands the attributes and benefits of the product in question.

The *Trial Close* is comprised of a series of questions you ask after you have completed the presentation of the product or service. With a trial close you are not asking the prospect to make the decision to buy—You are simply asking for feedback, and seeking confirmation. A trial close might include the following types of questions:

- *"Is that what you were looking for?"*
- *"Does this make sense for you?"*
- *"What do you think?"*

Close the Sale

Getting the customer or client to say, "Yes" is one of the most difficult steps in the personal selling process. The first thing you must do, prior to attempting to close the sale is, establish a dialogue with the customer/client, listen very carefully, and ask open-ended questions in order to accurately identify their needs. "These days, many salespeople have come to think of 'the close' a little differently. The goal is not so much to sell anything just for the sake of making a sale. The goal is to book sales that truly help satisfy a customer, and that create a mutually-beneficial, long-term relationship."[13]

The *Follow-Up is* the final step in the personal selling process and is designed to ensure that the needs and satisfaction of the customer have been fully realized.

PROMOTION: ITS STRATEGIC IMPORTANCE

As a student you have probably given little thought, once you have completed your education, as to how you will promote yourself to prospective employers. Although it may sound somewhat dispassionate, your education, life experiences, skills, and talent, which represent your Unique Selling Proposition, is what will determine whether or not you get the job! Determining how you will promote yourself as the most viable candidate represents the same challenge a company faces when trying to promote and sell its products or services.

Promotion is one of the four primary strategic components of the marketing mix and is used to support the other three elements of product, place and pricing. Promotion communicates the unique selling proposition of your product, its availability, and its value at a particular price. Effective promotion is a key component of the marketing mix, as it is the element that helps you attract customers, convinces them to buy your product, and lastly generates loyalty.

For every student it is essential to understand that your career begins today and that an essential step in the process of preparing for the transition from student to working professional is the development of a promotional strategy that effectively communicates the development of your unique and singular story. Good luck on your journey!

> "Our job is to make change. Our job is to connect to people, to interact with them in a way that leaves them better than we found them, more able to get where they'd like to go. Every time we waste that opportunity, every page or sentence that doesn't do enough to advance the cause, is waste." —Seth Godin

ENDNOTES

1. Mycoskie, Blake. Start Something that Matters. New York: Spiegel & Grau, 2011.
2. Staff, Entrepreneur. "Unique Selling Proposition (USP)." *Entrepreneur*, <www.entrepreneur.com/encyclopedia/unique-selling-proposition-usp.>
3. "What Is Content Marketing." *Content Marketing Institute*. 927 Sept 2012 < http:contentmarketinginstitute.com/what-is-content-marketing>
4. Keller, K 2009, 'Building strong brands in a modern marketing communications environment', Journal of Marketing Communications vol. 15, no. 2, pp. 139–155.
5. Berger, Jonah. Contagious: Why Things Catch On. Simon & Schuster. 2013.
6. Ankeny, Jason. "How These 10 Marketing Campaigns Became Viral Hits". Entrepreneur. May 2014 <https://www.entrepreneur.com/article/233207#>
7. Holt, Douglas. "Branding in the Age of Social Media" Harvard Business Review. Mar 2016 <https://hbr.org/2016/03/branding-in-the-age-of-social-media>.
8. Mintz, Laurel. "How to Determine the Perfect Marketing Budget for You Company". Entrepreneur.

11 Mar 2015. <https://www.entrepreneur.com/article/243790>

9. Colley, Russell H. Defining Advertising Goals for Measured Advertising Results. New York: New York Association of National Advertisers, 1962.

10. E. K. Strong, Jr. "*The Psychology of Selling and Advertising.*" New York 1925, p. 349 and p. 9.

11. "Public Relations Defined: PRSA's Widely Accepted Definition." Public Relations Society of America. 2011. <http://www.prsa.org/AboutPRSA/PublicRelationsDefined/>

12. Pink, Daniel. *To Sell is Human: The Surprising Truth About Persuading, Convincing, and influencing Others.* (New York: Canongate Books, 2013)

13. "How to Close a Sale." Inc. May 2010 <http://www.inc.com/guides/2010/05/closing-the-sale.html>

SOURCES

1. Fig. 11.1: Source: https://en.wikipedia.org/wiki/File:Tom-Logo.jpg.
2. Fig. 11.4: Source: https://www.statista.com/statistics/273018/number-of-internet-users-worldwide/.
3. Fig. 11.6: Copyright © 2015 Depositphotos/Ieremy.
4. Fig. 11.7: Copyright © 2015 Depositphotos/Ieremy.
5. Fig. 11.9: Copyright © The Coca-Cola Company.
6. Fig. 11.10: Copyright © World Wildlife Fund.
7. Fig. 11.11: Copyright © DHL International.
8. Fig. 11.12: Copyright © Nike, Inc.
9. Fig. 11.13: Copyright © 2011 Depositphotos/Orson.
10. Fig. 11.16: Copyright © 2011 Depositphotos/Iqoncept.

Chapter 12

Accounting

Managing the Numbers

PROLOGUE

Accounting, because of generally accepted accounting principles (GAAP), is considered the universal language of business, spoken around the world by business and government leaders, investors, analysts, and others seeking to measure and understand the dynamics of business performance. Today, more than ever, businesses need employees who understand and can use financial data to improve the performance of their respective companies. "*Management of any business requires a flow of information to make informed, intelligent decisions affecting the success or failure of its operations. Investors need statements to analyze investment potential, Banks require financial statements to decide whether or not to loan money, and many companies need statements to ascertain the risk involved in doing business with their customers and suppliers.*"[1]

Accounting represents a critical function in business that serves a wide variety of users including but not limited to owners, creditors, managers and employees. It is a process wherein financial events and transactions are recorded, classified, summarized, and interpreted. All of these activities ultimately provide critical information to the owner, manager, creditor, and investor so as to insure that they make informed business decisions. According to Robert Kiyosaki, author of Rich Dad, Poor Dad, "*The only way to get out of the "Rat Race" is to prove your proficiency at both accounting and investing, arguably two of the most difficult subjects to master.*"[2]

The most common financial statements include the balance sheet, income statement, and statement of cash flows which provide a summary of the activities and changes in the financial status within a company over a given period of time. Management, labor, investors, creditors and government regulatory agencies use these statements as the means of keeping score. Accounting is the process that allows for the creation of financial reports that are utilized to:

- Compare the performance of a company with previous periods of operation.
- Compare performance with similar companies.
- Compare performance against industry standards

Accounting makes its functional contribution by providing the tools necessary for a company, and its management team, to accurately measure its revenues, assets, costs, money, expenses, and capital. The various accounting activities of (a) collecting, measuring and recording financial data; (b) organizing the data using agreed-upon accounting rules and methods to create useful information about a company's financial performance; (c) analyzing this information and reporting and communicating the results in financial reports and statements enables managers, investors, and creditors to evaluate whether or not the business model being utilized is producing a sufficient return on the capital invested.

MAJOR AREAS OF ACCOUNTING

Managerial Accounting

This area of accounting provides information and analyses for internal use by entrepreneurs and managers within the organization to assist them in decision making and eventually the allocation of scarce resources. Managerial accounting, also referred to as cost accounting, deals with information that is not made public. Information involving salary costs, cost of goods produced, profit targets, and material controls are key data points needed by managers to effectively control the operations of the company. The knowledge supplied by managerial accounting is normally used by department heads, division managers, and supervisors to help them "keep score" of the day-to-day operations of the business. Accountants assist managers in formulating policies for their respective business organizations, provide critical information for decision-makers and establish the structure for making those decisions. Managerial accountants:

- *Measure and report costs of production, marketing, etc.*
- *Determine which business activities were least profitable.*
- *Estimate future revenues.*
- *Prepare budgets.*
- *Determine whether the organization is staying within their budgets.*
- *Design strategies to minimize tax obligations.*

Applications of Accounting Information
• Evaluate Operations of the Firm • Make Investment Decisions • Plan & Control • Use in Contract Negotiations • Evaluate Credit Ratings • Evaluate Tax Liabilities • Approve New Issues of Stocks & Bonds

Small Businesses Failure: Poor Cash Management

> "SmallBizTrends.com, a business news resource, offers this infographic which states that 40% of small businesses make a profit, 30% come out even, and the remaining 30% lose money.
>
> You must know, down to the last dime, where the money in your business is coming from and where it's going in order for your business to succeed ... Sometimes people start businesses with a dream of making money but don't have the skill or interest to manage cash flow, taxes, expenses, and other financial issues. Poor accounting practice puts a business on a path straight to failure."[3]

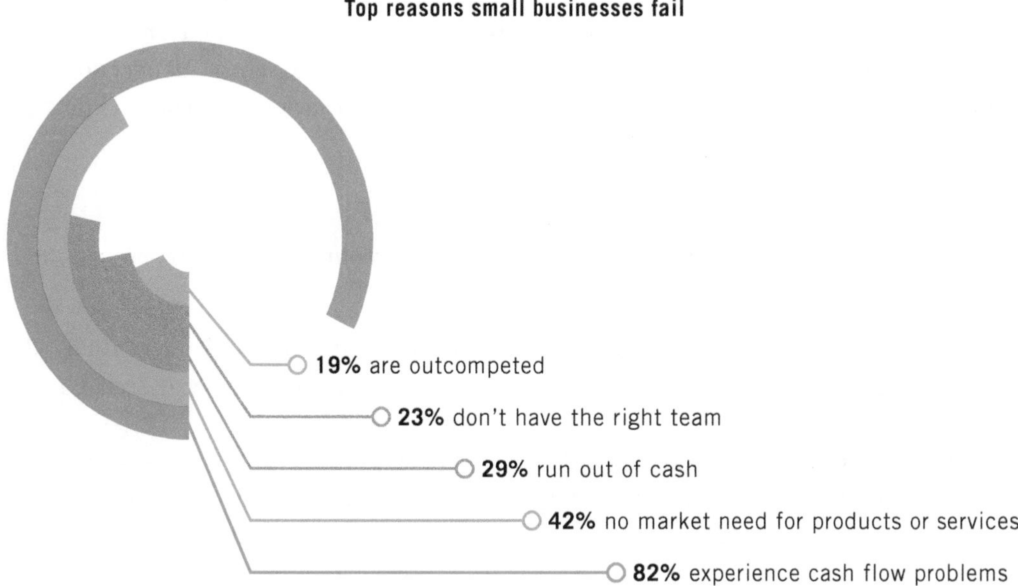
Top reasons small businesses fail
19% are outcompeted
23% don't have the right team
29% run out of cash
42% no market need for products or services
82% experience cash flow problems

Financial Accounting

Financial accounting is comprised of information that companies make available to the general public: stockholders, creditors, customers, suppliers, and government regulatory agencies. Using standardized guidelines (GAAP), transactions are recorded, summarized, and presented in various accounting statements (e.g. annual/quarterly reports, Income statements, etc.), to individuals outside the organization. The information is contained in a company's Annual Report and represents a yearly statement of the activities and financial condition of an organization in the previous year.

Users of Accounting Information
• Owners, stockholders, & potential investors • Management • Employees, union officials • Lenders, suppliers • Tax authorities • Government agencies

Financial Standards Accounting Board

The accounting profession has established, for the purpose of insuring the creation of consistent and accurate financial statements, a set of generally accepted accounting principles (GAAP) that guide the practice of financial accounting. These guidelines inform businesses how to properly record accounting information in a fair and consistent manner so as to ensure the reliability of the financial information provided to various stakeholders outside of the business.

Generally Accepted Accounting Principles (GAAP)

These principles serve as the guidelines that govern how accountants measure, process, and communicate financial information.

- The primary objective of financial reporting is to provide information useful for making investment and lending decisions. Useful information is relevant, reliable, and comparable.
- The Financial Accounting Standards Board (private sector), the Securities and Exchange Commission (public sector), and the American Institute of Certified Public Accountants (private sector) are all involved in determining how accounting is practiced.

Financial Accounting Standards Board (FASB)

"Since 1973, the Financial Accounting Standards Board (FASB) has been the designated organization in the private sector for establishing standards of financial accounting that govern the preparation of financial reports by nongovernmental entities. The FASB standards are officially recognized as authoritative by the Securities and Exchange Commission (SEC) ... Such standards are important to the efficient functioning of the economy because decisions about the allocation of resources rely heavily on credible, concise, and understandable financial information."[4]

Accounting Cycle

The accounting cycle consists of a series of steps that are designed to insure that a company accurately records all financial transactions and produces accurate financial statements.

Some data entry steps may occur at any time during the accounting cycle, while other transactions occur only during financial statement production. This process is repeated during every accounting period and provides managers with the information needed to track the revenues and expenses within their respective organizations. For purposes of simplifying the accounting cycle a shortened version of the cycle is presented here.

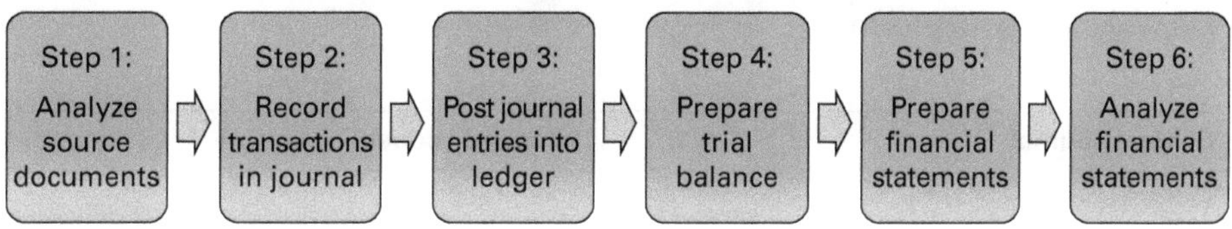

In reality, the accounting cycle is a ten-step process, illustrated below, rather than a six-step process.

Steps	Purpose	Timing
1. Analyze transactions	To determine accounts to be debited and credited	During the period
2. Journalize	To record the daily transactions	During the period
3. Post	To transfer the amounts from journal entries to the individual accounts affected by the record transaction	During the period
4. Prepare unadjusted trial balance	To summarize unadjusted ledger accounts and amounts	End of period
5. Journalizing and posting of adjusting entries	To bring the ledger accounts to adjusted balances	End of year
6. Prepare unadjusted trial balance	To summarize unadjusted ledger accounts and amounts	End of year
7. Preparing the statements	To report financial information	End of period*
8. Journalizing and posting of closing entries	To bring all temporary accounts to zero and the capital account up-to-date	End of year
9. Post-closing trial balance	To prove the accuracy of the adjusting and closing procedures	End of year
10. Reversing entries (optional)	To provide for recording in new fiscal period without consideration of accruals from previous periods adjustments	Beginning of new year

The ten step process[5] has been included here solely for the purpose of insuring accuracy of the information provided. Nonetheless, the accounting cycle basic purpose is to allow for the preparation of the balance sheet, income statement and statement of cash flows as "tools" for effectively managing a company.

Accounting Process

1. Collect Relevant Source Documents

Transactions—Receipts, invoices, and other source documents related to each transaction are assembled to justify making an entry in the firm's accounting records.

2. Verify Transactions

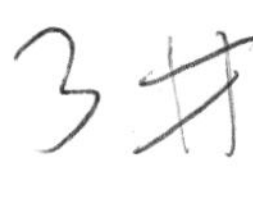

Classify and record transactions, usually electronically, into journals. A journal is the point of entry of every business transaction into the accounting system. It is a chronological record of the transaction, the date in which the transaction occurred, and includes a brief explanation of each transaction, the accounts affected, and whether those accounts are increased (debit/credit) or decreased (debit/credit), and by what amount. A general journal entry takes the following form:

General Journal

Date	Details	A/C#	Debit (Dr)	Credit (Cr)
1 May 2017	Cash	301	10,000	10,000
			Loan funds received	
10 May 2017	Cash	301	1000	
	Sales	101		1000
			Sale of inventory	
15 May 2017	Utilities Expense	201	500	
	Cash	301		500
			Expense Payment	
			Journals →	

General Ledger

Cash #301

Dr	Cr
10,000	500
1,000	

Loan #401

Dr	Cr
	10,000

Sales #101

Dr	Cr
	1,000

Utilities #201

Dr	Cr
500	

Posted → General ledger

3. Classify

Journal entries are transferred, or posted, usually electronically, to individual accounts kept in a ledger. The general ledger is a collection of the company's accounts. While a journal is organized in chronological order the ledger is organized by account. All entries involving cash are brought together in the ledger cash account; all entries involving sales are recorded in the ledger's sales account.

4. Summarize: Trial Balance

All accounts in the ledger are summarized at the end of the accounting period. If the journal entries are error-free and posted accurately to the general ledger, the total of all the debit balances should equal all of the credit balances. The total of the accounts is referred to as the trial balance. It is from the trial balance that the financial statements are prepared.

5. Prepare Financial Statements

Balance sheet | Income statement | Statement of cash flows

FUNDAMENTAL ACCOUNTING EQUATION

Assets are what a company owns, such as machinery, equipment, and inventory. Claims on these assets include liabilities and owner's equity. Liabilities consist of what the company owes, such as notes payable, bonds payable, and accounts payable. Owner's equity represents the claims of the owner's, based on their investment, against the assets of the business. The equation illustrates that the assets of a company must equal the claims against the company. Claims against the assets arise from both creditors of the company and the owners of the company.

Balance Sheet: Point Statement

The ***Balance Sheet*** supplies detailed information about the accounting equation factors:

Current Assets:
Cash and other liquid assets that can or will be converted to cash or used within one year.

Fixed Assets:
Plant, property, equipment, and other assets expected to last more than one year. These assets are subject to *Depreciation* which represents the cumulative value (usable life) of fixed assets that have been expensed or depreciated. Depreciation represents a non-cash expense that reflects the systematic reduction in the value of the firm's fixed assets.

Intangible Assets:
These assets have no physical form or clearly define value. Common examples include Goodwill, Copyright, and Patents.

Current Liabilities:
Claims (debts) of creditors that are due and payable within one year.

Long-Term Liabilities:
Claims (debts) that have due dates of one year or longer after the date on the balance sheet.

Shareholders' Equity:
Claims of the owner(s) against the assets of the business. The difference between total assets and total liabilities.

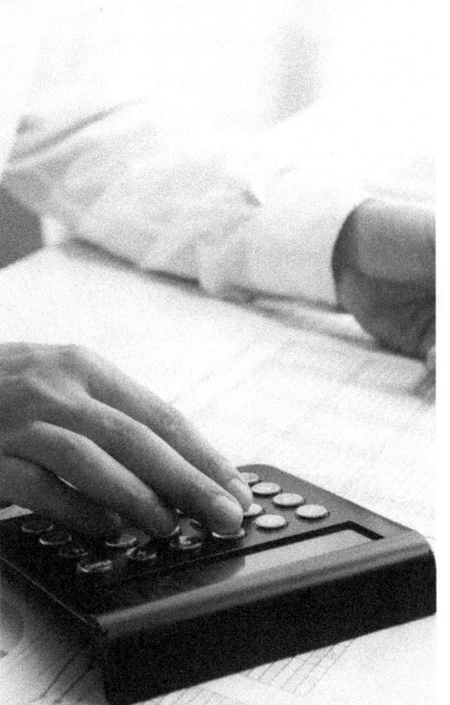

This financial statement is usually referred to as a "point statement" because it displays the status of assets, liabilities, and equities on a specific date. The balance sheet provides a picture of the financial health of a business at a given point in time. When used with financial ratios, the balance sheet can be used to identify warning signs of problems that could derail a business. The balance sheet is a vital financial statement that should be reviewed regularly because it changes with every transaction that occurs within the business.

BRC CORPORATION BALANCE SHEET AS OF JANUARY 31, 201X			
Assets			
Current Assets			
Cash		68777	
Accounts Receivable		108923	
Notes Receivable		84543	
Inventory		61400	
Total Current Assets			32364
Fixed Assets			
Land		741612	
Building		390463	
Less: Accumulated Depreciation	(100000)		
		290463	
Total Fixed Assets			1032075
Intangible Assets		18000	
Total Intangible Assets			18000
Total Assets			1082439
Liabilities & Equity			
Current Liabilities			
Notes Payable		53702	
Accounts Payable		33566	
Total Current Liabilities			87268
Long Term Liabilities			
Bond Payable		200000	
Mortgage Payable		500700	
Total L/T Liabilities			700700
Shareholder Equity			
Common Stock		249471	
Retained Earnings		45000	
Total Shareholder Equity			294471
Total Liabilities and Equity			1082439

Income Statement

Often referred to as a "period statement" this document displays the revenues, expenses and income before and after taxes from the operation of the business over a specific period of time.

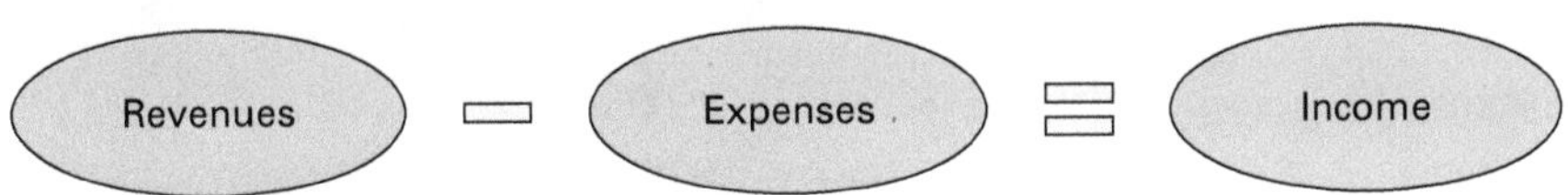

Income Statement (Period Statement)

Gross Sales/Revenues:
Funds received from the sale of goods and services or income received from investments.

Net Sales/Revenues:
This amount represents the revenue received after all returns, allowances, and discounts have been deducted from the gross sales revenues.

Cost of Goods Sold:
Cost of the merchandise or services that have been sold to generate the firm's sales revenues.

Operating Expenses:
The operating expenses can be classified in two categories-- Selling Expenses and General (G&A) Expenses. These expenses represent the costs involved in operating the business.

Net Income before Taxes (EBIDTA):
Gross income minus operating expenses equals Net Income. Net Income represents Earnings before Interest, Depreciation, Taxes, and Amortization.

Net Income after Taxes:
Sales minus total expenses minus taxes equals Net Income after Tax (Profit).

At certain points during the year, business owners and/or managers want to know how well the company is doing. Is it earning a profit? Is it losing money? How well is the company doing compared to other firms? Is it likely to earn a profit in the future? The Income Statement, also refered to as the Profit & Loss Statement, answers these questions and as such is one of the most relevant financial statements used by owners and managers to measure the performance of the company.

BRC CORPORATION INCOME STATEMENT YEAR ENDING DECEMBER 31, 201X			
Revenues			
Gross Sales		915247	
Less: Returns	22500		
Discounts	8312		
Net Sales		30812	884435
Cost of Goods Sold			
Beginning Inventory		174731	
Merchandise Purchased	50000		
Freight	6200		
Net Purchases		56200	
Cost of Goods Available for Sale	230931		
Less: End Inventory		–189000	
Cost of Goods Sold			–41931
Gross Profit			842504
Operating Expenses			
Selling Expenses			
Salaries	168550		
Advertising	15650		
Total Selling Expenses		184200	
General Expenses			
Office Salarie	78000		
Insurance	14900		
Rent	34000		
Utilities	8000		
Maintenance	12000		
Total General Expenses		146900	
Total Operating Expenses			331100
Net Income before Tax			511404
Less: Income Tax expense			117851
Net Income after Tax			393553

STATEMENT OF CASH FLOWS

Cash flow is simply the difference between cash flowing into the business and cash flowing out of the business. Starting with inventory and accounts receivables, if managers are able to maximize their cash flow, they can avoid running out of operating cash and exposing themselves to cash flow problems. The statement of cash flows reports cash receipts and disbursements involving the following activities:

- *Operations*
  - Operating cash flow is important because it measures the amount of cash generated by a company's normal business operations. It indicates whether a company is able to generate sufficient positive cash flow to maintain and grow its operations, or whether it may require external financing.
- *Investments*
  - These changes are a "cash out" entry because cash is used to buy new equipment, buildings or short-term marketable securities. The cash flow statement reports the aggregate change in a company's cash position resulting from any gains (or losses) from investments in the financial markets as well as changes resulting from amounts spent on investments on capital assets such as plant and equipment.

- *Financing*
  - Any changes in debt, loans or dividends are accounted for in cash from financing. *A category in the cash flow statement that accounts for external activities such as issuing cash dividends, adding or changing loans, or issuing and selling more stock.*

It is important to understand that profits and cash flow are two distinct factors used to assess the *liquidity* and *solvency* of a business.

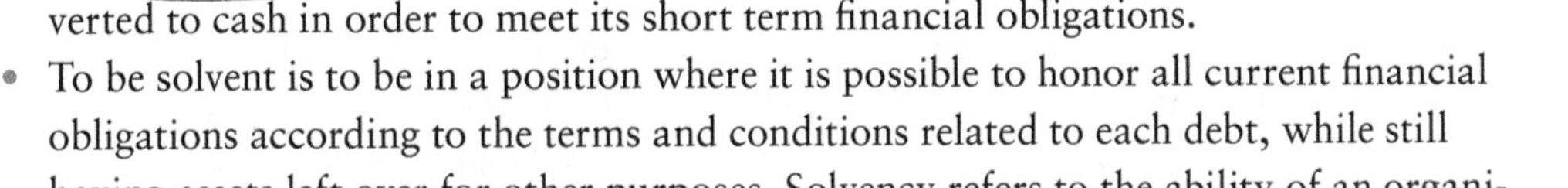

- An organization is considered to be liquid if it has the cash necessary to meet its immediate and short-term obligations and/or the assets that can be quickly converted to cash in order to meet its short term financial obligations.
- To be solvent is to be in a position where it is possible to honor all current financial obligations according to the terms and conditions related to each debt, while still having assets left over for other purposes. Solvency refers to the ability of an organization to meet its maturing long-term financial obligations as they come due.

The implications of solvency and liquidity are very different. A company that is insolvent must enter into bankruptcy; a company that lacks liquidity can also be forced to enter into bankruptcy even if it is solvent.

BRC CORPORATION STATEMENT OF CASH FLOWS YEAR ENDING DECEMBER 31, 201X		
Cash Flow from Operating Activities		
Cash Received: Customers	225000	
Cash Paid: Employees	(85000)	
Cash Paid: Suppliers	(12000)	
Interest Paid	(3000)	
Taxes Paid	(1900)	
Interest Income (Dividends)	1100	
Net Cash Flow from Operating Activities		124200
Cash Flow from Investing Activities		
Proceeds from sale of marketable securities	34000	
Net Cash Flow from Investing Activities		34000
Cash Flow from Financing Activities		
Repayment/Short Term Notes	(9000)	
Sale of Long Term Debt (Bond)	100000	
Cash Dividend: Shareholders	(50000)	
Net Cash Flow from Financing Activities		41000
Net Cash Change/Cash & Equivalents		199200
Cash Balance (Beginning of Year)		(43000)
Cash Balance (End of Year)		156200

Cash Flow Management

"Cash flow entails the movement of funds in and out of a business. This information should be tracked on a weekly, monthly or quarterly basis to identify where a business is currently from a financial standpoint and where it will be several months in the future.

Knowing when you'll receive and need to spend money is part of the budget process. The budget process, ultimately developed to help anticipate and create strategies for funding during shortages or investing during surpluses, helps a company know how much it will receive and spend at any point in time. Cash flow projections follow a similar structure to that of a company's budget.

To successfully project cash flow, organizations look at their prior year's checkbook as a basis of cash flow for the following year. Adjusting for any anticipated changes, this is often the more accurate way of projection. When looking over a previous year's expenses, a company would then factor in changes like new pricing, program offerings, funding sources and interest rate changes.

As the year unfolds, a company then updates cash flow projections to adequately reflect recent developments in expenses and profits. Comparing budgeted cash flows to actual deposits and expenditures will help in more accurately projecting cash flow in the following months. Even the most practiced of organizations find their forecasts change on a regular basis, thus prompting frequent revisiting."[6]

FINANCIAL RATIO ANALYSIS

Organizations and individuals use financial statements to spot problems and opportunities. Financial ratios provide the mechanism for measuring a company's performance and profitability. They provide useful information that often serves as benchmarks, to compare organizational performance over time and to compare the company to similar organizations within the same industry. Managers use financial ratios to understand how decisions involving pricing, product development, diversification, and downsizing might likely affect future profitability. Managers and outsiders also use ratio analysis to evaluate a company's performance in relation to the economy, the competition, and past performance.

Purpose of Ratio Analysis

1. Analyze Financial Statements
   Different users such as investors, management bankers and creditors use the ratio to analyze the financial situation of the company for their decision making purpose.
2. Judge Efficiency
   They help judge how well the company has been able to utilize its assets and earn profits.
3. Locate Weakness
   Accounting ratios can also be used in locating weakness of the company's operations even though its overall performance may be quite good.
4. Formulate Plans
   Although accounting ratios are used to analyze the company's past financial performance, they can also be used to help formulate the company's future plans.
5. Compare Performance
   It is essential for a company to know how well it is performing over the years and as compared to the other firms of the similar nature. Besides, it is also important to know how well its different divisions are performing among themselves in different years.

To perform ratio analysis most users look at historical trends and key ratios. Ratio analysis is simply a process of comparison. It requires managers to examine various financial aspects of a business against each other and against the backdrop of industry standards, in order to evaluate the overall performance of the company. There are four major classifications of ratios:

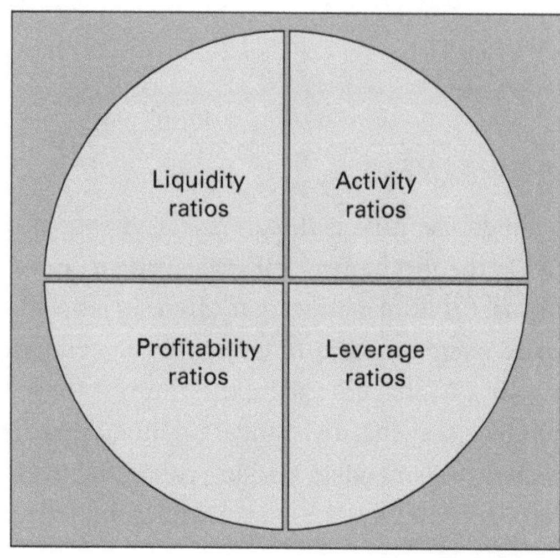

Liquidity Ratios

These ratios measure the firm's ability to meet short-term obligations. Because liquidity affects the ability of an organization to meet its short term obligations, and avoid bankruptcy, it represents a critical factor used to determine the financial health of a company.

Current Ratio

This ratio is mainly used to determine if a company has the ability to pay back its short-term liabilities (debt and payables) with its short-term assets (cash, inventory, receivables). A higher current ratio indicates that a company is capable of paying its obligations whereas a lower ratio, below 1:1, suggests that the company may be unable to pay off its short term obligations if they came due at that point in time.

$$\textit{Formula: } \frac{\textit{Current Assets}}{\textit{Current Liabilities}}$$

Acid-Test (Quick) Ratio

This ratio measures the ability of the firm to meet its short term obligations on demand. A more stringent indicator than the current ratio the acid test ratio indicates whether a company has sufficient short-term (liquid) assets available to meet its immediate short term liabilities without having to sell inventory.

$$\textit{Formula: } \frac{\textit{Quick Assets (Cash + Marketable Securities + Accounts Receivable)}}{\textit{Current Liabilities}}$$

- ***Marketable securities*** are securities or debts that can easily be converted to cash and include as such financial instruments as: government bonds, common stock or certificates of deposit.

Leverage Ratios

These ratios measure the extent a firm has relied on debt financing to sustain or grow its operations. A company's leverage ratio indicates whether or not a company has too much debt on its balance sheet. It also signals whether or not the company is in good financial health and presents less risk to its stockholders and debt holders. If a company is leveraged, having taken on too much debt, and if forced to file for bankruptcy, there exists a very strong probability that there will be nothing left over for its stockholders once the company has met its obligations to its debt holders.

Debt to Owners' Equity

Measures what proportion of equity and debt the company has used to finance the acquisition of company assets. A ratio greater than one means assets are mainly financed with debt, less than one means equity provides a majority of the financing. If a company's debt-to-equity ratio is too high, it's a signal that it may be in financial trouble and unable to pay its debtors. On the other hand if a company's debt-to-equity ratio is too low it indicates that a company is over-relying on equity to finance the business, which can be both costly and inefficient. This ratio varies based on the industry of each individual company.

$$\textit{Formula: } \frac{\textit{Total Liabilities}}{\textit{Owners' Equity}}$$

Profitability Ratios

These ratios provide an overall view of the financial performance of the company and its utilization of various resources to achieve profit.

Basic Earnings per Share (EPS)

The earnings per share ratio are most useful for publicly traded companies whose shares are traded on a public exchange. Earnings per share represents the portion of a company's profit that is allocated to each outstanding share of its common stock. The EPS from a previous quarter or year indicates the rate of growth a company's earnings on a per share basis.

$$\textit{Formula: } \frac{\textit{Net Income After Taxes}}{\textit{Common Shares Outstanding}}$$

Return on Sales (ROS)

This measure provides insight into how much profit is being produced per dollar of sales. It is best to compare a company's ROS over time to look for trends, and compare it to ratios of similar companies within your industry.

$$\textit{Formula: } \frac{\textit{Net Income}}{\textit{Net Sales}}$$

Return on Equity (ROE)

Measures how much was earned for every dollar invested by the owners/stockholders. *ROE* is both a measure of profit and a measure of efficiency. A rising ROE suggests that a company has the capacity to generate profit without needing as much capital. It also indicates how well a company's management is deploying the shareholders' capital. A high return on equity normally suggests that a company is capable of generating cash internally.

$$\textit{Formula: } \frac{\textit{Net Income}}{\textit{Total Owners' Equity}}$$

Activity Ratios

These ratios are used to determine the effectiveness of the firm's use of its resources.

Inventory Turnover Ratio

The inventory turn ratio measures how many times a company's inventory is sold and replaced over a period of time. It measures the speed of the inventory moving through a firm. A low turnover indicates poor sales and excess inventory, whereas a high ratio implies either strong sales or ineffective buying. This ratio is most useful when it is compared against industry averages.

$$\textit{Formula: } \frac{\textit{Cost of Goods Sold}}{\textit{Average Inventory}}$$

WHY DOES ANYBODY NEED TO UNDERSTAND ACCOUNTING?

"Sometimes it seems as if our lives are dominated by financial crises and failed reforms. But how much do Americans even understand about finance? Few of us can do basic accounting and fewer still know what a balance sheet is. If we are going to get to the point where we can have a serious debate about financial accountability, we first need to learn some essentials ... The German economic thinker Max Weber believed that for capitalism to work, average people needed

> to know how to do double-entry bookkeeping ... If we want stable, sustainable capitalism, a good place to start would be to make double-entry accounting and basic finance part of the curriculum in high school ..."[7]

Over the many years that I have been teaching, the one subject that often creates the most anxiety and fear is accounting. The vast majority of students automatically associate accounting with math. The assumption that students make is that if they are not "good" at math then there is no way they can ever learn accounting. The reality is that, if you can add, subtract, multiply and divide, you can perform the rudimentary functions associated with accounting. If you look at the example of the balance sheet again, you will see that it is nothing more than a series of numbers that have been added and/or subtracted from each category in order to arrive at a Balance: Assets = Liabilities + Owner's Equity. Ratio analysis is nothing more than the comparison (relationship) of two sets of numbers. In order to calculate any of the basic financial ratios depicted in the chapter you simply need to know how to divide! As a college student, now is the time to develop an understanding of accounting. Take control, to the extent that you can, of your financial future and learn how to manage the numbers so that you make the best financial decisions possible for you, your family, and even the economic well-being of the country.

ENDNOTES

1. "Understanding Financial Statements." Dun and Bradstreet. 2013 <http://www.dnb.com/customer-service/understanding-financial-statements.html>.
2. Kiyosaki, Robert. *Rich Dad, Poor Dad: What the Rich Teach Their Kids About Money That the Poor and Middle Class Do Not!* Paradise Valley, Ariz: TechPress, 1998. Print.
3. Kamo, Mike, et al. "6 Reasons Your Small Business Will Fail (And How to Avoid Them)." *Bplans Blog*, 12 May 2017, articles.bplans.com/6-reasons-your-small-business-will-fail-and-how-to-avoid-them/.
4. "Facts about FASB." Financial Accounting Standards Board. 2012. FASB. 30 Mar. 2012. <http://www.fasb.org/jsp/FASB/Page/SectionPage&cid=1176154526495>
5. Chiappetta, Shaw, and John J. Wild. Fundamental Accounting Principles, 20th Edition. New York: McGraw-Hill /Irwin, 2011.
6. Goodrich, Ryan. "Cash Flow Management: Techniques and Tools." Business News Daily 13 Jun 2013. <http://www.businessnewsdaily.com/4635-cash-flow-management.html>.
7. Jacob Soll, "No Accounting Skills? No Moral Reckoning." New York Times: Opinion Page April 27, 2014.

SOURCES

1. Fig. 12.2: Adapted from: Insurance Quotes, https://www.insurancequotes.com/business/why-do-businesses-fail.
2. Fig. 12.9: Copyright © 2014 Depositphotos/minervastock.
3. Fig. 12.11: Copyright © 2015 Depositphotos/vinnstock

Chapter 13

Finance

Putting Your Money to Work

PROLOGUE

Any decision that involves the use of money is a financial decision and normally results in costs and/or benefits. Finance involves the study of money and its management and is similar in many ways to accounting and economics. Finance explores how companies allocate scarce resources, in a rapidly changing business environment, over a period of time against the backdrop of whether or not the assumption of risk provides an adequate rate of return from the allocation and use of company resources. In the end financial managers are responsible for making decisions in a period of unprecedented change and uncertainty assessing both risk and return in order to assure the short- and long-term survival of the company.

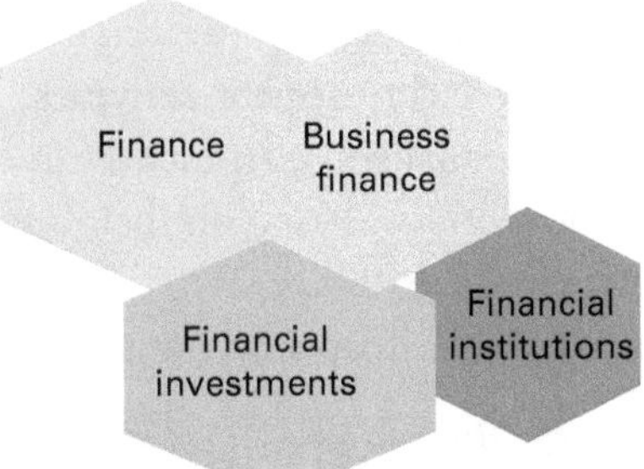

Although finance can be divided into three distinct areas of study, financial institutions, financial investments, and business finance, our discussion will center on the role of the financial manager and how they influence the acquisition, financing, and management of business assets. Financial managers are responsible for the investments, financing, and asset management decisions within a company and the result of their decisions directly influence the overall performance of a company.

"The fundamental success of a strategy depends on three critical factors: a firm's alignment with the external environment, a realistic internal view of its core competencies and sustainable competitive advantages, and careful implementation and monitoring."[1] Virtually every decision made within a company has some financial implication and the availability and use of financial resources are normally a major constraint adversely affecting the firm's ability to execute its strategic plan. The role of the financial manager is to manage the firm's resources so that the organization can meet its goals and objectives. At its most basic level finance involves:

- Strategic Planning
- Oversight of the daily operations of a business
- Budgeting and forecasting
- Maintaining adequate cash flows
- Reducing operational costs
- Establishment of practical control systems

"Being knowledgeable about money management, budgeting and finance is no guarantee of success in life. But ignorance about such concepts often comes at great cost. When it comes to financial literacy, however, the U.S. gets a failing grade at least by one count. The U.S. ranked 14th in a 2015 global study conducted by Standard & Poor's Ratings Group and others, with a financial literacy rate of 57%."[2]

ROLE OF THE FINANCIAL MANAGER

The primary role of the financial manager is to increase the firm's value by planning and controlling the acquisition and dispersal of its financial assets. Almost every firm, government agency, and organization has one or more financial managers who oversee the preparation of financial reports, direct investment activities, and implementation of cash management strategies. Financial managers, particularly in business, engage in ongoing data analysis and make recommendations, based on their analysis, to senior managers on strategies to improve and/or maximize profits.

Financial managers are responsible for carrying out the following tasks:

- *Establish Financial Goals for the Business*
- *Develop and Implement a Financial Plan*
- *Raise Capital (Debt vs. Equity)*
- *Determine the Most Advantageous Sources of Capital*
- *Determine the Allocation and Expenditures of Available Capital*
- *Collect Overdue Payments and Minimizing Bad Debt*

"The role of the financial manager is more than simply the person who, as the accountant of years ago, tallied the assets and liabilities of a corporation. The finance manager is part financial wizard, and part strategic planner, as well as someone keenly aware of industry trends and standards. The financial manager must understand all aspects of the business so they are able to adequately advise and support the chief executive officer in decision-making and ensuring company growth and profitability into the future."[3]

CAUSES OF FINANCIAL FAILURE

The greatest cause of financial failure may actually be attributable to a general lack of financial knowledge and awareness. Managers often struggle to understand and more importantly recognize when a business is struggling compared to when it is failing, especially if they have no understanding of basic financial principles. There are many reasons why some companies grow and why others regress and then slowly fade away.

External factors often cause businesses to fail and can include, but are limited to: a shrinking market, rising unemployment, advances in technology, declining consumer sentiment, and increased competition. There are also a multitude of internal factors that impact the success of a company and may include, inefficient operations, employee turnover, and ineffective leadership. In every industry, there are companies that grow and dominate, while others stagnate, shrink, and ultimately fail. The primary reason for the failure of most companies can be attributed to three broad factors.

- Undercapitalization
  - When a company is undercapitalized it lacks sufficient funds to launch, sustain and grow the operations of the business. Due to a lack of funding a company is then likely to seek out borrowed monies, which contribute to the insolvency of the business and ultimately its demise.
  - Most small-business owners underestimate how much money they're going to need, not merely to get through start up, but also to sustain the company as it struggles to establish a commercial foothold. Norman Scarborough, an associate professor of business administration at Presbyterian College in South Carolina, says, "Once you start out undercapitalized, that can start a downward spiral from which you can never catch up."
- Poor Cash Flow
  - A healthy cash flow is an essential part of any successful business. If you fail to have enough cash to pay your suppliers, creditors, or your employees, you're out of business! "A cash flow statement shows if a business is running out of money, even if it is profitable at the same time. One of the most important numbers that business owners and their stakeholders should know is the company's cash flow from operations, which is often overlooked in lieu of the income statement and balance sheet numbers. Being able to internally generate sufficient cash is key to maintaining a healthy business. A Statement of Cash Flows serves as a map that tells where cash came from and where it went, and is a crucial planning tool for any business's long term success."[4]

- Inadequate Expense Control
  - A common tendency is to underestimate cash disbursements, which can result in a cash crisis. The timing of payables is just as crucial to proper cash management as the timing of accounts payable. To make solid determinations as to what expenses can be eliminated, you should understand and track monthly expenditures. "Create a monthly budget and stick to it. You cannot manage what you cannot measure. While two thirds of owners agree that they are responsible for cost control, according to a survey of owners by National Foundation of Independent Business (NFIB), many don't have monthly budgets."[5]

FINANCIAL PLANNING

A financial plan is a document that specifies the funds needed by the firm for a precise period of time, indicating the inflows and outflows of cash, and the most appropriate uses of capital. The plan answers three vital questions:

- *What funds does the firm require during the next period of operations?*
- *How will it obtain the necessary funds?*
- *When will additional funds be needed?*

In order to answer these questions, it is essential to follow the steps in the financial planning process.

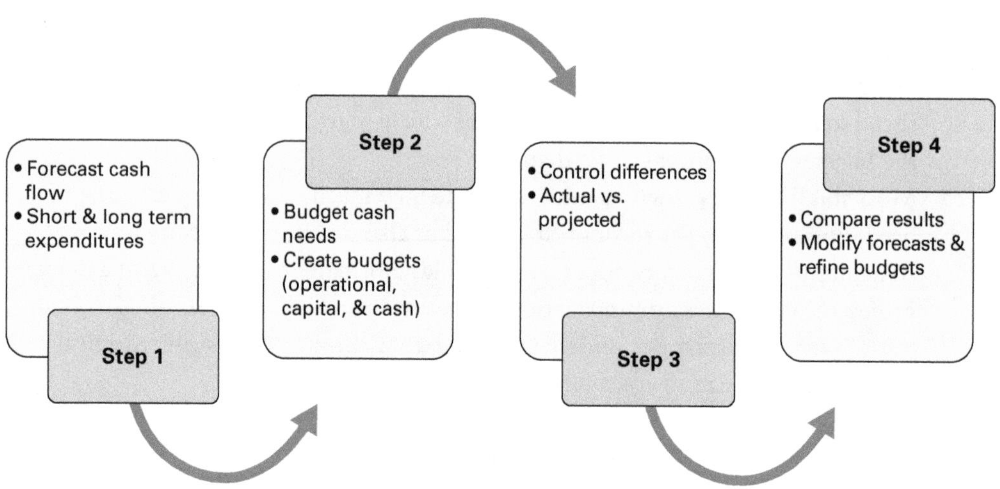

FINANCIAL PLANNING PROCESS

Step 1: Forecasting

Forecasting is fundamental to all businesses, whatever the size, since every organization must spend money in order to survive. Forecasts should be based on credible information applied to a consistent process that ultimately shapes and supports a company's business strategy. This requires financial managers, on a regular basis, to project the short term and long-term financial needs of the organization taking into account the dynamic changes within the internal and external environments of the company.

Short-Term Operating Expenditures (One Year or Less)

An expenditure, which is an expense, is incurred as a result of a company carrying out the ordinary and necessary day-to-day activities of the business and are not directly associated with the production activities of the company. Operating expenditures can include, but are not limited to, such things as: rent, repairs and maintenance, marketing, taxes, and payroll. These expenses, as discussed in the previous chapter, are subdivided into two different categories, selling expenses or general expenses. Examples of short-term expenditures include:

- Accounts Payable–unpaid bills plus wages and taxes due within the upcoming year.
  - Rent and rates
  - Utility bills (electricity, telephone, gas)
  - Maintenance, repairs & decorations
  - Depreciation expense
  - Accounting, legal or any other professional fees
  - Advertising and marketing costs
  - Insurance and premiums paid
  - Supplies and office equipment

Most businesses need short-term ***working capital*** at some point in their operations. This creates a need for working capital to fund inventory, accounts receivable and operating expenses.

- Working Capital
  - Working capital represents the money needed to fund the short-term, normal, day-to-day operations of a business. It ensures that a company has sufficient cash to pay its debts and expenses as they fall due.
  - Working capital is calculated by adding inventories (raw materials, work-in-process, and finished goods on hand) and accounts receivable (minus accounts payable).
    - *Current Assets – Current Liabilities = Working Capital*

Long-Term (Capital) Expenditures (One Year or More)

Also referred to as capital expenditures, these funds are used by a company to upgrade or acquire physical assets that have a long term lifespan. These fixed assets are normally not easily converted into cash, require a very large investment, and represent a long-term legally binding commitment of company funds that may continue for many years into the future. Long-term expenditures, those with a lifespan of greater than a year, include:

- Property
- Buildings
- Vehicles

- Equipment
- Machinery

Step 2: Developing Budgets

This is the portion of the financial plan that allocates resources based on projected revenues and expenses. Dave Ramsey, in his book *The Total Money Makeover*, says that "A budget is telling your money where to go instead of wondering where it went." Budgets are used to determine how to use financial resources to reach organizational goals. There are three types of budgets:

- Operating Budget
  - An operating budget is a detailed projection of all estimated income and expenses, based on forecasted sales projections, during a specific period of time, normally one year. The operating budget projects dollar allocations to various costs and expenses needed to run the company. This budget is used to summarize the operating, capital, and cash budgets.
- Capital Budget
  - The capital budget outlines the spending plans for capital assets (fixed assets) whose returns are expected to occur over an extended period of time--more than a year.
- Cash Budget
  - Cash budgets are used to estimate whether or not a company has a sufficient amount of cash to fulfill regular operations. The cash budget is a detailed projection of cash inflows and outflows incorporating both revenue and capital items. It is thus a statement in which estimated future cash receipts and payments are tabulated in such a way as to show the forecasted cash balance of a business at defined intervals.

Step 3: Establish Financial Control

This step in the financial planning process allows managers to determine how well the organization has followed its financial plan and is meeting its financial goals. This means comparing *actual* revenues, costs, and expenses with *projected* revenues, costs, and expenses. "Driving the bottom line through profitable revenue growth likely is the objective of virtually every company. This should be the number one focus, of course. If you're not growing, you're dying. But companies also need to focus on controlling costs. Without constant vigilance, companies can find themselves in an uncompetitive situation with bloated overhead. The episodic slashing and burning that then becomes necessary can significantly damage a company."[6]

Operating Funds

The need for operating funds never ceases and sound financial management is essential because the monetary needs of businesses change over time. Funds must be available to finance specific operational needs. Operating Funds must be available to finance specific operational needs. The typical operational needs include:

- Managing Daily Business Operations
  - Funds must be available to meet daily cash requirements without jeopardizing the firm financial strength and stability.
- "Time Value of Money"
  - "This principle suggests that a certain amount of money today has different buying power than the same amount of money in the future."[7] In other words, money today is more valuable than a year from today. This principle requires financial managers to minimize cash expenditures whenever possible and convert excess cash into interest-bearing accounts.
  - *Interest* is typically referred to as a percentage earned on money (principal) deposited or invested. Interest is normally divided into two distinct categories:
    - Simple Interest – "interest earned on the interest earned in prior periods is called compound interest. If interest is not earned on interest, we have simple interest."[8]
  - Understanding the value of your money, based on the (interest) rate of return at some point in the future, requires financial managers to understand the basic principle of "*Future Value.*" The formula for calculating the future value of money, applying simple and compound interest, is as follows:
    - *Using simple interest*
    - $FV_1 = P_0 (1+i)^1$ *(Simple Interest)*
    - *Using simple interest of 7% on a \$1000 deposit*
    - $FV_1 = \$1000\ (1.00 + .07) = \$1{,}070$
    - *Using compound interest based on the above information:*
    - $FV_2 = \$1000\ (1.00 + .07)^2 = \$1{,}144.90$
- Managing Accounts Receivable
  - Accounts receivable management is a significant factor affecting a business's financial health. It's important to establish a formal process to ensure the timely invoicing of your customers as well as a regular practice of reviewing your accounts receivable. Accounts receivable is money owed to a company by its customers for goods or services that have been delivered or used, but not yet paid. It is possible to minimize the cost of accounts receivable and whenever practical provide incentives to speed up the payment of accounts receivable. For example, providing billing terms that incentivize your customers to pay in advance of the due date may look like:
    - 2/10/n30
    - "2" represents the percentage amount of the discount offered.
    - "10" is the total number of days (0-10) from the invoice date which the buyer is eligible to receive the discount.
    - "n/30 represents the total time allowed to pay the net invoice amount providing the buyer does not pay the discounted invoice amount within 10 days.
- Obtaining Needed Inventory
  - Maintaining adequate inventory ties up a significant amount of cash. A sound inventory policy helps managers maximize profitability by reducing the funds

companies tie up in inventory. A commonly used method for managing inventory is the Economic Order Quantity (EOQ). The EOQ allows managers to minimize the total cost of carrying and processing inventory on an annual basis. The total annual inventory costs are the sum of ordering costs and carrying costs. These annual costs can calculated by using the Ordering Costs (OC), Number of Units Sold (S), Size of each Order (Q), and the Cost per Order (F).

- Financing Major Capital Expenditures
  - Capital expenditures are major investments in long-term assets that require a significant portion of the organization's funds. Decisions involving capital expenditures are based primarily on the cash flows they will generate at some point in time in the future. An investment in plant or equipment may produce negative cash flows at the initial stages of the project before generating positive cash flows. The key factor to be considered when determining the types of financing for major capital expenditures is: Will cash flows improve and ultimately create long-term benefit for the company?

SOURCES OF CAPITAL

The most appropriate sources of capital for an organization depend on the stage of development of the company. If the company is a start-up the challenges in acquiring financing are much more difficult than an established company with a proven track record of success. There are two methods of raising capital necessary to fund the operations of a company. These include:

Debt Financing

Debt includes both secured and unsecured loans. Before a debt can be made, both the debtor and the creditor must agree on the manner in which the debt will be repaid, known as the standard of deferred payment. Debt refers to funds raised through various forms of borrowing that have the following characteristics:

- Repayment of the principal (amount of loan) with interest
- Established due date (maturity) for repayment
- Often collateralized (secured with some assets of the debtor)
- Provide the creditor (lender) with a reasonable rate of return

Leverage = Debt

Financial leverage is the degree to which a business is utilizing debt (borrowed money) rather than equity to fund its operations. It reflects the amount of debt used in the capital structure of the company and is used to magnify the rate of return on shareholders' equity. If the company's earnings are larger than the interest payments on the funds borrowed, stockholders earn a higher rate of return than if equity financing were used.

Leverage – Selling Bonds		*Equity – Selling Stock*	
Common Stock	*$250,000*	*Common Stock*	*$700,000*
Bonds (@10%)	*$450,000*	*Bonds (@10%)*	*0*
Funds Raised	*$700,000*	*Funds Raised*	*$700,000*
Earnings	*$325,000*	*Earnings*	*$325,000*
Less: Bond Interest	*$ 45,000*	*Less: Bond Interest*	*0*
Total Earnings	*$280,000*	*Total Earnings*	*$325,000*
Return to	*$280,000*	*Return to Stockholders =*	*$325,000*
Stockholders =	*$250,000 = 112%*		$700,000 ≈ 46%

Financing for Your Future—The Five C's of Credit

*"It's the most common question business owners ask their banker: '**What are you looking for from me and my business if I need to borrow?**' While each lending situation a bank reviews is unique, most banks utilize some variation of "The Five C's of Credit" when making credit decisions.*

- ***Character**—Banks want to put their money with clients who have the best credentials and references.*
- ***Capacity**—What is your company's borrowing history and track record of repayment? How much debt can your company handle? Will you be able to honor the obligation and repay the debt?*
- ***Capital**—How well capitalized is your company? How much money have you invested in the business?*
- ***Conditions**—What are the current economic conditions and how does your company fit in? If your business is sensitive to economic downturns, the bank wants to know that you are good at managing productivity and expenses.*
- ***Collateral**—Collateral represents assets that the company pledges as an alternate repayment source for the loan. Most collateral is in the form of real estate and office or manufacturing equipment. Your accounts receivable and inventory can also be pledged as collateral. Unless you're a business with a proven payments track record, you will almost always be required to pledge collateral."*[9]

There are a multitude of sources of debt available for businesses today. Rather than trying to include all the various sources of debt available to businesses within this discussion; instead the most common sources of debt financing will be highlighted. Debt capital always represents funds obtained through borrowing.

Common Methods of Debt Financing		
Trade Credit	**Loans**	**Bonds**
Open account where businesses buy goods now and pay for them later. A typical invoice of 2/10/n30 means that: The buyer can take a 2% discount from the net amount by paying within 10 days of pay the toal amount (net) in 30 days.	There are numerous types of loans available that normally fall into one of two categories: secured or unsecured. A secured loan is backed by tangible assets such as property. An unsecured loan requires no collateral.	In finance, a bond is an instrument of indebtedness of the bond issuer to the holders. It is a debt security, under which the issuer owes the holders a debt and, depending on the terms of the bond, is obliged to pay them interest (the coupon) and/or to repay the principal at a later date, termed the maturity.[10]

Short-Term Financing

In every organization the day-to-day operations require management to meet the short-term financial needs of the firm. Firms typically borrow short-term funds to finance the purchase of inventory or to meet the recurring expenses that occur each month in the operation of the business. Short-term funds are those monies due and payable within one year from the date of issue.

Trade Credit

Trade credit transactions between business intermediaries (wholesaler to retailer) that normally involve short-term (e.g. 2/10/n30) delayed payment of purchases of intermediate goods or services. Through delayed payment, trade credit suppliers are effectively funding their clients with short-term debt containing three main unique differences from conventional corporate debt.

1. Suppliers lend *in kind*[11]; they seldom lend cash.
2. In contrast to bonds or loans, trade credit is frequently not subject to specific, formal contracts between the lender and the borrower.
3. A non-financial (bank) firm issues trade credit.

In the event that a business (borrower) seeking trade credit does not have a strong credit history the issuer (business intermediary) would require that the borrower sign a *Promissory Note* wherein all the terms pertaining to the indebtedness by the issuer are explicitly stated. These would include the amount to be repaid, interest rate, repayment schedule, maturity date, consequences of default, date and place of issuance, and issuer's signature.

A company should attempt to, whenever possible, take advantage of the cash discount offered for early payment. Failing to take advantage of the discount will normally result in higher opportunity costs and diminish the effective use of capital. The formula for determining the effective interest rate that you are offering customers through your early payment discount terms. The formula steps are:

1. Calculate the difference between the payment date for those taking the early payment discount, and the date when payment is normally due, and divide it into 360 days. For example, under 2/10 net 30 terms, you would divide 20 days into 360, to arrive at 18. You use this number to annualize the interest rate calculated in the next step.
2. Subtract the discount percentage from 100% and divide the result into the discount percentage. For example, under 2/10 net 30 terms, you would divide 2% by 98% to arrive at 0.0204. This is the interest rate being offered through the credit terms.
3. Multiply the result of both calculations together to obtain the annualized interest rate. To conclude the example, you would multiply 18 by 0.0204 to arrive at an effective annualized interest rate of 36.72%.

Thus, the full calculation for the cost of credit is:

$$\frac{\text{Discount \%}}{(1-\text{Discount \%})} \times \frac{360}{(\text{Full allowed payment days} - \text{Discount days})}$$

Commercial Bank: Loans

Banking occupies one of the most important positions in the modern economic world. It is necessary for trade and industry. Hence it is one of the great agencies of commerce. Although banking in one form or another has been in existence from very early times, modern banking is of recent origin. It is one of the results of the Industrial Revolution and the child of economic necessity. Its presence is very helpful to the economic activity and industrial progress of a country.[12]

For most banks, loans represent the principal way in which they earn income. Loans are typically made for fixed terms, at fixed rates and are typically secured with real property. There are numerous methods to acquire funding from a commercial bank. The most common forms include:

- Unsecured Loans
  - *An unsecured loan is one that is obtained without the use of property as collateral for the loan. These loans are normally based on the company's reputation and are typically very difficult loans to acquire.*

- *Secured Loans*
  - Backed by specific assets (collateral) of the borrower. If the borrower should default on the loan, fail to repay the loan, the creditor has the legal authority to take possession of the asset used as collateral and may sell it to regain some or all of the amount of money originally lent to the borrower.
- *Pledging*
  - *Requires organizations to use accounts receivables as security. Because receivables are highly liquid assets, they are attractive as collateral to commercial banks and finance companies.*
- *Inventory Financing*
  - This financing option requires organizations to use their inventory as collateral. This form of financing is useful for businesses that must pay their suppliers in a shorter period of time than it takes them to sell their inventory to customers.
- *Line of Credit*
  - A *closed end* [13] line of credit establishes a formal agreement between the bank and the subject business in which a specific amount of debt, both secured and unsecured, is provided at specified periods of time throughout the calendar year.
- *Revolving Line of Credit*
  - This *open-end*[14] line of credit is a guaranteed and legally binding agreement. This commits the bank to lend a specified amount of money on demand to a company up to a predetermined amount. The most familiar form of a revolving line of credit is your credit card wherein you are assigned a credit limit and are able to purchase any product or service as long as your credit limit is not exceeded.

Commercial Paper

This is essentially a promissory note issued to major corporations who maintain high credit standing and back the loan solely with the reputation of the company. Commercial paper is in essence a promissory note that matures at various periods of time ranging from 5 days to 270 days[15]. Normally issued in higher denomination, between $100,00 and $1,000,000, commercial paper is only available to large established companies with a high credit rating. Other companies like banks, insurance companies, financial institutions, and pension funds wanting to invest in short term securities purchase commercial paper.

Long-Term Financing

Businesses require long-term financing in order to acquire new equipment, fund Research & Development, enhance cash flow, and support company expansion. Long-term loans are used to purchase fixed assets (capital items) and normally must be repaid over a period of five years or more. Rather than include an exhaustive list of the long-term financing options available to businesses, we will instead focus our discussion on the two most common forms of financing options used: Term Loans and Corporate Bonds.

Term Loans

This type of loan represents a promissory note that requires the borrower to repay the loan in specified installments over a specific period of time. Term loans are available to established businesses that can provide lenders with sound financial statements as well as a demonstrable capacity to produce sufficient cash flows to meet the monthly payment obligations and total costs of the loan. Term loans normally require collateral and are subject to a rigorous approval process by the lender. Bankers classify term loans into two broad categories:

- **Intermediate-Term Loans**
  - The duration of these loans is typically less than three years and are generally repaid in monthly installments, sometimes with a balloon payment, from monies derived from a company's cash flow.
- **Long-Term Loans**
  - These loans are for periods of time greater than three years with most having maturities between three and ten years. Long-term loans are collateralized by a business's assets and typically require quarterly or monthly payments derived from profits or cash flow.

Corporate Bonds

Bonds are long-term debt sold to investors by companies that require a fixed-sum payment, sometimes annually, at the date of maturity. Bonds issued by corporations provide no claim of ownership and pay no dividend payments to bondholders. The proceeds of the bond issue are used for many purposes, including operational expansion. Investors purchase bonds with the understanding that the company will pay back the principal plus any interest (coupon rate) that is due at a date (maturity date) specified in the bond agreement. There are two general categories of bonds: local municipalities (state or city), or the federal government. The issuer of a bond is

- ***Secured Bonds***
  Secured bonds represent a debt instrument, which is secured by specific assets, or other collateral, of the company. These assets, in the event of default, are then assigned (transferred) to the bondholder. Because these bonds offer the pledge of specific assets of the issuer to the bondholder they are considered less risky than unsecured bonds and as a result normally provide a lower rate of return to an investor.
- ***Unsecured Bonds***
  Also called *Debenture Bonds* these represent unsecured debt backed solely by the creditworthiness and reputation of the company issuing the bond. These bonds are not secured by any physical asset or collateral of the firm. Large, financially strong companies with excellent bond ratings are usually the only entities capable of issuing debentures.

EQUITY FINANCING

Equity represents money generated from within the firm, from operations, or through the sale of ownership in the firm. "If an entrepreneur obtains venture capital financing early in the life of a business, it is typically at a huge cost. In exchange for this financing, the start-up's founders will have to sell part of their company, thereby diluting their ownership. The decisions entrepreneurs make at this stage can have wide ramifications, not only for their future success but also for their profits."[16]

These are funds acquired through the sale of stock (assets) or through additional investment by the owners (stockholders) of the company. Equity capital represents money invested into a company in exchange for an ownership position in that company. Unlike debt, equity capital does not require repayment according to a specific schedule nor do the assets of a company secure the money of investors. An equity investor expects that, at some point in time in the future, the ownership percentage that he/she holds will be worth more than the original amount invested.

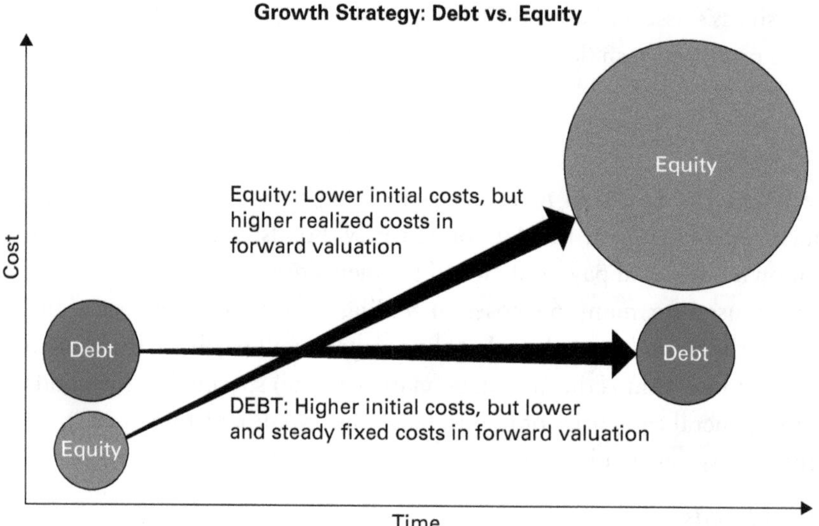

Sources of Equity Financing

For many small businesses, the prime source of small business financing is from money invested by the founding members of the company. Obviously, the sources of equity financing are different for different types of businesses whether the company is a startup versus public corporation. Nonetheless, there generally are two primary methods of raising equity; either internally, generated from financial sources within the company; or, externally generated through an expansion of ownership.

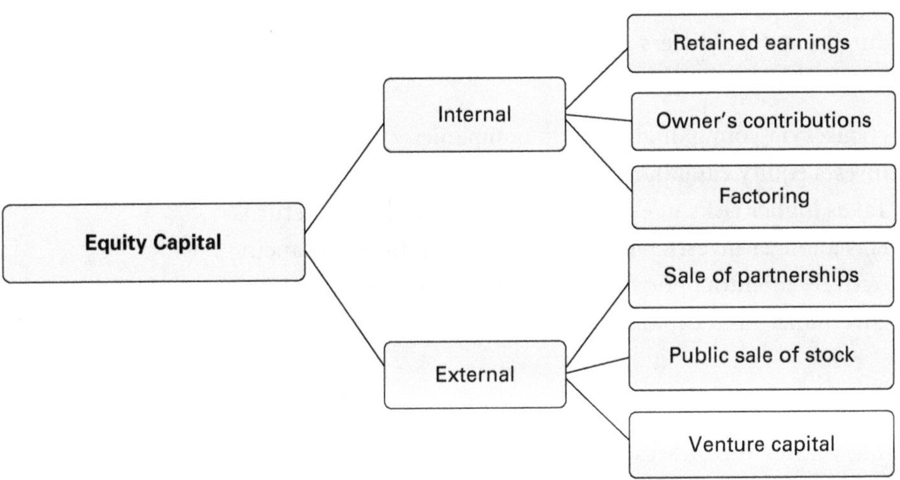

Stock

Companies fall into two broad categories of ownership: private and public. When a privately-held company elects to become a public company it essentially sells off of assets (ownership) in the form of stock certificates. New issues of shares are offered to the public, for the first time, through an Initial Public Offer (IPO). Often the issuing companies are rapidly growing startups that have previously relied on venture capital to fund their operations.

It is very unlikely that investors will purchase shares of stock in a private company. Conversely public companies attract investors to buy stock by engaging in the IPO process. This IPO process requires a company to disclose all of its financial statements for public view. This is also referred to as "going public."

Retained Earnings

Profits from the firm's operation that are reinvested back into the company. Retained earnings are often the most utilized form of financing because there is no interest payments required, no dividend payments, and no new segment of ownership created.

Venture Capital

The most difficult time to raise capital is during the start-up phase of a new business. Venture capitalists invest money in new and emerging high-tech, high-growth companies that are determined to have the greatest profit potential. Generally a venture capitalist wants a "stake" in the company and, because of the high degree of risk, requires a significantly higher rate of return on their investment.

About Venture Capital

"Venture capital is a type of equity financing that addresses the funding needs of entrepreneurial companies that for reasons of size, assets, and stage of development cannot seek capital from more traditional sources, such as public markets and banks. Venture capital investments are generally made as cash in exchange for shares and an active role in the invested company.

Venture capital differs from traditional financing sources in that venture capital typically:

1. Focuses on young, high-growth companies
2. Invests equity capital, rather than debt
3. Takes higher risks in exchange for potential higher returns
4. Has a longer investment horizon than traditional financing
5. Actively monitors portfolio companies via board participation, strategic marketing, governance, and capital structure."[17]

Factoring

Factoring allows businesses to get almost all of their invoices paid by a third party. This frees the company from having to "chase payments" for their accounts receivable and instead focus their time and attention on building future revenues. There are two types of factoring available to businesses who carry large amounts of accounts receivable:

1. *Non-recourse factoring* occurs when the accounts receivable are sold at an agreed-upon price, for cash and the factor assumes all of the risk for collecting the accounts. This process usually works in the following manner:
   a. *The factor purchases accounts receivable at a discount (usually 60–80% of face value) at the time of the sale.*
   b. *A fee is assessed, normally 0.3-2% of face value.*
   c. *Once sold, the factor is responsible for collecting outstanding accounts receivables.*
2. *Recourse factoring*, wherein the factoring firm does not guarantee the credit-worthiness of the client's accounts, and the client remains responsible for losses occurring as a result of any uncollected receivables.

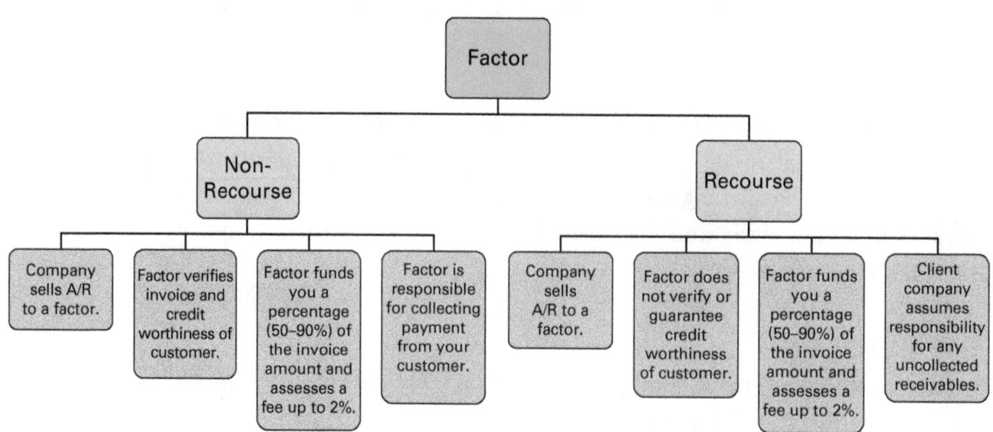

FINANCE AND YOUR FUTURE

Virtually every decision you make, and the decisions made by the company you work for, has some financial consequence. For businesses, as well as college students, financial analysis is the process used to measure the efficacy of your economic/monetary decisions. Just like any financial manager today you too need to understand how to put your money to work. Understanding how to develop a financial plan, evaluate sources of capital, create budgets, manage inventory and receivables, and understand the concept of the time value of money are all critical to the success of any organization. Developing an understanding of these financial concepts will allow you to:

1. Ask the right questions
2. Intelligently assess risk
3. Understand causal relationships
4. Maximize profit
5. Create wealth
6. Make a difference!

The truth is, financial literacy is a requisite skill you must develop if your goal is to build wealth and enjoy financial security. Now is the time for you to take control of your financial future. Your knowledge of finance will serve you well as you go out into the world and attempt to carve out a living for yourself. Make sure that "at the end of the day" your money is working harder than you are as you attempt to create financial independence and wealth.

ENDNOTES

1. M.E. Porter, "What is Strategy?" *Harvard Business Review*, 74, no. 6 (1996).
2. "Should College Students Be Required to Take a Course in Personal Finance?" Wall Street Journal 19 March 2017. <https://www.wsj.com/articles/should-college-students-be-required-to-take-a-course-in-personal-finance-1489975500>
3. Mann, Thea. "The Role of the Finance Manager." Yahoo Voices 25 Apr 2006. <http://voices.yahoo.com/the-role-finance-manager-67611.html>.
4. Walters, Sherry. "Don't Overlook the Cash Flow Statement." Shepard Schwartz & Harris, LLP. 12 Dec 2012. <http://www.ssh-cpa.com/newsroom-publications-dont-overlook-the-cash-flow-statement.html>.
5. "Cut, Budget, Compare and Control your Expenses and Maximize Your Cash Flow." 1040 Accountants Accessed August 30, 2013. <http://1040accountant.com/wpcontent/uploads/2010/07/CutBudgetCompare.pdf>.
6. Odland, Steve. "5 Ways to Control Costs." Forbes 15 Feb 2012 <http://www.forbes.com/sites/steveodland/2012/02/15/5-ways-to-control-costs/>.
7. "Time Value of Money." <http://en.wikipedia.org/wiki/Time_value_of_money"Time>.
8. Brigham, Eugene F., and Joel F. Houston. Fundamentals of Financial Management. Ohio: South-Western Cengage Learning, 2009.
9. "Financing for your Future: The Five C's of Credit." PNC. 2012. 12 Apr. 2012 <https://www.pnc.com/webapp/unsec/ProductsAndService.do?siteArea=/pnccorp/PNC/Home/Small+Business/Financing+Your+Future/The+Five+Cs+of+Credit >
10. O'Sullivan, Arthur, and Steven Sheffrin. Economics: Principles in Action. New Jersey: Pearson Prentice Hall, 2003.

11. adj. Referring to payment, distribution or substitution of things in lieu of money. LAW.COM 2013 < http://dictionary.law.com/Default.aspx?selected=965>.

12. Higginbottom, Sam. "Retail Banking: The New Buzzword of Today's World of Banking." Journal of Banking Financial Services and Insurance Research 1,8 (2011) <http://www.newagepublishers.com/samplechapter/001636.pdf>.

13. "Lines of Credit." Debt.org. 2013. <http://www.debt.org/credit/lines/>.

14. ibid

15. Mayo, Herbert B., Basic Finance: An Introduction to Financial Institutions, Investments and Management. Ohio: South-Western Cengage 2012.

16. "The Wisest Entrepreneurs Know How to Preserve Equity." US Capital Partners. 2013 <http://uscapital.squarespace.com>.

17. "Venture Capital." U.S. mall Business Administration. 2013 <http://www.sba.gov/content/venture-capital>.

SOURCES

1. Fig. 13.8: Source: Sweeney, 2013, http://infrapm.blogspot.com/2013/11/debt-vs-equity-financing.html.

Chapter 14

Securities & Investing

Getting Into the Game

PROLOGUE

The securities market is an important part of the U.S. economy and plays a fundamental role in the growth of both business and commerce. It is precisely because of its impact on the overall economy that the government and central banks pay close attention to the actions of the securities market.

A securities market is an exchange where the sale and purchase of securities transactions are conducted. The Securities market encompasses equity markets and bond markets and serves as a source of new capital investment for new and emerging companies. Additionally securities markets provide the necessary liquidity mechanism, to varying degrees, for securities traded within its domain (NYSE, NASDAQ, OTC). It is through the sale of stocks and bonds that businesses are able to access long-term funding as well as a place for private investors to buy and sell securities/investments such as stocks, bonds, commodities, Exchange Traded Funds (ETF's) and mutual funds.

When companies need to raise funds for the expansion or creation of a new business venture they either borrow money from a financial institution or they seek capital through the securities market. The securities markets are generally categorized as either money markets or capital markets. Investors use money markets for short term borrowing or lending and are typically seen as a safe place for investors to put money due to the liquidity of the securities and short maturities. Capital markets serve as a source of long-term funds by bringing together investors who are holding capital, and companies seeking capital, through various equity or debt instruments. In addition capital markets provide a mechanism, the secondary market, where investors can purchase/sell stocks and bonds.

The securities market represents one of the primary sources for raising funds for business expansion. If a company wants to raise equity capital it can issue new shares of stock (IPO) through the ***primary market.*** To issue new shares of stock a company must be listed on a stock exchange and in doing so can then sell shares of stock in order to raise capital.

In the case of an already listed public company, they would issue more shares of stock to the market as a means of acquiring the additional funds needed for business expansion. This is the primary function of the securities market and the important role it plays in the growth of business and commerce in the country. That is the reason that a rising stock market signifies a healthy, growing industrial sector and a robust, growing economy.

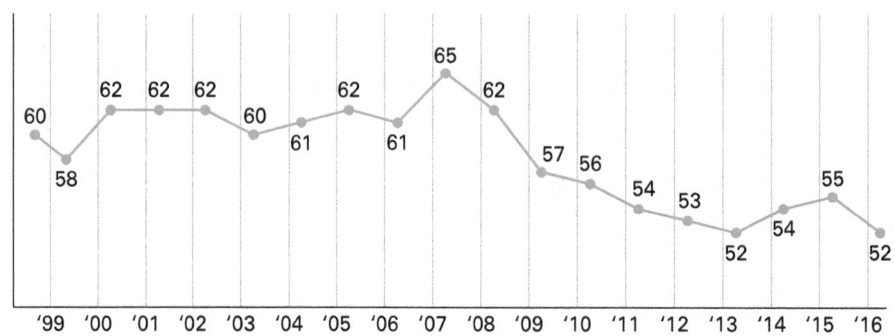

http://news.gallup.com/poll/190883/half-americans-own-stocks-matching-record-low.aspx

SECURITIES AND EXCHANGE COMMISSION

The Securities Act of 1933 protects investors by requiring full disclosure of financial information by firms selling new stocks or bonds. The ***Securities and Exchange Commission*** *(SEC)* is the federal agency that has responsibility for regulating the various exchanges. Companies trading on the national exchanges must register with the *SEC* and provide annual updates. When issuing bonds or stock, companies must follow established specific guidelines such as filing a prospectus.

> "The mission of the U.S. Securities and Exchange Commission is to protect investors, maintain fair, orderly, and efficient markets, and facilitate capital formation.
>
> The world of investing is fascinating and complex, and it can be very fruitful. But unlike the banking world, where deposits are guaranteed by the federal government, stocks, bonds and other securities can lose value. There are no guarantees. That's why investing is not a spectator sport. By far the best way for investors to protect the money they put into the securities markets is to do research and ask questions."[1]

DOW JONES INDUSTRIAL AVERAGE

> "Roughly two-thirds of the DJIA's 30 component companies are manufacturers of industrial and consumer goods. The others represent industries as diverse as financial services, entertainment and information technology. Even so, the DJIA

today serves the same purpose for which it was created – to provide a clear, straightforward view of the stock market and, by extension, the U.S. economy."[2]

1. 3M	16. Johnson & Johnson
2. American Express	17. JPMorgan Chase
3. Apple	18. McDonald's
4. Boeing	19. Merck
5. Caterpillar	20. Microsoft
6. Chevron	21. Nike
7. Cisco Systems	22. Pfizer
8. Coca-Cola	23. Procter & Gamble
9. DuPont	24. Travelers
10. ExxonMobil	25. United Health Group
11. General Electric	26. United Technologies
12. Goldman Sachs	27. Verizon
13. The Home Depot	28. Visa
14. IBM	29. Walmart
15. Intel	30. Walt-Disney

The DJIA contains 30 stocks of the most highly-capitalized and influential companies in the U.S. economy. The "Dow" is also the most referenced U.S. market index and remains a financial barometer of general market trends. The Dow is price weighted and each of the 30 companies has a weightage share in the index depending upon the price of its stock.

SECURITIES MARKET

The Securities Market, or more commonly the Stock Market, is an organized exchange, marketplace, where shares, options and futures on stocks, bonds, and commodities are traded in the secondary market. A stock exchange is comprised of members who can buy and sell (exchange) securities for the public. Brokerage firms, including "The big five brokerages" of TD Ameritrade, Etrade, Fidelity Investments, Charles Schwab, and Scottrade, purchase membership seats on the various stock exchanges (NYSE, NASDAQ).

Before a company can begin trading on an exchange, it must meet certain initial requirements or "listing standards." The various exchanges set their own standards for listing and continuing to trade a stock. The four largest exchanges include:

New York Stock Exchange (NYSE)

Also known as the Big Board or the Exchange, the NYSE has 1,366 exchange members who "own" seats on the exchange. The NYSE minimum requirements[3] for companies wishing to apply for listing include:

Initial Listing Standard 1

1. *Size*—Stockholders' equity of at least $4,000,000.
2. *Income*—Pre-tax income from continuing operations of at least $750,000 in its last fiscal year, or in two of its last three fiscal years.
3. *Distribution*— Minimum public distribution of 500,000, together with a minimum of 800 public shareholders or minimum public distribution of 1,000,000 shares together with a minimum of 400 public shareholders.
4. *Stock Price/Market Value of Shares Publicly Held*— $3,000,000 aggregate market value of publicly held shares

National Association of Securities Dealers Automated Quotation (NASDAQ)

The NASDAQ now contains about 3,200 publicly traded companies, and is the second largest stock exchange (in terms of its securities' values) and the largest electronic stock market. The NASDAQ trades shares in a variety of types of companies — including capital goods, consumer durables and nondurables, energy, finance, healthcare, public utilities, technology, and transportation — but it is most well-known for its high-tech stocks.

To be listed on the NASDAQ National Market, companies must meet specific financial criteria. They must maintain a stock price of at least $1, and the value of outstanding stocks must total at least $1.1 million. For smaller companies unable to meet the financial requirements, there is the NASDAQ Small Caps Market. NASDAQ will shift companies from market to market as eligibility changes.[4]

Over-the-Counter (OTC)

Dealers in the OTC market act as "market makers" by quoting prices at which they will buy and sell a security or currency. Trading in the OTC is done almost exclusively through dealers who buy and sell their own inventories. Unlike exchanges, OTC markets have never been a "place" since they have no physical location. They are less formal, although often well-organized, networks of trading relationships centered around one or more dealers. Dealers act as market makers by quoting prices at which they will sell "ask" or "bid" to other dealers and to their clients or customers. That does not mean they quote the same prices to other dealers as they post to customers, and they do not necessarily quote the same prices to all customers. Moreover, dealers in an OTC security can withdraw from market making at any time, which can cause liquidity to dry up, disrupting the ability of market participants to buy or sell. Exchanges are far more liquid because all buy and sell orders as well as execution prices are exposed to one another.[5]

Primary Markets

In the primary market shares of stock are brought to the market and sold to individual and institutional investors through an *Initial Public Offering (IPO)*.

Institutional Investors

These investors represent a group of investment professionals who trade large volumes of securities for individuals, businesses, and even the government. Included in this group are institutions such as banks, life insurance companies, mutual funds, retirement and pension funds and hedge funds. "The growth in the proportion of assets managed by institutional investors has been accompanied by a dramatic growth in the market capitalization of U.S. listed companies. For example, in 1950, the combined market value of all stocks listed on the New York Stock Exchange (NYSE) was about $94 billion. By 2012, however, the domestic market capitalization of the NYSE was more than $14 trillion, an increase of nearly 1500%. This growth is even more impressive if you add the $4.5 trillion in market capitalization on the NASDAQ market, which did not exist until 1971. The bottom line is, that as a whole, institutional investors own a larger share of a larger market.[6]

Individual Investors

Individual investors use and manage their investments as they plan for the best use of their capital prior to and during retirement. Stated another way, any investors who aren't institutional are individual investors. Obviously this includes virtually everyone who buys and sells debt, equity or other investments through their broker, banker, or real estate agent.

The primary market is where securities are created. Most companies that engage in an *IPO* are small, fast growing companies that require large sums of additional capital to continue or further their expansion. There are numerous steps that a company must complete in order to receive the approval of current shareholders, investors, and the *Securities and Exchange Commission*. One of the early steps in the process involves the filing of a registration statement with the SEC called a *prospectus*.

Prospectus

This is a document that must be filed with the *Securities and Exchange Commission* when a company issues stock to the public. This document is used in the *IPO* process to gain approval of the *SEC* as well as providing the investment community with a detailed statement involving the key issues of the subject company including; management, financial position, operations, and investment plans for the future. The issuer must provide, according to SEC regulations, the official documents to potential purchasers of a new securities issue prior to approval of the *SEC*.

Investment Bankers

Investment Banking is a form of banking, which finances major capital requirements of a business enterprise. These capital requirements are include but are not limited to the following forms of financial assistance: launching an *Initial public offering (IPO)*, Bonds, and Mergers and Acquisitions.

Global IB Revenue by Bank – H1 2017				
Rank	Bank	Rev. $m	% Share	H1 2016
1	JPMorgan	3,299	8.3	1
2	Goldman Sachs	2,728	6.8	2
3	Bank of America Merrill Lynch	2,615	6.6	3
4	Morgan Stanley	2,401	6.0	4
5	Citi	2,335	5.8	5
6	Barclays	1,862	4.7	6
7	Credit Suisse	1,718	4.3	7
8	Deutsche Bank	1,371	3.4	8
9	RBC Capital Markets	953	2.4	11
10	UBS	872	2.2	10

Source: http://www.dealogic.com/insight/key-trends-h1-2017/?utm_content=buffercac91&utm_medium=social&utm_source=twitter.com&utm_campaign=buffer

The investment banker acts as a middleman in the process of raising funds and, in most cases, assumes the risk by ***underwriting*** the issues of new securities. The *underwriting* process involves purchasing all of the securities of a firm and then assuming the risk of reselling them to the public. The investment banker agrees to the purchase of firm's securities at a fixed price and in doing so serves an important link between the original issuer and the securities markets. By assuming much of the risk through the underwriting process the investment banker enables corporations and others to find needed capital while at the same time providing investors with the opportunity to participate in the ownership of securities in the secondary market.

Secondary Markets

The secondary market is often referred to as the aftermarket because it is the market where securities are traded after they have been issued. The secondary market involves the purchase and sale of existing shares that are traded among investors and does not involve, or benefit, the corporation that issued the securities. In the aftermarket an investor is able purchase from, or sell to, a security to another investor. The secondary market provides the mechanism for:

- The continuous pricing of securities
- The ease of transfer of ownership among investors/traders in the market

Investing Objectives: Four Key Questions

Prior to investing money into stocks and bonds, an investor would first be well advised to consider the following four key questions:

Question #1: Tax Implications
Tax regulations are constantly changing. As with any type of investment, when you realize a capital gain it is considered income. A capital gain is profit resulting from the sale of investments such as stocks, bonds, or real estate, which exceeds the purchase price.

Question #2: Risk vs. Return (Yield)
The risk-return continuum is the relationship between the amount of return gained on an investment and the amount of risk you are willing to undertake. Yield refers to the amount of money your investment will earn for you. The formula for calculating yield is:

Dividend/Price of Stock = yield (%)

Question #3: Duration (Investment Horizon)
How much time will your money be committed to an investment?

Question #4: Liquidity
How quickly will you need to convert your investment into cash? An asset with a high degree of liquidity can be sold quickly without a significant price concession.

STOCKS

Equity financing refers to the acquisition of funds through the sale of ownership in a corporation. Stocks represent a type of security, units of individual ownership in a corporation, and entitle each stockholder to part of a corporation's earnings and assets. There are two common classifications of stocks, *Common* and *Preferred.*

Common Stock

These are securities that represent ownership in a corporation. Each share of common stock represents a proportional (fractional) share of ownership in the company. They also give the holder a pro rata share of anything paid out, in the form of dividends, by the company. Typically, stockholders of common stock receive one vote per share allowing them to vote on important company matters. Examples of the type of issues that holders of common stock would vote on would include, electing members of the Board of Directors, stock splits, and mergers and acquisitions.

Common stock is considered a permanent form of long-term financing and unlike preferred stock has no maturity date. Common stock can move up and down sharply over time and returns vary greatly. Common stock provides the stockholder with:

- A residual claim, last claim, to the company's earnings or assets.
- Voting rights involving major corporate decisions.
- Greater risk and speculation than either bonds or preferred stock.

Types of Common Stock

The stock market offers a wide range of stocks, from those that provide the least amount of risk to those that are highly speculative. Investors will generally seek out stocks that align with their investment objectives and level of risk they are willing to assume. Common stocks attract a wide range of investors because they are a source of stable income (dividends) as well as provide an attractive rate of return. The following represents a short list of common stock choices available to today's investor.

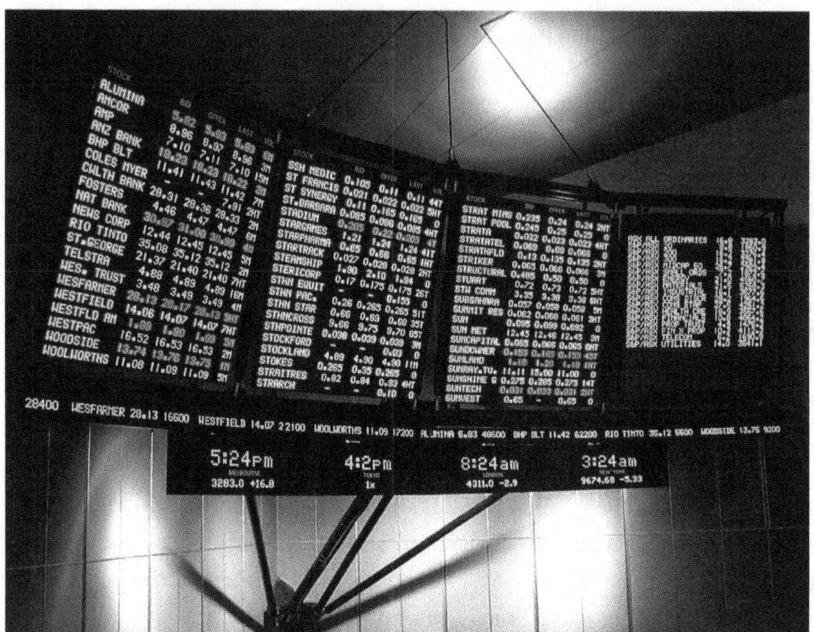

Growth Stocks

Corporate stocks with high P/E Ratios whose earnings are expected to grow faster than other stocks or the overall economy. Because of the growth prospects of these stocks investors are more willing to buy them at higher prices. Investors are motivated to purchase growth stocks because of their potential for capital appreciation. "A good growth stock might exhibit a sustained growth in earnings of 15% to 18% per year ... Generally speaking, established growth companies combine steady earnings growth with high returns on equity."[7]

Income Stocks

Well-established companies that have a record of stable earnings and solid financial outlook are typically referred to as income stocks. For companies in the mature stages of their industry life cycle it is unlikely that they will see a sustained and rapid increase in the price of their stock. In order to maintain interest in their company stock these established companies pay regular, often steadily increasing dividends that offer a higher yield; Dividend/Stock Price = Yield.

In general income stocks have lower levels of instability than the overall stock market, and offer higher-than-market dividend yields.

Blue Chip Stocks

Blue-chip stocks are comprised of companies with a long history of sustained earnings and dividend payments. These are established, highly regarded, profitable companies that have carved out leadership positions in their respective industries. Good examples of blue chip stocks include those companies listed in the Dow Jones Industrial Average.

Penny Stocks

Penny stocks are highly speculative (risky), low-priced, stocks that normally trade on the over-the-counter (OTC) market. These stocks usually sell for less than $2 per share and reflect the uncertainty surrounding the liquidity and future operations of the company. "Low-priced, small-cap stocks are known as penny stocks. Contrary to their name, penny stocks rarely cost a penny. The SEC considers a penny stock to be pretty much anything under $5. And while there are sub $5 stocks trading on big exchanges like NYSE and NASDAQ, most investors don't think of these when asked to describe a penny stock. Most individual investors look at penny stocks like Wall Street's Wild West, an untamed world of investing detached from all the glitz and media coverage that comes with stocks that are traded on major exchanges. While the gains and losses can be pretty impressive in the penny stock world, they're not often heard about elsewhere."[8]

Preferred Stock

Preferred stock represents ownership in a corporation, just like common stock, but is listed separately from common stock and trades at a different price. Preferred stockholders are not entitled to voting rights, but they do have a higher claim on assets and earnings than do common shareholders. Preferred stock shares many of the same characteristics of both a stock and a bond. Like bonds, they have a relatively high fixed-rate payment. Like common stock, they are generally listed on a stock exchange. A preferred stock is an equity that may or may not have maturity. Preferred stockholders are paid returns after bondholder claims are satisfied but before common stockholders. Preferred stock gives the holder preference in the payment of dividends (which are fixed) and in the event of liquidation; preferred shares maintain their issue price. The most basic characteristics of preferred stock include:

- *Holder has no voting rights.*
- *Typically has no specified maturity, but are often callable by the issuer.*
- *Dividend payment is fixed.*

Types of Preferred Stock

Cumulative

If stock dividends are not paid in any (one) year they accumulate and must be paid before any payment is made to common stockholders.

Non-Cumulative

Stock whose holders must forgo dividend payments when the company misses a dividend payment.

Convertible

Provides the holder with the option of converting to common stock at a specific price that has been stated in the prospectus.

Convertible preferred stock: An example

Let's assume you purchase 100 shares of XYZ company convertible preferred stock on June 1, 2012. According to the registration statement, each share of preferred stock is convertible after January 1, 2013, (the conversion date) to three shares of XYZ Company common stock. (The number of common shares given for each preferred share is called the conversion ratio. In this example, the ratio is 3.0.)

If after the conversion date arrives XYZ company preferred shares are trading at $50 per share, and the common shares are trading at $10 per share, then converting the shares would effectively turn $50 worth of stock into only $30 worth (the investor has the choice between holding one share valued at $50 or holding three shares valued at $10 each).The difference between the two amounts, $20, is called the conversion premium (although it is typically expressed as a percentage of the preferred share price; in this case it woould be $20/$50, or 40%).

By dividing the price of the preferred shares ($50) by the conversion ratio (3), we can determine what the common stock must trade at for you to break even on the conversion. In this case, XYZ Company common must be trading at a minimum of $16.67 per share for you to seriously consider converting.

STOCK SPLIT

When a stock split occurs, the corporation calls in its outstanding shares and issues two or more new shares in exchange for each of the old ones. Splits can be accomplished at any ratio and are the result of the following:

- *The company develops a recapitalization strategy.*
- *The company will split a single share of stock into multiple shares.*
- *The split increases the number of shares that each stock certificate represents but does not increase the value of the stock at the time of the split.*
- *The split will attract new investors, which translates into increased capital available to the company.*
- *A stock split is usually indicative of good financial health of the company offering the split.*

2-for-1 Split	Pre-Split	Post-Split
Number of Shares	1000	2000
Share Price	$10.00/Share	$5.00/Share
Market Cap	$100 Million	$100 Million

BUYING AND SELLING STOCK

Market Order

This represents an order to buy or sell a stock immediately at the best available current price. Because market orders are simple and straightforward, they are the most frequently used order and are often the lowest-commission.

Limit Order

A limit order is an order to buy a stock at or below a specified price or to sell a stock at or above a specified price. For instance, you could tell a broker "buy me 100 shares of XYZ Corp at $8 or less" or to "sell 100 shares of XYZ at $10 or better." The customer specifies a price and the order can be executed only if the market reaches or betters that price. A limit order is a conditional trading order designed to avoid the danger of adverse unexpected price changes.

Margin Call

A margin call occurs when a brokerage demands an investor to deposit additional funds into their account to maintain margin requirements. This occurs when an investor's account falls below some defined percentage, which then requires a deposit of additional funds or the sale of shares in the account necessary to comply with the margin requirements of the brokerage firm.

For example:

Suppose you account has a 50% margin requirement and a 30% maintenance margin. You have $20,000, and with a 50% margin buy 800 shares of stock in XYZ Corporation totaling $40,000. After you buy the stock the price falls to $35/share. The total value of your position falls to $28,000 (800 × $35). You still owe the broker $20,000 so your account equity is $8,000 ($28,000 – $20,000). Your margin therefore is $8,000/$28,000 = .286, or 28.6%. You are below the 30% maintenance margin requirement and are now subject to a margin call to bring your account back into conformity with the maintenance margin of 30%.

BONDS

Bonds represent a written promise that the borrower will repay the lender, at some future date, the principal and stated, predetermined, rate of return (coupon rate).

Coupon Rate

Adding the total amount of coupons paid per year and dividing by the bond's face value will allow you to calculate the coupon rate. For example, if a bond has a face value of $10,000 and a coupon rate of 5%, then it pays total coupons of $500 per year.

A bond represents a contract of indebtedness issued by a corporation or government unit and places each bondholder in a preferential claim position to the assets and earnings of the company. All bonds are characterized according to this credit quality and therefore fall into one of two categories of bonds:

Investment Grade

These are bonds issued by low- to medium-risk lenders. A bond rating on investment-grade debt usually ranges from AAA to BBB. Investment grade bonds might not offer huge returns, but the risk of the borrower defaulting on interest payments is much smaller.

Junk Bonds

These are the bonds that pay high yields to bondholders because the borrowers don't have any other option. The credit ratings of the company issuing junk bonds are less than perfect, making it difficult for them to acquire capital at an inexpensive cost. Junk bonds are typically rated at BB/Ba or less.

Bond Evaluation

Bond evaluation normally requires a careful examination of the degree of risk and the interest rate (yield) inherent within any bond issue. The evaluation of a bond normally involves three main risks: 1) the interest rate risk (the risk that interest rates could rise thus reducing the rate of return of the bond); 2) purchasing power risk (the risk an increase in inflation will lessen the value of bond); 3) the credit risk of the issuer which translates into a diminished capacity of the bond issuer being able to meet their debt obligations. The first two risks require the individual investor to conduct a significant amount of research on his/her own. Credit risks on the other hand are relatively easy to assess since the level of risk is usually reflected in a bond's rating provided by Moody's and Standard and Poor's.

Moody's

Moody's Investors Service is a monthly publication containing data on corporate, convertible, government and municipal bonds, and ratings on commercial paper and preferred stock. Corporate bond information includes the interest coupon, payment dates, call price, Moody's rating, and yield to maturity. (http://www.moodys.com)

Standard & Poor's

The Bond Guide has the same format as the Stock Guide. A monthly publication in booklet form, it presents data on corporate and convertible bonds. The Standard & Poor's rating is presented along with other information. All the conversion data are presented with bond prices and common stock prices. (http://www.standardandpoors.com)

BOND RATING		GRADE	RISK
Moody's	Standard & Poor's		
Aaa	AAA	Investment	Lowest Risk
Aa	AA	Investment	Low Risk
A	A	Investment	Low Risk
Baa	BBB	Investment	Medium Risk
Ba, B	BB, B	Junk	High Risk
Caa/Ca/C	CCC/CC/C	Junk	Highest Risk
C	D	Junk	In Default

Bond Features

Sinking Fund Bond

These bonds include a provision that requires a corporation to set up a custodial account and wherein it is required to make periodic payments into a trustee-managed account. In most cases, the sinking fund requires the issuer to actually retire a portion of the debt on a prearranged schedule so that all of the debt is retired by the maturity date.

Callable Bond

These bond issues have a call provision allowing the issuer to buy back all or part of its outstanding bonds at a specified call price sometime before the bonds mature.

Convertible Bond

Convertible or redeemable bonds are bonds that can be redeemed or paid off by the issuer prior to the bond's maturity date. When an issuer calls its bonds, it pays investors the call price (usually the face value of the bonds) together with accrued interest to date and, at that point, stops making interest payments. Call provisions are often part of corporate and municipal bonds, but usually not bonds issued by the federal government.[9]

Secured Bonds

In the event a corporation goes out of business or defaults on its debt, bondholders, as creditors, have priority over stockholders in bankruptcy court. However, the order of priority among all the vying groups of creditors depends on the specific terms of each bond, among other factors. One of the most important factors is whether the bond is secured or unsecured. If a bond is secured, the issuer has pledged specific assets (known as collateral) that can be sold, if necessary, to pay the bondholders. If you buy a secured bond, you will "pay" for the extra safety by receiving a lower interest rate than you would have received on a comparable unsecured bond.[10]

Mortgage Bond

These bonds represent debt issued with a lien on specific property, usually real estate, pledged as security for the bonds.

Collateral Trust Bonds

These bonds are characterized by a pledge of financial assets as security for the bond issue. These bonds are normally issued by holding companies that pledge the stocks, bonds, or other securities issued by their subsidiaries as collateral for their own bond.

Equipment Trust Bonds

These bonds represent debt issued by a trustee to purchase heavy industrial equipment that is leased and used by railroads, airlines, and other companies with a demand for heavy equipment. Under this financial agreement, a trustee holds the title to the equipment until the loan is paid off, and the investors who buy the certificates usually have a first claim on the equipment.

Unsecured Bonds

Any assets owned by the corporation do not back these bonds. If bankruptcy occurs, repayment is not guaranteed by the corporation's future revenue stream, equipment, or property. An unsecured bond is only backed by the full faith and credit of the issuing institution.

Debenture Bonds

These represent the most frequently issued type of corporate bonds. Additionally the federal government can issue debenture bonds. An example of a government debenture would be any government-issued Treasury bond or Treasury bill. T-bonds and T-bills are generally considered risk-free because the governments can print off more money or raise taxes to pay these types of debt.

Debentures are backed solely by the reputation and credit history of the issuing corporation rather than by specific pledges of assets. However, in the event of default by the issuing corporation, the bondholders' claim extends to all corporate assets as specified in the indenture agreement.

- Indenture
  - This agreement (contract) contains all the terms and conditions applicable to the bond issue and outlines the specific promises made to bondholders. A trustee, usually a commercial bank or some other financial institution, appointed by the issuing firm to represent the rights of the bondholders, ensures that the terms of the indenture are fulfilled.

Junk Bonds

Often referred to as "High-Yield Bonds," these bonds are characterized by a speculative or low grade rating, those rated Ba or lower by Moody's or BB or lower by Standard & Poor's, that are offset by a higher yield premium offered to compensate for higher credit risk.

From a technical point of view, a junk bond is exactly the same as a regular bond. Junk bonds are an IOU from a corporation or organization that states the amount it will pay you back (principal), the date it will pay you back (maturity date) and the interest (coupon) it will pay you on the borrowed money. Because of the poor credit quality of their issuers they are required to pay high yields to bondholders because the issuer doesn't have any other option.

MUTUAL FUNDS

At the most basic level, a company that pools funds obtained from individual investors and invests them in diversified holdings is called an *Investment Company*. In other words, an investment company is a business that specializes in managing financial assets for individual investors. All mutual funds are, in fact, investment companies.

> "Picking individual stocks can be intimidating to new investors. Investing in mutual funds, however, eases some of the pressure of building a stock portfolio.
>
> 'Mutual funds are good choices for first-time investors,' says Jeremy Torgerson, CEO of Denver-based nVest Advisors. 'You're diversified across dozens or even hundreds of investments from your very first dollar in a fund that's been professionally selected to fit the specific objectives of the fund's investors.'
>
> That, Torgerson says, takes much of the guesswork out of answering a question novice investors often have – does this stock give me what I want? Although mutual funds are an all-in-one investing package, newbies can still choose the wrong ones thanks to some common mistakes."[11]

Two Types of Funds

As you might suspect mutual funds come in a wide variety of types including, but not limited to, funds that specialize in municipal bonds and various types of equities. Any decision regarding mutual funds normally comes down to the question every investor has to answer: Why not simply invest in stocks or bonds directly? The greatest advantage to a mutual fund is that it allows the individual investor to achieve greater diversification, generate a more attractive rate of return, and have access to the advice of professional money managers.

Open-End Fund

The fund itself will sell new shares to anyone wishing to buy and will "buy back" shares from anyone wishing to sell. There are no restrictions to the amount of shares that a fund will issue. When an investor wishes to buy shares in an open-end fund the fund simply issues shares and then invests the money received. When someone wishes to sell their shares of open-end fund the fund sells some of its assets and uses the cash to redeem the shares.

Closed-End Fund

The number of shares is fixed and never changes. Because closed-end funds trade like stock, you must buy (or sell) them from another investor, and as a result must use a broker to buy shares via a stock exchange. The number of fund shares do not fluctuate based on investor demand and the fund does not issue new shares.

EXCHANGE TRADED FUNDS

Exchange-traded funds (ETFs) are a relatively new investment opportunities that offer investors, including those with limited knowledge and capital, the opportunity to purchase shares in a diversified pool of securities at a competitive price. An exchange-traded fund is an investment company that offers investors a proportionate share in a portfolio of stocks, bonds, or other securities. Like individual equity securities, ETFs are traded on a stock exchange and can be bought and sold throughout the day through a broker-dealer.

> Most ETFs are index-style investments, similar to index mutual funds. That means the ETF simply buys and holds the stocks or bonds in a market gauge like the Standard & Poor's 500 stock index or Dow Jones Industrial Average. Investors therefore know what securities their fund holds, and they enjoy returns matching those of the underlying index. If the S&P 500 goes up 10 percent, your SPDR S&P 500 Index ETF (SPY) will go up 10 percent, less a small fee. Many investors like index products because they are not dependent on the talents of a fund manager who might lose his touch, retire or quit.[12]

GETTING IN THE GAME

Obviously the securities market and your involvement as an investor is not a game! Instead the securities market represents numerous opportunities for an investor, investment companies, corporations and the government to engage in a process of capitalization and wealth creation. The challenge for every student today is to ask themselves: How do I invest money as a means of securing my financial future? The answer to this question requires rigorous "due diligence," specialized knowledge, the ability to understand financial information, a capacity to assume risk, and a proactive approach. The time to begin developing your financial investment plan begins today! Make sure your journey is not based on happenstance and luck but instead a pragmatic understanding of the nuances and risks of a dynamic securities market. Good luck as you begin your journey.

ENDNOTES

1. "The Investor's Advocate: How the SEC Protects Investors, Maintains Market Integrity, and Facilitates Capital Formation." U.S. Securities and Exchange Commission. 12 May 2012 <http://www.sec.gov/about/whatwedo.shtml>

2. "Dow Jones Industrial Average." Dow Jones Indexes: A CME Group Company. 2012 A CME Group Company. 15 May 2012 < http://www.djaverages.com/?go=industrial-overview>

3. "NYSE MKT Company Guide." Wallstreet.cch.com. 14 May 2012 <http://lynn.libguides.com/content.php?pid=58823&sid=449599>.

4. Horn, Elaine J. "What is NASDAQ?" Business News Daily 9 Nov 2012 <http://www.businessnewsdaily.com/3403-nasdaq.html>.

5. Dodd, Randall. "Markets: Exchange or Over-the-Counter." International Monetary Fund 28 Mar 2012 <http://www.imf.org/external/pubs/ft/fandd/basics/markets.htm>.

6. "Institutional Investors: Power and Responsibility." U.S. Securities and Exchange Commission. 2013 <https://www.sec.gov/News/Speech/Detail/Speech/1365171515808#.UitWVRb3CRs>.

7. Gitman, Lawrence J. , Michael D.Joehnk, and Scott B. Smart. Fundamental of Investing. Boston: Pearson/ Prentice Hall, 2011.

8. Elmerraji, Jonas. "How to Buy Penny Stocks (For Beginners)." The Street. 27 Sep 2011. <http://www.thestreet.com/story/11260181/1/penny-stocks.html>.

9. "Callable or Redeemable Bonds." U.S. Securities and Exchange Commission. 2008 <http://www.sec.gov/answers/callablebonds.htm>.

10. "About Corporate Bonds: Understanding Collateralization." The Security and Financial Markets Association. 2010 <http://www.investinginbonds.com/learnmore.asp?catid=10&subcatid=47&id=181#sthash.rPjPSYmw.dpuf>.

11. Lake, Rebecca. *3 Costly Mistakes First-Time Mutual Fund Investors Make.* 24 Oct 2017 <https://money.usnews.com/investing/funds/articles/2017-10-24/3-costly-mistakes-first-time-mutual-fund-investors-make>

12. Brown, Jeff. "ETF's? Here's What You Should Know." CNBC. 21 May 2013 <http://www.cnbc.com/id/100754770>.

SOURCES

1. Fig. 14.1: Source: http://news.gallup.com/poll/190883/half-americans-own-stocks-matching-record-low.aspx.

2. Fig. 14.3: Source: http://www.dealogic.com/insight/key-trends-h1-2017/?utm_content=buffercac91&utm_medium=social&utm_source=twitter.com&utm_campaign=buffer.

3. Fig. 14.5: Source: https://commons.wikimedia.org/wiki/File:E-ticker.jpg.

CPSIA information can be obtained
at www.ICGtesting.com
Printed in the USA
LVHW01s1817090818
586398LV00003B/10/P